Letters from Red Farm

OTHER BOOKS FROM BRIGHT LEAF

House Stories
The Meanings of Home in a New England Town
BETH LUEY

Bricklayer Bill
The Untold Story of the Workingman's Boston Marathon
PATRICK L. KENNEDY AND LAWRENCE W. KENNEDY

Concrete Changes
Architecture, Politics, and the Design of Boston City Hall
BRIAN M. SIRMAN

Williamstown and Williams College
Explorations in Local History
DUSTIN GRIFFIN

Massachusetts Treasures
A Guide to Marvelous, Must-See Museums
CHUCK D'IMPERIO

Boston's Twentieth-Century Bicycling Renaissance
Cultural Change on Two Wheels
LORENZ J. FINISON

Went to the Devil
A Yankee Whaler in the Slave Trade
ANTHONY J. CONNORS

At Home
Historic Houses of Eastern Massachusetts
BETH LUEY

Black Lives, Native Lands, White Worlds
A History of Slavery in New England
JARED ROSS HARDESTY

At Home
Historic Houses of Central and Western Massachusetts
BETH LUEY

Flight Calls
Exploring Massachusetts through Birds
JOHN R. NELSON

Lost Wonderland
The Brief and Brilliant Life of Boston's Million Dollar Amusement Park
STEPHEN R. WILK

Legends of the Common Stream
JOHN HANSON MITCHELL

I Believe I'll Go Back Home
Roots and Revival in New England Folk Music
THOMAS S. CURREN

Minds and Hearts
The Story of James Otis Jr. and Mercy Otis Warren
JEFFREY H. HACKER

Combat Zone
Murder, Race, and Boston's Struggle for Justice
JAN BROGAN

Letters from Red Farm

The Untold Story
of the Friendship between Helen Keller
and Journalist Joseph Edgar Chamberlin

ELIZABETH EMERSON

BRIGHT LEAF
Amherst and Boston
An imprint of University of Massachusetts Press

Letters from Red Farm has been supported by the Regional Books Fund, established by donors in 2019 to support the University of Massachusetts Press's Bright Leaf imprint.

Bright Leaf, an imprint of the University of Massachusetts Press, publishes accessible and entertaining books about New England. Highlighting the history, culture, diversity, and environment of the region, Bright Leaf offers readers the tools and inspiration to explore its landmarks and traditions, famous personalities, and distinctive flora and fauna.

Printed in the United States of America

ISBN 978-1-62534-617-9 (paper); 616-2 (hardcover)

Designed by Deste Roosa
Set in Typeka and Bulmer
Printed and bound by Books International, Inc.

Cover design by Deste Roosa
Cover photos: (foreground) by Charles Whitman, *Helen Keller at Edge of Water*, 1909. Courtesy of Perkins School for the Blind Archives, Watertown, MA. (background) A page from an article written by Helen Keller entitled "My Recollections of Boston, The City of Kind Hearts." Copyright © American Foundation for the Blind, Helen Keller Archive.

Library of Congress Cataloging-in-Publication Data
Names: Emerson, Elizabeth, 1957– author.
Title: Letters from Red Farm : the untold story of the friendship between Helen Keller and journalist Joseph Edgar Chamberlin / Elizabeth Emerson.
Description: Amherst : University of Massachusetts Press, 2021. | Series: Bright leaf | Includes bibliographical references and index.
Identifiers: LCCN 2021017179 (print) | LCCN 2021017180 (ebook) | ISBN 9781625346162 (hardcover) | ISBN 9781625346179 (paperback) | ISBN 9781613768921 (ebook) | ISBN 9781613768938 (ebook)
Subjects: LCSH: Chamberlin, Joseph Edgar, 1851–1935—Friends and associates. | Journalists—United States—Biography. | Keller, Helen, 1880–1968—Friends and associates. | Deafblind women—United States—Biography.
Classification: LCC PN4871.C43 E44 2021 (print) | LCC PN4871.C43 (ebook) | DDC 070.92 [B]—dc23
LC record available at https://lccn.loc.gov/2021017179
LC ebook record available at https://lccn.loc.gov/2021017180

British Library Cataloguing-in-Publication Data
A catalog record for this book is available from the British Library.

To
Martha Bennett Stiles,
who generously showed me how an author lives,
and my family

I wish you knew Mr. Chamberlin better. I think you would find much to admire in his character. He runs through Life's maze of joys and woes so peacefully, and with such kindliness towards all living things that [one] cannot be with him and not feel something of his gentle influence.

—Helen Keller to a friend, 1898

CONTENTS

Preface xi

Introduction 1

PART I

Chapter One 7
The Road to Boston

Chapter Two 26
Helen and Annie

Chapter Three 40
The Move to Red Farm

Chapter Four 46
Ed Chamberlin Steps In, 1892

Chapter Five 62
Helen's Story

PART II

Chapter Six 77
Away and Back to Boston, 1894–1896

Chapter Seven 99
The Cambridge School

Chapter Eight 108
The Gilman Affair

Chapter Nine 126
"The Happiest Months"

Chapter Ten 137
Radcliffe Aspirations

PART III

Chapter Eleven 159
Dreams and Challenges

Chapter Twelve 168
Battle Lines

Chapter Thirteen 179
Crisis

Chapter Fourteen 191
Upheaval and Recovery

Chapter Fifteen 202
The Intervening Years, 1901–1915

PART IV

Chapter Sixteen 227
Souls Tried and Greatened

Chapter Seventeen 233
Reconnection

Chapter Eighteen 245
A Gentle Influence

Afterword 252

Acknowledgments 253

Notes 257

Index 281

Photo gallery follows page 136

PREFACE

As it turns out, our family's best memory-keeper was a deafblind girl named Helen Keller.[1]

Like many families, ours has always been serious about genealogy and family trees. We can trace our lineage back for centuries, and we thought it was all thoroughly documented. But there is a difference between documenting ancestry and telling the story. For the story, in a certain generation, we have Helen.

I grew up fascinated by books about Helen Keller. I was captivated by the story of the "wild child" who could neither see nor hear and whose inner potential and delightful personality were revealed by her teacher Annie Sullivan. While millions around the world also read those stories, I had a unique and personal relationship to them: books about Helen frequently mentioned times she spent with a family named Chamberlin at their home called Red Farm in Wrentham, a suburb of Boston. As I read, I knew that she had spent those happy hours with my great-great-grandparents Joseph Edgar ("Ed") and Ida Chamberlin and their children. Ed and Ida's fourth child and second daughter was Elisabeth, my great-grandmother.

The fact that Helen spent parts of her childhood with my ancestors was the extent of my knowledge of the relationship until a few years ago when I came across copies of two letters that had been passed down to me through four generations of my family. One was the letter of sympathy Helen wrote in 1935 on hearing that her "Uncle Ed" had passed away. The other Helen had written to Ed a year earlier, a long and intimate document that illustrated a lengthy history and close relationship of more than forty years. It was clear that not only were they friends but that the bond between them was deep and lifelong. And like many friendships, theirs appeared to have weathered good times and tumultuous times. I felt compelled to find out more.

My research started in earnest in January 2012 when I called the American Foundation for the Blind (AFB) in New York City, where most of Helen Keller's personal letters and papers are archived.

From an online search, I knew there existed a box of letters related to the Chamberlins in their collection.

I reached Helen Selsdon, the head archivist at the AFB. I began by telling her that I was the great-great-granddaughter of Joseph Edgar Chamberlin, a man who had been a journalist in the Boston area and friends with Helen Keller for many years, and I was interested in doing some research.

I could hear the phone being jostled, repositioned. "Say that again?"

I repeated my story. "Oh my goodness!" Ms. Selsdon said. "The Chamberlins were huge in Helen's life. It's so amazing to hear from you. Are you really of the family?"

She was eager to help me. Five days later I received a twenty-page list of hits in the foundation database that involved the Chamberlins.

It was immediately obvious from the entries that the narrative revealed would not be the one I had expected. Somehow I had imagined I would discover a pleasant, straightforward tale about my friendly family who invited Helen and Annie for dinners and holidays at their home. Instead, what I found was a complex and multilayered story that told of joys and talents but also of controversy, tragedy, and personal and systemic failings. It was clear that I had something bigger on my hands than merely a collection of family anecdotes.

Six months after my first call, I visited the AFB offices in New York City. The Helen Keller Archive file room was filled floor to ceiling with neatly labeled boxes of letters and photographs, movie reels, and monographs related to Helen Keller and Annie Sullivan. Ms. Selsdon had already identified key boxes where she thought I should begin my research. She loaded my arms, then her own, with folders and showed me to a cubicle where I could read and flag items I wanted copied.

The hundreds of letters were organized by author and in chronological order.[2] The first folder contained letters from Ed to Helen and Annie. Most appeared to have been written to Helen, but the earliest was a March 1892 letter from Ed to Annie asking if Helen was giving thought to an earlier request from him to write "a little written account of her instruction" for the popular periodical he edited called the *Youth's Companion.*

I was thrilled to see for the first time the small, flowing handwriting of my great-great-grandfather, written on *Youth's Companion* letterhead. It was clear that Helen and her teacher were already acquainted with him, for he wrote, "You know me, I do not want a long story."

At this point in my research, I knew I would have time only to skim the dozens of letters before me, so I moved on. The next correspondence was from Ed, dated December 13, 1892, and addressed to "My dear Helen." The letter was long and chatty. He wrote about having received a "most pleasant and interesting little note" from her and then talked in charming detail about his children.

Those files provided the perfect starting point, but I would subsequently find countless other sources. The AFB documents led me to the Alexander Graham Bell Family Papers archived at the Library of Congress, which provided copies of many more letters and even more illuminating details. Joseph P. Lash's epic work, *Helen and Teacher,* and Kim E. Nielsen's 2009 biography of Annie Sullivan, *Beyond the Miracle Worker,* were both recommended by Helen Selsdon and served as important references, filling in critical story details not provided by the letters.

As a journalist for more than sixty years, Ed Chamberlin left a long and rich trail of his own. I was fortunate to have access to his autobiography covering his first eighteen years and a brief biography written by Samuel M. Waxman, both of which appeared posthumously in an anthology of Ed's *Boston Evening Transcript* columns called *Nomads and Listeners.* Online searches provided reprints of many of Ed's newspaper and magazine articles, as well as several of his published books. A number of biographies of the avant-garde artists and writers who frequented Red Farm mentioned the Chamberlin family and aspects of their life. The Perkins School Archive, with its carefully kept scrapbooks of over a hundred years of newspaper clippings, was also invaluable.

But the writer who gave the most consistent breadth and detail of life in the Chamberlin household was Helen Keller herself. She was a prolific and generous letter writer, and in reading her vivid descriptions it is easy to forget that she was deafblind. Words were everything to her; when spelled into her hand by her companions, they were her window to what was happening around her, and when spelled or written by her to others, they were her primary means for telling what she was thinking and feeling.

In Ed Chamberlin, a man she met when she was just eight years old, who lived "in the service of words" and cared deeply about people and social issues and the natural world, Helen found a most sympathetic and understanding friend, mentor, and advocate.

This is their story.

Letters from Red Farm

INTRODUCTION

At some point in time, the place became known as Red Farm. It was an idyllic spot, just a short train ride out from Boston, in the village of Wrentham, Massachusetts. In the late 1800s, it was a working farm situated on thirty or so acres of open fields that straddled the crest of a hill and overlooked a small lake called King Philip's Pond. The property featured a large, red-painted farmhouse with a wide front porch that commanded a clear view of the lake below. Multiple red barns and outbuildings peppered the property, and a tall windmill on scaffolding dominated the front yard. To the rear, a deep, vine-covered ravine dropped away from the house and main barn. Several large trees close to the house provided shade in summer months.

For those at Red Farm, it was little trouble to shift from farming pursuits to boating and swimming in summer, or ice skating and sledding in winter, simply by crossing the dirt lane in front of the house and strolling down the embankment to the lake. It was a perfect combination of waterfront resort and rural farm life.

Red Farm cast a spell over its residents and guests. Over many years, it was the gathering place for a lively and diverse crowd of intellectuals and creative minds—drawn to the location and the hospitality of Boston journalist Joseph Edgar Chamberlin, his wife Ida, and their children. Poets and writers, artists and musicians, naturalists, theologians, social reformers, and celebrities all flocked to Red Farm, captivated by its brilliant and stimulating atmosphere. Guests were invited to help with farm chores and meals if so inclined, before gathering in the evening for readings and performances by young and old alike—indoors in front of a large stone fireplace in cold weather or outside on the lawn in summer. Chamberlin presided over these assemblages, gently encouraging and mentoring aspiring or established writers, or reading his own works.

From about 1889 until 1901, Red Farm was the preferred weekend and holiday destination for arguably one of the most famous girls in the world: deafblind Helen Keller. She had come to Boston to attend the Perkins Institution for the Blind, the premier program for the deafblind in the United States, and she was a media sensation, with national and international newspaper and magazine coverage of her accomplishments.

So much has been written about Helen Keller, and the story of her early years is perhaps the best-known aspect of her life. She was born in 1880 in Tuscumbia, Alabama, and while exceptionally healthy in infancy, she contracted a serious illness at nineteen months of age that left her without the ability to see or hear. Also unable to speak, she showed her frustration at not being understood through violent tantrums, until her realization at the water pump on her parents' property—as water poured over her hand—that letters spelled into her hand were her teacher's attempt to communicate with her. Everything had a name. The realization electrified her and unlocked a desire to learn that was palpable and unquenchable.

Far fewer people know the history of how Helen was educated, first at Perkins and later at other private schools; how she excelled in school despite many obstacles and much systemic resistance; and how she went to Radcliffe—again, despite many barriers—and became a prolific writer on many subjects, often political and controversial. Most significantly, though, her strongest and most enduring work was as an advocate for people with disabilities, particularly those who were blind.

One cannot know Helen's story without knowing that of Annie Sullivan, the young woman who overcame extreme poverty and her own adversities and challenges to become Helen's lifelong teacher and companion, the woman who unlocked the mystery of language and communication for Helen through techniques learned at Perkins. The story of how Annie communicated the mystery of language to Helen was later immortalized in a Broadway play in 1959 and then in the 1962 movie *The Miracle Worker,* both starring Patty Duke as Helen and Anne Bancroft as Annie. Countless books have been written about Annie's life as well, and her name is synonymous with exemplary teaching, self-sacrifice, and devotion.

But history has a way of forgetting the modest and the humble, thus the role of Joseph Edgar Chamberlin in Helen's life is virtually unknown. When they met in 1888, he was already well known as "The Listener" columnist for the *Boston Evening Transcript* and as an editor for the nationally distributed *Youth's Companion* magazine. He was a gentle, self-educated man with formidable intelligence. One writer described Chamberlin as "a lay saint, beloved and venerated by all those with whom he came into contact. He was also something of a sage with his encyclopedic knowledge of history, arts and letters, and nature. . . . He had the soul of a poet and he gave a poetic touch to everything he said or wrote."[1]

To Helen, he was her "dear Uncle Ed," and to him she was "my dearest Helen." Over their forty years of friendship, Helen and Ed wrote many tributes to one another in personal letters, books, and periodicals. This book offers a new perspective on what is known about Helen, the child who captivated the world with her courage and determination in overcoming her disabilities, and explores her friendship with the man she met when she was eight years old and he was almost forty.

This retelling also brings Ed Chamberlin and his Red Farm world to life, largely through Helen's letters. Helen herself acknowledged that, like most journalists, Ed often preferred to remain anonymous, instead allowing his work to speak for itself, which it did with a voice and clarity that made him beloved and respected. But Helen also dearly wanted to immortalize the influence that "had sweetened her life" and the lives of others whom he mentored and helped to literary and artistic success.[2] With Helen's words as a guide, this work seeks to accomplish that.

The power of the written word to connect, enlighten, entertain, and persuade was Helen and Ed's shared delight.

But on July 6, 1935, at the age of eighty-three, Ed Chamberlin's pen finally halted, his kind and expansive heart ceased beating, and his restless soul found peace. In his final days, though not religious himself, he asked for his mother's Bible and her portrait and to be sung some of the German songs he had heard during his boyhood in Wisconsin. Even during those last days, he continued to write, dictating his thoughts when writing became too difficult.

Of the hundreds of condolence messages doubtless received from his wide circle of friends by his third wife and widow, Jenny

LeRoyer Chamberlin, the only one history preserves is the letter Helen wrote on July 7, the day after Ed's death. The letter begins,

Dear Aunt Jenny:

I received with tender sorrow, up here in the Catskills, the telegram with the news of dear Uncle Ed's death. When I last saw him, so brave and interested in everything, I could not think that he would leave us so soon. If I could take you and the others who loved him in my arms, you would feel the sympathy no words can utter. I realize that there can be no consolation for the loss of one whose life was a part of your own, but affection will speak—the affection my teacher and I have had for Uncle Ed during many years.

We remember how he always understood and appreciated us both. The tears come as I think how bound up he is with the fateful experience of our lives.[3]

PART I

CHAPTER ONE

The Road to Boston

By the time Joseph Edgar Chamberlin met young Helen Keller and her teacher Annie Sullivan, he had quietly and unintentionally become famous. Writers, artists, and thinkers of the day—both aspiring and established—wanted to know him, for in his roles as magazine editor, critic, and newspaper columnist, he had the ear of many, commanded a broad readership, and circulated among the wealthy and powerful of Boston and the Northeast.

Those roles brought Ed, as he was called by family and friends, into the social orbit of eight-year-old Helen Keller and Annie Sullivan, most likely sometime in the summer or autumn of 1888. Helen and Annie were already celebrities in local society and beyond. Truly, it seemed that all of Boston was clamoring for even a glimpse of the famous pair, and they were overwhelmed by invitations to teas and events.

Although no documents record details of their first meeting, Ed probably waited patiently in the background while others—many whom he knew—pressed forward to meet Helen and her remarkable teacher. Michael Anagnos, director of the Perkins Institution for the Blind, had offered to make the introduction and was eager for Chamberlin, the popular "Listener" columnist of the *Boston Evening Transcript,* to meet his school's new star.

From his vantage point near the back of the room, Ed would have been able to observe Helen with her glowing, inquisitive face that lit up as information was spelled into her hand. She was tall for her age and vigorous in appearance. Beside her, Annie was primly dressed and attentive. She was undoubtedly impatient at having to endure such an event in the name of fundraising for Perkins. Annie had no tolerance for what she called "witless dramas and social inanities."[1] Ed Chamberlin, a close observer of human nature, surely noticed her forced smile and impatient manner.

Upon introduction toward the end of the event, none among the three could possibly have foreseen a friendship that would reach forward more than four decades. It was an unlikely pairing: the balding, bespectacled father of five who was nearing forty, and the deafblind child and her twenty-two-year-old teacher. What made the friendship even more unlikely was that Ed was a newsman, a member of the species already making life difficult for Annie Sullivan.

But Ed's gentle and unassuming manner must have appealed to Annie. Even in early conversations, she likely found his family history of abolitionism and social activism significant, as she herself was outspoken on such topics and had quarreled with Keller family members about slavery and the Civil War soon after her arrival at the Keller home in Tuscumbia in 1886.[2] Indeed, Ed may originally have come to be familiar with Perkins because its founding director, Dr. Samuel Gridley Howe, in addition to his work in education, was an ardent abolitionist and had been one of the secret conspirators and supporters of the infamous John Brown prior to the Civil War. His example had inspired Ed's abolitionist parents and a generation of northern activists.

Ed Chamberlin's and Annie Sullivan's conversation might soon have turned to his home and family. The invitation for Helen and Annie to visit the Chamberlin home at Red Farm, any time, was almost certainly extended.

Ed and his wife Ida Atwood Chamberlin were not members of the semi-aristocracy of old, Harvard-educated Boston families called the Brahmin that had evolved by the late 1800s. They could, however, claim a legitimate American colonial pedigree, and they were well enough connected through Ed's position in the literary and intellectual community to feel comfortable in Boston society. Access to the Brahmin class, without actually belonging, enabled Ed to be an objective observer and narrator of life among the intelligentsia of the city. At the same time, he had a keen interest and heart for the poor and disadvantaged and could circulate in those quarters as well. Together, those attributes and opportunities allowed for a peripheral vantage point that suited him, and, according to his biographer Samuel M. Waxman, meant that Ed could "live in the world, but a little apart from it, as befits a listener who writes the record of an epoch with which he is not entirely in sympathy."[3]

Ed and Ida were both descended from families that were first established in Massachusetts in the early 1600s and later migrated to different towns in Vermont. Over generations, the families became established as citizens and leaders. Ed's was one of the founding families of the town of Newbury, Vermont, on the Connecticut River, having come there originally from Braintree, Massachusetts.

The day of the Chamberlins' arrival in Newbury in 1762 is recorded in subsequent written histories: "In June, one day about noon, came Richard Chamberlin and wife . . . in boats. Seven of their thirteen children came with their parents, the rest afterward. Before night they had erected a rude hut of posts and bark, in which they lived three months. A large stump in the middle, covered with a board, served for a table" until the family built a cabin that offered more protection.[4] Vermont was still a wilderness; "bear and wolf tracks in the snow greeted the family many mornings outside their cabin, and family members recalled that wolves would often lift the curtain that hung over the door and thrust their heads inside."[5] Ed's ancestors bought property, built homes, and prospered as farmers and tradesmen. Patriotism led his great-grandfather Joseph to serve as a soldier in the French and Indian War from 1757 to 1758 and to enlist as a minuteman in Captain Thomas Johnson's company from Newbury, serving at Ticonderoga and other locations during the Revolutionary War. He also held many "positions of trust" in the town.[6]

But the success of those early ancestors was not "universally repeated" by subsequent generations. As Ed wrote, "My forebears were all good people from the British Isles, and their offspring and the original immigrants had the good sense to settle in Massachusetts and Vermont until I was born on a shelf of fairly good ground gloriously overlooking the Connecticut River Valley and the White Mountains. I am proud of that, but it would have been better for me if my ancestors had had a keener faculty for picking up pounds, shillings, and pence."[7]

Born on August 6, 1851, Ed was by far the youngest of Abner and Mary Haseltine Chamberlin's seven surviving children. His eldest sister, Martha Ann, was twenty-four years old at the time of his birth. Of his parents, Ed wrote, "By the time I was born they had drifted to an old square house on a farm, whence they looked out on one of the loveliest panoramas of valley and mountain in the world; but it was a stony old farm, and my father developed there a hankering for some land where he could run his plough for as much as a few rods through clear mellow level ground, and where, when he went out to the barn in winter, he would not be up to his middle in snow."[8]

Ed was six years old in 1857 when his parents left Vermont and followed the railroad west to the town of Spring Prairie, near Burlington, Wisconsin, where an advance party of two older sons had found the land more hospitable for farming.[9] Many migrating Vermonters already had homes there. Not all the Chamberlin offspring made this westward journey; eldest son Preston was newly married and remained behind to start his own family. Another daughter, Adaline, was also married and stayed in Vermont.

The journey west required following seven rail lines that connected the country in short legs, with passengers switching trains many times. Ed later remembered that he spent nights sleeping with his head in his mother's lap. The last leg of the family's journey was conducted by covered wagon.

When he wrote of his family's new property in Wisconsin, Ed described it as "God's country" and "as near to Paradise as any life could be." Further, it was "a lovely land where all you had to do, in order to get along comfortably, which was all we had ever done, was to work hard."[10]

Ed was brought up immersed in the large, close-knit Chamberlin family's sense of social activism and community involvement. His father was a hardworking man, though gentle and amiable in spirit, who held several town offices and a position in the local militia. The family was Republican and staunchly abolitionist, even lodging itinerant speakers who came to the area to arouse opposition to slavery before the outbreak of the Civil War. Ed wrote passionately about his days as a watchful and attentive young boy among socially conscious adults:

Daily I heard talk of the wickedness of human slavery and the struggle among my countrymen to put an end to it; and I was drawn into keen sympathy with that struggle. I read, with eight- or ten-year-old eyes, the story of the captivity and sufferings of Uncle Tom, and my young heart alternately bled and was filled with the knowledge of the gathering cloud of war over the country. My father was an active anti-slavery man, according to his opportunities engaged in the propaganda work of the party which was bent on extinguishing the institution of slavery, and the names of Lincoln, Fremont, Greely, John Brown, and John C. Potter were those of the heroes whose fame nourished my childish passions. John C. Potter, the representative in Congress . . . came to our house to lodge on his speaking tours. It was a diet of fire and sword on which my soul was nourished.[11]

In his childhood home, Ed witnessed philosophical debates, became exposed to individuals from a variety of backgrounds, and developed an appreciation for keeping quiet and listening. He saw the adults around him resisting constrictive social structures and how those structures could be changed through political movements. Advocacy for a cause would come easily in the future to the boy raised in this atmosphere.

The family regularly attended services at Plymouth Congregational Church in nearby Burlington. Congregationalists across the country at that time were bound in the tenets of the antislavery movement, and support was particularly strong in Midwestern regions such as the Burlington area.[12] These were people of faith who believed in "activism against slavery versus just words."[13] Although the Underground Railroad network of safe houses, through which freedom-seeking African Americans were helped to reach safety in the northern United States and Canada, was of necessity highly secretive—and information remains scant and scattered to this day—historians acknowledge that the movement received substantial aid by emigration from New England homes to western prairies. It was probably no coincidence that the Chamberlins had moved to Burlington. While direct evidence does not exist as to their involvement in the Underground Railroad, the family was known to be committed to the cause and came from Newbury, Vermont, a town that was active on the network since it was strategically located on the Connecticut River, which divided Vermont and New Hampshire.[14] They had also uprooted their lives during this time of controversy and were now living on a major travel route known to be a Canadian-bound path of the Underground Railroad.[15]

Once war came, Ed's father, too old to join the military, did his part by serving as an enroller for the Burlington area, offering his own home as a mustering station. Three of Ed's older brothers, Preston, George, and Everett—twenty-nine, twenty-four, and twenty-two years old respectively at the start of the war—fought for the Union in Vermont and Wisconsin brigades. Preston and Everett were present but unharmed at the Battle of Gettysburg. While their Vermont brigade was, in Ed's words, "decimated in the front rank on Cemetery Hill," the brothers prior to the battle were deployed instead to defend a depot at the rear of the battlefield against an expected attack that never occurred, which probably saved their lives. The third brother, George, served in the malaria-ridden Neuse River basin of North Carolina throughout the war, guarding against Confederate blockade runners.[16] Young Ed spent anxious years at home with his mother and father, waiting for news from the front about his brothers.

During the war, the family openly gave refuge to a freedom-seeking enslaved person from Mississippi named Job. Everett Chamberlin, then a captain with a Wisconsin regiment, was encamped in Tennessee when he met Job. "Finding the man, who was forty years old, evidently a good and steady man," Everett gave him train fare to Wisconsin to work with Abner Chamberlin, for whom help had grown scarce on the farm. Job lived with the Chamberlin family and ate at their table. Young Ed worked side by side with Job in the fields, listening to tales and songs of the plantation and trying without success to teach the eager man to read. At war's end, with three hundred dollars of savings given to him by Ed's mother, Job departed for Mississippi and was not heard from again, but Ed learned much through the experience, saying later, "Job taught more than he was taught."[17]

At last the "war wore to an end," and shortly afterward the news reached the family that President Abraham Lincoln had been shot. Ed was working in a field with his father when they were told of the assassination.[18] He was devastated, writing that "for the patriotic young boy, the tragedy quite equaled what the loss of a brother would have been. It was a sorrow profound and ineffaceable. The April anniversary each year ever brought back tears and renewed its pang."[19]

Ed's three brothers survived the war, though, as he wrote, "they suffered physically for their service for the remainder of their lives." He described his brother George as "wrecked in health" from malaria contracted in the swamps of North Carolina. Still, all would return to civilian life and do their part to contribute to the good of society: George became a newspaperman in Minnesota and then served in the Minnesota House of Representatives until poor health forced him to return to Vermont and his extended family in 1893. Preston became a Vermont legislator. Everett, the youngest Chamberlin to serve, had been a teacher before the war but returned to become city editor of the *Milwaukee Sentinel.* He moved to Chicago for editorial work with the *Chicago Evening Post* prior to 1868.[20]

Life was difficult for the Chamberlin family on the edge of the frontier, "dominated by hard and necessary work, but was not without its rewards." Ed described hunting small game, skating on frozen rivers, and "pulling bass and pickerel out of glassy lakes in the woods" with his friends, while covered wagons of emigrants heading west rattled past the family's door.[21]

His mother Mary's strict Puritan understanding of the Bible also influenced him spiritually, though not in ways she had intended. He respected her intelligence and deep knowledge and spent many hours listening to her debates with the family's frequent clerical and political guests. A debate between Mary and a visitor over the doctrine of "infinite punishment for finite sin" caused Ed eventually to reject her faith, though he allowed that his mother had been "the superior reasoner and a clever disputant."[22]

Early on, she had marked Ed for a future as a preacher. At her knee, he learned "all the particulars of the Puritan Theology, including the peril of eternal torment," but he could not accept the harsh, unforgiving doctrine of Calvinism and believed it was "altogether probable that daily respectful association with one to whom this peril seemed to have no terrors, to wit, with his father, had an effect to lighten the burden of the fear of hell." Unlike his wife, Ed's father "had never worried about his soul or taken any interest in theology, always attended the church services, and generally slept amiably and silently through the sermon."[23] Ed's job was to wake him if he began to snore.

Hardworking German immigrant families also populated the Burlington area. In his autobiography, Ed told of listening every day "to the talk of the German hired men, most of whom were peasants but some few of whom had been students and all of whom could sing songs."[24] He would hum or whistle those songs to himself to his dying day.

Throughout his childhood and into his youth, Ed attended school in a one-room schoolhouse near his home, where he excelled in every subject except math. With the anticipated departure of their last child from home, his parents moved in 1867 from their farm outside of town into Burlington proper, where they purchased and ran the multistory Chamberlin Hotel. Longing to become a teacher, Ed dreamed of attending nearby Beloit College, but by the time he reached the age of seventeen, the family's fortunes did not allow it. He was bitterly disappointed.

Ed eventually "cast his lot," as he said, with his older brother Everett, now established in Chicago as a newsman. Everett was the editor of the musical and dramatic sections of the *Chicago Evening Post,* and through his help, Ed was offered entry-level work as a proofreader's "holder." He left home in a blizzard one December morning in 1868 and took the train "for good and all, for Chicago and the service of the press."[25]

Referring to himself in the third person, Ed described his early days in the newspaper business:

It was not much, that job in the EVENING POST, *but something to begin with. The boy sat at a table in a dark room up against a gaslight, with a green shade over his eyes, and held the copy, which meant that the proof-reader read aloud what was in the proofs, while the "holder" followed the copy and called out when there was any deviation. Sometimes for a change, he read the copy, instead of the reader reading the proof, and he had to read it rapidly and accurately. To the boy, it was agreeable work. It was the service of words, and it poured the story of the world daily into his brain. On the side, it was part of the boy's duty, when the paper went to press, to descend to the press room and get a dozen of the first copies that came off the press and carry them upstairs to the editors. This was a glorious duty, for it brought the boy into daily contact with the editor and the editorial writers and established an acquaintance, of some sort, with them.*[26]

Although he was denied the opportunity to attend college, Ed now demonstrated a zeal for learning that would define his life, writing of himself, "When a boy passionately desires an education, unquestionably he obtains it in some sort, college or no college." In his free time, he took advantage of the resources of the newly opened Chicago Public Library to obtain a self-guided, classical education: "The books of the world were at the boy's command, and he conducted courses of reading for himself with many authors as his teachers."[27]

Ed also began to write everything he could think of to offer to the editor of the paper. He ultimately believed that "it was probably a matter of personal favor to his brother that now and then one of the boy's pieces was printed." Regardless, before his eighteenth birthday he was transferred from the proof-room to the news desk, launching his career as a newspaperman. He was now what he called "an apprentice in the service of words."[28]

In addition to the opportunity to work with his brother, the *Evening Post* also brought Ed into a collegial relationship with another reporter and native Vermonter named Charles Atwood, already a friend of Everett and a man who would figure prominently in Ed's professional and personal life.

Ed's adopted city was infinitely different from the small towns of his rural upbringing, and Ed's fresh eyes took it all in. Over 300,000 inhabitants made Chicago home in 1870, many of them immigrants. It was a booming city of busy streets, railroad yards, and ships in port, of tenements as well as grand mansions, all overcast by the stench of slaughterhouses and a polluted river.

The vibrancy of life in Ed's new city also brought hazards. Shortly after his move to the *Evening Post* news desk, the cub reporter was singularly launched in his chosen career by an epic disaster: the Great Fire of 1871.

Thanks to a dangerous mix of wooden buildings, kerosene lanterns, and a steady wind, fires were a near-daily occurrence in Chicago in the mid-1800s. These were generally managed by local fire brigades until the inauspicious date of Sunday, October 8, 1871, during a drought year, when a fire ignited at 137 De Koven Street around 8:30 p.m. A series of errors and missteps meant the city fire department's response was confused and delayed. By ten o'clock, the blaze was out of control.

Ed's accounts of the Great Chicago Fire were the first to go out to the world, as he was at the scene in a few minutes. He described the involved part of town as "thickly studded with one-story frame dwellings, cow stables, pig sties, corncribs, sheds innumerable; every wretched building within four feet of its neighbor, and everything of wood."[29] Fanned by strong winds, the fire grew rapidly and residents began to panic and flee. By midnight, crowds jammed the thoroughfares. The raging fire leapt the Chicago River. Gasworks exploded. Bridges presumed safe began to burn and became impassable.

Throughout the night, the fire consumed the city. By daylight, residents had fled east as far as they could go to the edge of Lake Michigan, with "people, belongings, and animals trapped on the shoreline."[30] Behind them, Michigan Avenue blazed. North Side residents moved en masse toward the prairie. At daylight, the center of the city was in rubble, the ground too hot to stand on. Fires still burned on the North Side.

The Great Fire continued unabated into the next day. By noon, federal troops led by General Philip Sheridan began blowing up buildings, hoping to halt the inferno's progress. The townspeople streamed north, ahead of the blaze. Twenty-four hours after it began, there was no rest. Citizens later reported feeling the heat of the monumental blaze at their backs as they evacuated.

Through it all, Ed worked tirelessly, constantly in harm's way, to report from the scene. His firsthand experiences and vivid descriptions would make his accounts crucial to the historical record.

Like those around him, Ed was breathing in scorching hot air and running for his life. He observed, "The noise of the conflagration was terrific. To the roar which the simple process of combustion always makes, magnified here to so grand an extent, was added the crash of falling buildings and the constant explosions of stores of oil and other like material. The noise of the crowd was nothing compared with this chaos of sound. All these things—the great, dazzling, mounting light, the crash and roar of the conflagration, and the desperate flight of the crowd—combined to make a scene of which no intelligent idea can be conveyed in words."[31]

Finally, rain fell "on Monday night, extinguishing some of The Fire, which eventually died out. The scale of devastation was enormous." In the end, 73 miles of city streets and over 17,000 buildings were destroyed. Deaths numbered between two and three hundred. An estimated ninety thousand people—a third of the population—were left homeless.[32]

The Great Fire was a pivotal point in Chicago's history, but while agonizing and destructive for most, ironically for Ed Chamberlin it provided an opportunity to ascend to the next level of the newspaper industry. His name was now widely known.

Following the fire, Ed moved briefly to Indianapolis to work as city editor of the *Daily Journal,* but a few months later he returned to work as assistant editor for the *Chicago Times.* Ed's friend Charles Atwood was now working for that paper as the night editor. And Atwood happened to have a lovely daughter named Ida.

On June 26, 1873, at the age of twenty-two, Ed married sixteen-year-old Ida Elizabeth Atwood at the home of her father. Details of the afternoon event were reported in the *Chicago Sunday Times,* which noted that "the groom and father of the bride are both well-known in local newspaper circles, and the good wishes of the fraternity will be united with those of . . . other friends in wishing the pair a smooth and merry voyage over the sea matrimonial." The couple then took the northern-bound train over the Chicago and Northwestern Road for a "brief bridal tour."[33]

A small, wood-framed studio photograph of Ida taken by a Chicago photographer around the time of the marriage portrays a pretty, fair-haired young woman with elegantly coiffed hair, fashionably dressed in a light-colored jacket with braided trim and a modest ruffled blouse. She wears several brooches and necklaces over her jacket and a small locket on a thin black ribbon around her neck.

Ida was very proud of her American colonial lineage. The first Atwood on record in America came on the *Mayflower,* with others following thereafter. Ida's great-great-great-grandfather George Hammond had served in the Revolutionary War as commander of a company of volunteers from Plymouth, Kingston, and Duxbury, Massachusetts.[34]

Ida's father, Charles Atwood, was born in 1833 in Barnard, Vermont, the third of twelve children. The Atwoods loved literature and the arts, and it was a boisterous and loving household in which nearly everyone played musical instruments.[35]

An attractive man with many talents, Charles moved to Bay City, Michigan, in his early twenties to teach music. There, in 1855, he married Helen Beebe, whose parents were also from Vermont. Their daughter, Ida, was born in 1856. By 1859, Charles was serving as the first recorder of the newly established Bay County. Life progressed contentedly for the young Atwood family until 1861, when Helen Beebe Atwood died, leaving behind her husband and five-year-old Ida.

On April 18, 1865, when Ida was nine, Charles married a twenty-five-year-old Irish-born woman named Sophia Gilman, with whom he would have five more children over the next thirteen years. Soon after their marriage, the couple moved with young Ida to Chicago, where Charles began work for the *Evening Post* as a reporter, bringing him into a close working relationship with the established writer and editor Everett Chamberlin.

When Everett's youngest brother, Ed, also joined the paper in 1868, the three developed a strong friendship. Their offices were located on Randolph Street in the business district of Chicago in a "dingy basement, in the front part of which was located the business office, and in the rear the editorial, the news and the press departments, jumbled together in one confused mass." With a new owner in 1865, the *Post* expanded to another floor along Dearborn Street to house the massive printing press, which Ed described as a "magical apparatus of public intelligence."[36]

In 1870, Charles Atwood moved on from the *Post* to become an editor for the *Chicago Times*, a paper with a Vermont-born owner named Wilbur F. Storey.[37]

The move to Chicago with his new wife and daughter around 1865 also brought Charles Atwood closer to his own extended family: his younger sister Nancy Ann had married fellow Vermonter Albert Arnold Sprague three years earlier and moved to Chicago with her husband. Their household was vibrant and social and focused on a love of music and the arts. Charles's and Nancy's youngest sister, Lucia, eventually married Albert Sprague's younger brother Otho, and they too moved to Chicago.

Albert and Otho Sprague, along with their partner Ezra J. Warner, built the highly successful Sprague, Warner & Co. grocery business, and the families became some of the wealthiest in Chicago. Nancy Ann and Albert Sprague's mansion, with its turreted brick and stone exterior on Chicago's Gold Coast, was designed by the renowned architect Charles Burnham.[38] Nancy Ann would eventually leave behind a philanthropic legacy across the Midwest and northeastern United States through countless major contributions to health care and the arts. The Albert Arnold Sprague Memorial Hall, her gift in 1917 to her husband's alma mater, Yale University, still stands today and has nurtured generations of students in the Yale School of Music. Their daughter, Elizabeth Sprague Coolidge, was a concert pianist and generous patron of the arts who left her own lasting legacy. Equally wealthy were the Otho Spragues. Their daughter, Lucy Sprague Mitchell, eventually founded what became the Bank Street College of Education in New York City.

Nancy Ann Sprague was described by one of her daughter's biographers as having had "an abundance of executive energy and an uninhibited tongue."[39] She would play a vital role in Ida Atwood's life as a mother figure and generous and affectionate "Aunt Nan."

Thus, young Ida was privileged to spend her later childhood and adolescence in the embrace of her large, wealthy, socially connected, and confident extended family in Chicago, finally coming into the orbit of her future husband, Ed Chamberlin.

With his marriage to the lively and sociable Ida Atwood, daughter of a friend, colleague, and mentor, Ed's personal and professional lives were now densely intertwined.

Chicago journalism was a tough and grinding world in the 1870s, with newsmen working long hours and tirelessly striving to gain a competitive edge over rival newspapers. But the first few years after his marriage to Ida were promising for Ed. His solid career at the *Times* allowed the couple to purchase a home in the up-and-coming neighborhood of Irving Park. Soon Ida was expecting their first child, Helen, who was born in 1874.

Unfortunately, the bright glow of Ed and Ida's early family life was shortly cast into shadow. Everett Chamberlin left the *Post* in Chicago to work at the *Tribune* before ultimately joining Ed and Charles Atwood at the *Times.* After the Great Fire, he had published his first book, a compilation with Elias Colbert entitled *Chicago and the Great Conflagration.* But in 1873, "compelled by delicate health to relinquish all editorial work," he went to California, then Colorado, and finally Florida in quest of better health. He died on February 19, 1875, of tuberculosis, leaving behind a wife and four children.[40]

Ed's beloved older brother Everett, the Civil War veteran and accomplished writer, the role model and brilliant personality whom Ed described as the "torchbearer of his generation," had died. Ed would speak with sadness about the "prince" of the family, "to them like an angel or prophet. When he died at age thirty-six, it seemed to us that the light of our life had gone out, that our star had been extinguished in abiding gloom."[41]

Everett's passing marked the first of several years of sadness and loss in Ed and Ida's life together. That same year, Ed's oldest sister, Martha Ann, died in Minnesota. In September 1877,

Ed's mother died after a long illness at the age of sixty-nine. A few months later, Ed's father moved back to Vermont, where his son Preston and daughter Adaline had remained two decades earlier. The Chamberlin family compass was slowly shifting back toward the east.

There was one bright spot for Ed and Ida during this dark time: in September 1876, they had their first son, named Charles after Ida's father and called Charley by the family. While outwardly healthy during his first few months, Charley would terrify his doting parents before his first birthday by developing a syndrome called marasmus, a wasting disease. Mysteriously but fortuitously, the disease resolved itself and in time he was restored to health.[42]

The years leading up to 1880 continued to be difficult for Ed as work pressures mounted. This was a very challenging time to be working for the *Times*. As historian Justin E. Walsh described it, "The ten years between 1871 and 1881 marked the wildest period in the stormy career of its owner Wilbur F. Storey, and in American journalism."[43]

After losing his wife in January 1873, Wilbur Storey fell into a deep depression that led many to believe he suffered from early dementia. He began to find ways to attack institutions in Chicago on a daily basis: "During that decade the *Chicago Times* established a tyranny throughout Cook County and beyond, crucifying politicians, the medical profession, the law, and the judicial system and private reputations with total abandon."[44]

Walsh's extensive history of Storey's tenure notes, "In the spring of 1875, there were so many libel cases pending against the *Times* that an exact count cannot be determined."[45] Each new sensation caused a ripple through Chicago, and the counter paper, the *Tribune*, worked to respond to every attack. The war among the papers was waged on a daily basis.

Even as the *Times* was criticized, it grew "increasingly bolder with shock and sensation. It pioneered in its approach to news and features, making it one of the most advanced journals of the day." Despite so many controversies, the paper and its popularity soared. In 1876, what became known as "The Alice Early Libel Suit" against the paper involved Charles Atwood, who published a false story after believing he recognized the signatures of three gentlemen he knew on letters detailing the "seduction of a young lady by a prominent citizen." Although the *Times* immediately issued an apology after discovering that the signatures were forged, the article spurred a major lawsuit and trial that carried on for three years and caused significant personal embarrassment for Atwood.[46]

By 1876, Storey, suffering from documented dementia, began to back off from his executive role. In early 1880, he suffered a stroke and officially left the paper. His departure occurred simultaneously with other major events in Ed's life and perhaps helped hasten a personal crisis for Ed.

In 1879, Ed and Ida adopted a son, Philip.[47] This event was soon overshadowed, however, when in August 1880, Ida's father and Ed's colleague, Charles Atwood, passed away at the age of forty-seven.

Ed, now almost thirty years old, experienced a physical and emotional crisis that his biographer described in later years as a "nervous breakdown," as the accumulated stress of work, the death of his father-in-law and friend, and other familial losses finally caught up with him. As his biographer related, "He was not the stuff of which managing editors are made. His gentle, sensitive soul, housed in a delicate body, made him suffer keenly while he held this position, and a nervous breakdown taught him that he could not be happy holding executive positions on large newspapers."[48]

Ed's career path was irrevocably altered. The theme of loss, overwork, exhaustion, crisis, and "escape" would be repeated throughout his life—and he never again sought a role as an executive manager of a large paper. The emotional breakdown spurred the young family to leave Chicago and, as Ed's father had done several years previously, move eastward.

For Ida, the move from Chicago meant leaving her extended family—with aunts, uncles, and cousins in close proximity—and its accompanying social whirl. She left behind many memories, as well as the home she and Ed had established in Irving Park.

After leaving Chicago, Ed sought newspaper positions that were more literary than executive. Over the next seven years, he served as editor at small papers such as the *Daily Herald* of Newport,

Rhode Island, and the *Daily News* of Fall River, Massachusetts. Eventually he settled in Boston, where he began working as an editor for the *Evening Record* and *Daily Advertiser*.[49]

In 1887, Ed joined the *Boston Evening Transcript* as a writer and columnist. At the time, it was the largest daily paper in New England, having grown in stature and importance from its "tentative" first issue in 1830, when Boston was a busy but small port city with just over sixty thousand residents, sailing ships dotting the harbor, and "air teeming with great ideas." By the 1880s, the paper had a printing press that was capable of turning out five thousand papers in an hour and informed a city of more than 350,000 that was "the community of Emerson, of Longfellow, of Holmes, of Hawthorne, and of the old mercantile families [of] genteel Boston." The *Transcript* "was a force, as well as a delight, in an environment which was itself a power in the nation and the world."[50]

At the *Transcript,* Ed wrote a daily column called "The Listener." This was divided into "The Listener in the Town," which featured astute and sensitive observations of human nature and life in the city, and "The Listener in the Country," which allowed him to share his love for and observations of nature. Many years later, he would add "The Nomad" on topics of travel and politics to his regular columns. The paper was published each afternoon except Sunday. As a distinguished "newspaper of record," it had a large circulation, and its editorial writing and newsgathering were considered authoritative and of the highest standard.

The *Transcript* offices were located at the corner of Washington and Milk Streets, in the area of town known as "Newspaper Row." The granite, mansard-roofed, five-story building anchored one end of the lineup of other prominent newspapers of the time, including the *Boston Globe, Boston Post,* and *Boston Journal.* The latest news was delivered daily to the populace from Washington Street, with information exchanged among those on the street. It was a noisy, bustling part of town on an average day, and even more so when some particular report of events or elections was expected. Then, large crowds gathered on the street outside the newspaper offices, with breaking news often posted on large blackboards or broadcast via megaphone before the papers were printed and distributed.[51]

In addition, Ed soon began working for the *Youth's Companion* as associate editor. He considered this editorial work and writing to be his principal job. The *Companion* had recently changed from a youth-oriented periodical to a more entertaining and family-oriented focus. The new iteration was touted as "An illustrated Family Paper published every Thursday of the year," and its masthead read, "The Best of American Life in Fiction, Fact, and Comment." The *Youth's Companion* was "temperate," advocating against the use of alcohol.[52]

The journal's change in focus resulted in an exponential increase in circulation. It became a leading national magazine by the 1890s, featuring articles over the years by such still recognizable names as Grover Cleveland, Theodore Roosevelt, and Booker T. Washington. It also helped establish Mark Twain, Emily Dickinson, Jack London, and others as popular writers. In September 1892, *Youth's Companion* first published the Pledge of Allegiance by staff writer Francis Bellamy, as part of a campaign to promote American flags in public schools. The magazine was published by the Perry Mason Company, which author Erle Stanley Gardner, an avid reader of the periodical as a youth, later borrowed for the name of his famous fictional attorney.[53]

Working for both the *Transcript* and *Youth's Companion,* Ed had a uniquely influential role. His positions as writer and editor enabled him to guide contemporary thought, garner support for large and small social causes, and gain access to significant people of the day. Having been raised in an unusual circle of men and women of strength and conviction, he was not intimidated by social status or position. Among his own parents and older siblings he could count town leaders, legislators, and newspaper editors. In his childhood home he had listened with rapt and objective attention to nationally known politicians, heroes, social agitators, and theologians.

Ed possessed a rare, innate ability to see all sides of any conflict, though he tended to side with the apparent targets of criticism. It was this compassionate and objective nature that ruled his life. His gentle manner and tone were advantageous and effective tools in service of his work. As the *Transcript*'s "Listener," he could write on any topic he chose, couched as observations about people, places, social phenomena, and the human condition. He also helped shape the content and commentary that families across the United States read weekly in the *Youth's Companion.*

The self-educated, Vermont-born boy, raised in a patriotic, abolitionist household in the woodlands of Wisconsin, had paid his dues in the hardscrabble journalism world of a major Midwestern city and worked his way from there to the top echelon of literary circles on the East Coast. He had become an established thought leader for New England society and beyond.

Ed and Ida set up household in the Boston area, first in Somerville, where their daughter Elisabeth was born in February 1886. Another daughter, Corda, would arrive three years later, making the Chamberlins a family of seven, with three girls and two boys. They also resided in Medford and for a time in Newton Lower Falls.

Although his career brought him a measure of success, above all else Ed considered himself a family man, and he loved nothing better than to be at home reading to his children.[54] Ed and Ida adhered to progressive ideals of childrearing in which family time together was focused on the children.[55] They had both grown up accustomed to large extended family circles and frequent houseguests of many backgrounds.

In their home, Ed and Ida merged the best experiences of their own childhoods, and children were always included in adult gatherings. Ed described the proud experience of watching their son Charley entertain their friends: "Even in his childhood, he was a fit companion of mature minds—an exceptional writer and inventor of fairy tales. His improvisations of stories, in the group of writing people who came to our house, were sometimes an astonishment; original and thrilling, they enraptured his audiences, while his dark eyes blazed with the fire of composition." Further, Charley was a leader among his age-mates and companions at home, and "when Charley led, the sport was new, original and on a grand scale."[56]

It was into the boisterous, nurturing, and inclusive atmosphere of the Chamberlin home that Helen Keller and Annie Sullivan were welcomed and embraced.

CHAPTER TWO

Helen and Annie

The year 1880, when Ed and Ida returned to the East, was also an auspicious one in the lives of Helen Keller and Annie Sullivan.

Helen Keller was born in Tuscumbia, Alabama, on June 27, 1880, the first child of Captain Arthur Keller and his wife, Kate. That same year, fourteen-year-old Annie Sullivan was rescued from a squalid existence in an almshouse in Tewksbury, Massachusetts, and allowed to attend the Perkins Institution for the Blind in South Boston.

An orphan who had spent four years at Tewksbury after she and her younger brother Jimmie were abandoned by her widowed father, Annie had suffered from trachoma, a bacterial infection, and resulting near-blindness since childhood. When Frank B. Sanborn, the Massachusetts state inspector of charities, visited Tewksbury in 1880, Annie saw her opportunity and threw herself at his feet, beseeching him to release her from the almshouse and send her to school.

Sanborn was a close friend of Perkins's late founder, Dr. Samuel Gridley Howe. A bold and compassionate man, Sanborn must have seen something promising in the sobbing girl with afflicted eyes, as he then used his influence to convince the current director of Perkins, Howe's Greek-born son-in-law Michael Anagnos, to accept Annie as a pupil. She was discharged from Tewksbury in February 1880 and enrolled at Perkins later that year.[1] Once there, Annie's eyesight was partially restored through several operations and she began her formal education. She was feisty, ignorant of manners, and frequently rude to her teachers. Still, though years behind her peers, she caught up to them, excelling and graduating as valedictorian of her class six years later through sheer determination. Anagnos described her accomplishment, writing, "She was obliged to begin her education at the lowest and most elementary point; but she showed from the start that she had in herself the force and capacity which insure success."[2]

Howe had opened the New England Institution for the Education of the Blind, the first such school in the United States, in his father's house in 1832. A year later it was renamed the Perkins Institution when Boston financier and merchant Thomas H. Perkins offered his large home for the school. Howe, a Harvard-trained physician, fiery mercenary soldier, and revolutionary in many arenas, had returned from years abroad in Greece and France with a passion to improve the lives of blind and deaf children in America through instructional techniques he had observed in France. He developed an embossed alphabet called Boston Line Type in 1835, and then commissioned a printer, Samuel Preston Ruggles, to design a press that could produce embossed books in Line Type which could be read by people who were blind.[3] In 1837, he began working with a deafblind girl named Laura Bridgman and successfully taught her to communicate and gain significant education, an accomplishment that attracted much attention, including, years later, that of Alexander Graham Bell, inventor of the telephone and a noted expert on matters related to the deaf.[4] As Helen Keller would write many years later, Howe, Bell, and other Perkins leaders "transmuted their pity of their fellow-citizens . . . into a sense of responsibility for their rehabilitation. Their activities brought new hope to the blind and the deaf."[5]

Others noted these accomplishments as well: following a visit to America in 1842, the British author Charles Dickens wrote about Bridgman and the work being done at Perkins in his book *American Notes.* He described her as having been left "blind, deaf, and dumb; destitute of smell; and nearly so, of taste" from childhood illnesses and a raging fever that had all resolved by the time she was four years old but left her in a "bewildered" state. During his visit to Perkins, Dickens described her as "radiant with intelligence and pleasure."[6] He found her case extraordinary, and his account was widely read on both sides of the Atlantic.

In 1886, more than twenty years after first publication of the article in *American Notes,* Kate Keller sought the same sort of miracle. She read Dickens's description of Bridgman's transformation at Perkins and also of the work of Dr. Bell.[7] She was desperate to find help for her daughter Helen, who was now deafblind. The Keller family had been dealing with the challenges of Helen's disabilities since early 1882, when the nineteen-month-old toddler was stricken with a high fever, called at the time a "congestion of the brain," that left her without the ability to see or hear. The family contacted Bell in Washington, DC, hoping he could help.

The Keller family was not wealthy, having suffered like many southern landowners following the Civil War. Arthur Keller had been a paymaster in the Confederate Army and was then variously employed in printing, lumber, and cattle before being appointed as U.S. marshal in 1885, which then provided a steady but modest income.[8] He also owned a local weekly newspaper, the *North Alabamian*. He was a widower with two sons and twenty years older than his second wife, Kate, who had been a pampered Memphis belle before her marriage to Keller and was ill-prepared for life on a working farm in a small town in Alabama. She was described as "an aloof person, very private, fastidious, whom an error of taste offended more than a real fault." But with another baby, named Mildred, born in 1886, she had begun "to press her husband that something must be done for Helen as her thwarted passion to communicate produced increasingly violent tantrums."[9]

Thus, in the summer of 1886, Captain Keller traveled with six-year-old Helen to Washington to meet Bell, who found "the evidently intelligent child" an "interesting case" and suggested the Kellers contact Perkins for a teacher for Helen.[10]

Keller wrote to Michael Anagnos, asking if he could recommend a teacher for his daughter. Anagnos responded on August 16 that Keller's description of Helen reminded him "forcibly of Laura Bridgman," and "it would give him great pleasure to aid in securing the services of a competent person to give [Helen] the necessary instruction." He asked Keller, however, to first describe "what compensation he could provide."[11] Keller responded that he could offer twenty-five dollars per month and board.[12]

Anagnos wrote again on January 21, 1887, that he had found "an excellent and most reliable guide" for the Kellers.[13] He chose Annie Sullivan, one of Perkins's recent graduates, to go to the Keller home to work with Helen. As an orphan without family to return to, and with limited professional opportunities available to a young woman at the time, Annie had few prospects after graduation, so she took the Keller family posting.

During Annie's education at Perkins, she had known of the methods of Dr. Howe. Upon acceptance of the Kellers' offer and prior to going to Alabama, she studied the methods with a new purpose—in particular the manual alphabet originally developed for deaf people in which letters are spelled into the palm of the hand. She also lived briefly in the house at Perkins where the adult Laura Bridgman resided, in order to further master Howe's techniques.[14]

Annie left for Tuscumbia believing she was prepared for her young pupil.

On March 3, 1887, after an exhausting journey of several days by train, Annie arrived at the Keller home. She described her first encounter with Helen in a letter to Anagnos written three days after her arrival:

Somehow I expected to see a pale, delicate child—I suppose I got the idea from Dr. Howe's description of Laura Bridgman when she came to the Institution. But there's nothing pale or delicate about Helen. She is large, strong, and ruddy, and as unrestrained in her movements as a young colt. She has none of those nervous habits that are so noticeable and so distressing in blind children. Her body is well formed and vigorous, and Mrs. Keller says that she has not been ill a day since the illness that deprived her of her sight and hearing. . . . Her face is hard to describe. It is intelligent, but lacks mobility, or soul, or something. . . . You see at a glance that she is blind. One eye is larger than the other, and protrudes noticeably. She rarely smiles; indeed, I have seen her smile only once or twice since I came.

One thing that impresses everybody is Helen's tireless activity. She is never still a moment. She is here, there, and everywhere. Her hands are in everything; but nothing holds her attention for long. Dear child, her restless spirit gropes in the dark. Her untaught, unsatisfied hands destroy everything they touch because they do not know what else to do with things.[15]

It soon became apparent that Annie's first challenge with Helen was to figure out how to "discipline and control her without breaking her spirit."[16] She wrote to Anagnos after one week in the household, "I find considerable trouble in controlling her. She has always done just as her fancy inclined and it is next to impossible to make her obey. However I think I shall succeed."[17]

The Keller family balked at Annie's corrective approach to her pupil—an approach that included slapping—but Annie insisted her method was essential to Helen's education. It took some time to convince the Kellers that it was necessary, but Annie was able to retreat with Helen to a small cottage on the family property where the pair could live by themselves without the interference of her parents. After several more weeks of struggle and frustration, in a dramatic moment at the water pump, a breakthrough occurred, and the dark and silent world in which Helen existed was breached through the manual alphabet. Helen suddenly understood that her teacher was trying to communicate with her: letters that formed words were being spelled into her hand.

In April, barely more than a month after her arrival, Annie wrote to Anagnos:

I see an improvement in Helen from day to day, almost from hour to hour. Everything must have a name now. Wherever we go, she asks eagerly for the names of things she has not learned at home. She is anxious for her friends to spell, and eager to teach the letters to every one she meets. She drops the signs and pantomime she used before, as soon as she has words to supply in their place, and the acquirement of a new word affords her the liveliest pleasure. And we notice that her face grows more expressive each day.[18]

On May 23, Annie provided another update for Anagnos, writing, "My little pupil can now read every word she can spell, and spends hours each day finding them in her books. When she touches a word she knows her face grows radiant, and if by any chance she finds part of a sentence that conveys any meaning to her mind her joy is unbounded."[19]

Soon after, on June 2, Annie again wrote to Anagnos. She was becoming concerned about the fame that was developing around her pupil: "Already people are taking a deep interest in Helen. No one can see her without being impressed. She is no ordinary child, and people's interest in her education will be no ordinary interest. Therefore let us be exceedingly careful what we say and write about her. I shall write freely to you and tell you everything, on one condition. It is this: you must promise never to show my letters to any one. My beautiful Helen shall not be transformed into a prodigy if I can help it."[20]

Annie's fears were well founded. The news media was fascinated with Helen and fed the public's thirst with frequent reports on her activities and schooling. Many of the reports absurdly exaggerated her successes.

Affection between Helen and Annie was also growing. By early May, Annie reported to Anagnos that Helen was becoming attached to her and she could "see that she obeys more from love than because she thinks she must."[21] Later in life, Helen would describe her love for Annie at that time "as a child's for its mother—innocent and unconditional." Although she could not see Annie, Helen developed a mental picture of her that was confirmed by the descriptions of others. According to Helen, she "loved to put [her] hand on [Annie's] face, it was so beautifully expressive, sensitive, and alive with interest in people and things. An adorable, wistful sweetness imprinted its loveliness upon her mouth, and my frequent childish kisses and her eager response, remembered, warm me like sparks nurtured in the embers."[22]

For Annie, Helen satisfied emotional needs for love and purpose. She had lost the only remaining person who mattered in her life, her younger brother Jimmie, when he died shortly after their arrival as orphans at the Tewksbury Almshouse. Now experiencing the unconditional love of Helen, Annie noted, "It is a great thing to feel that you are necessary to somebody. Helen's dependence on me for almost everything makes me strong and glad."[23]

Over the next year, under Annie's tutelage, Helen's knowledge of the world grew exponentially and she demonstrated precocious mastery of academic subjects. Anagnos and others followed Helen's progress from afar with great interest, and Annie made regular reports by letter. Some of these were published by Anagnos in Perkins newsletters and reports. Despite Annie's request for confidentiality, he could not resist the publicity her success could garner for his school, and as a former journalist himself prior to coming to the United States with Howe, he knew how to use the media to advantage.[24]

Anagnos was eager for Annie and her young pupil to come to Boston so he might feature them among New England society. A visit for Helen, Annie, and Kate Keller was arranged for late May 1888. Seven-year-old Helen's childish anticipation and unbridled excitement were palpable in her later description of the trip:

At last the time came for us to leave for Boston. I had talked incessantly about Boston for three weeks, since I was told we were really going to Boston. Boston was at the beginning or end of every sentence. Boston was the Land of Promise—the place where I knew I would meet many little blind girls who could spell on their fingers. . . .

On the eventful day of our departure I followed my mother and Miss S. about the house. . . .

I kept running out to the yard where the carriage was, to see if old Charlie was hitched up. After what seemed ages . . . old Joe . . . carried the trunks out to the mule-wagon, and I followed them, most certainly getting in their way. Then I ran back into the house, and there were my mother and Miss S. still in their dressing-gowns! My teacher sat me down in a chair and spelled very emphatically, "Keep still, or you shall not go to Boston. . . ."

Finally everybody came into the hall, and they had their hats on. My father took me by the hand and led me out to the carriage. . . .

My heart jumped into my mouth as the carriage moved, and I felt old Charlie going down the lane at a trot—we were really going to Boston, and no mistake. . . .

The station was reached in the middle of eternity, and my father led me to the platform. I listened with my feet to the rumble of the train. I had been on the train several times, and knew what to expect. People were there to see us off.

When the train rumbled into the station, I kissed everybody on the platform, friends and stranger alike, and was lifted up on the train. "Now you must not bother people, you must sit in your own compartment," my mother insisted. I could not amuse myself as other children do looking out of the train window, and that is why I intruded upon my fellow-passengers. They were all very kind and gentle to me.

I thought everybody on the train was going to Boston. When the conductor came, I gave him our tickets, bursting with satisfaction, and he allowed me to feel him punch them. Everything about the train interested me, and I learned new words by leaps and bounds. . . .

I am afraid my mother and Miss S. had no rest or enjoyment on the trip, I never stopped asking questions, hardly even in my sleep.[25]

Along the way, the trio made a stop in Washington, where they met with Dr. Bell, who "rejoiced in Helen's progress." They also received an invitation to visit President Grover Cleveland, which they accepted and whom Helen described as "living in a very large and beautiful white house."[26] But despite the dignitaries and fanfare, Helen was impatient to get to their real destination.

Boston and its accompanying experiences did not disappoint. The trip was a resounding success for both Annie, the proud and capable returning Perkins graduate, and Helen, the new "darling" of the school.[27] Helen delighted in the company of other blind children and told of her great joy at being with them, writing later, "I joined the little blind children in their work and play, and talked continually. I was delighted to find that nearly all my new friends could spell with their fingers. Oh, what happiness! To talk freely with other children! To feel at home in the great world!"[28]

There was intense fascination with Helen among prominent Bostonians. Philanthropists, intellectuals, society ladies, and literary figures extended invitations to prestigious social events.[29] That so many should know about Helen was not a surprise: Perkins was adept at cultivating donors and supporters, and in addition to leadership by four directors and twelve trustees representing the elite of Boston, each year the school nominated selected individuals as "Members of the Corporation." In 1887, the list of over five hundred members included *Little Women* author Louisa May Alcott, then in her mid-fifties, as well as representatives of some of Boston's most prominent families, including the Cabots, Endicotts, Peabodys, and Lodges. All of these constituents were apprised of Helen's story and progress in a lengthy report that was also released to the news media.[30] Helen was a celebrity, a phenomenon, and even a "miracle." The story of how she was overcoming her disabilities captivated the popular imagination. In addition, she possessed a natural sweetness, and her personality charmed and drew people to her.

Helen was welcomed to Boston by an eager community. Years later, in a letter to Ed Chamberlin, she described some of the influential men she met during her early days in the city: "In Boston it was my privilege to know and talk with men of genius. They opened their hearts to me, and their conversation widened the world for me. I discovered Boston in the happy atmosphere of childhood. I cannot recall a single person I met . . . who did not add something to my sum of knowledge, and whom it is not a pleasure to remember."[31]

Foremost among those Helen told of meeting was the prominent minister Phillips Brooks, who was described as "a towering figure in Boston's religious life, both as a preacher and physically—for he was six feet four inches tall." He was the minister of Boston's Trinity Church on Copley Square.[32] Helen later wrote, "Only those who knew Phillips Brooks can appreciate the preciousness of his friendship." She "loved to sit on his knee, clasping his great hand with one of mine, while Miss Sullivan spelled into the other his beautiful words about God and love and being good. His religion seemed to spring from an abundant joy of life. I never left Phillips Brooks without carrying away a fine thought that has deepened in meaning and beauty with the years."[33] Brooks guided her spiritual development throughout her childhood, responding gently to her many questions and inquiries about God. When a new baby was born to the Kellers in 1891, Helen persuaded her parents to name him Phillips Brooks Keller.[34]

Equally important to Helen among those she met was the "immensely loved" and also physically imposing Unitarian minister and social reformer Reverend Edward Everett Hale. Hale was the minister of the Unitarian South Congregational Church in the South End.[35] Reverends Hale and Brooks were distant cousins, and both were charismatic leaders as well as members of the Perkins Corporation. Hale had written to Helen prior to her visit to Boston, claiming kinship with her, as Helen's mother was of Everett family lineage, and expressing great pride in "his little cousin."[36]

Hale met Helen, Annie, and Kate Keller soon after their arrival in town, reporting to his personal assistant Harriet E. Freeman—who was herself from a prominent Boston family and also a member of the Perkins Corporation—"Little Helen Keller has come. I saw her mother and Annie Sullivan yesterday." He noted that he would "make a State call" the next day and added that "the mother is a pleasing person, glowing with happiness, as indeed she may be, in presence of a constant miracle."[37]

A few days later, Hale described Helen's attendance at the Perkins School commencement: "Our dear little Helen [was] the light and life of the whole thing. Every now and then the exercises would be broken in upon with a coo—oo—oo of laughter from her, or a stream of kisses on Mr. Anagnos or Annie Sullivan, because Helen was quite too delighted to hold in. She read, very prettily, before the Assembly, Annie Sullivan interpreting. She fairly dances across the stage, life is such a joy to her. . . . Did I tell you Annie always calls her 'Baby'?"[38]

Soon after the commencement, Reverend Hale and his wife, Emily, gave what he called "a famous party for Helen" at their home, inviting five little girls to meet her. "Darling child, she fascinated us all," he wrote.[39] Hale again came to see Helen on June 27, her eighth birthday. Of the visit, Helen later reported,

I remembered well his interest in my rag doll Nancy. I told him she had been very ill, and I must sit by the sofa and watch her all day. I loved him for the child-like spirit with which he entered in the situation, telling her stories to keep her quiet. From that day to the

day of his death I relied on Dr. Hale's friendship. He stood staunchly by Miss Sullivan and me in the trials and sorrows which came to us in later years. He was never too busy to answer our letters, or come to us when we needed his counsel. He gave a personal touch to his letters to me by pricking his signature in braille.[40]

Other literary giants in Boston likewise became her friends, among them Oliver Wendell Holmes. She later described her visits with him, writing that "after learning to speak . . . I frequently visited Oliver Wendell Holmes, and in his library recited for him 'The Chambered Nautilus,' 'The Opening of the Piano' and 'Dorothy Q,' which I had learned by heart. I would stand beside him as he sat in a great arm-chair by a window looking out on the river Charles, or by an open fire when it was cool, and haltingly repeat the last poem I had learned. The tapping of his hand on my arm was like an accompanying music, and gave me confidence."[41]

Helen told of meeting the poet John Greenleaf Whittier "at his quiet home on the Merrimac." He expressed his admiration of Dr. Howe's work: "He placed my hands on the statue of a slave, from whose crouching figure the chains were falling. 'God is in all that liberates,' said he, 'She is thy spiritual liberator [referring to Annie].' What she and Dr. Howe have done strengthens my faith that some day all fetters shall be broken which keep the minds and hearts of men in bondage."[42]

It was sometime during their first months in Boston that Helen and Annie also met Ed Chamberlin, friend and admirer of both Hale and Anagnos, and popular newspaper columnist and magazine editor. Although modest and self-effacing, Ed had significant stature in the literary world.

It was a fortuitous introduction. Despite meeting many notable figures in those early days, throughout her life Helen would say that it was on meeting Ed that the pair's "robust education in literary ways" began.[43] Perhaps he simply invited the trio to his house for Helen to play with his children or to enjoy the rural setting as an antidote to life in the city, but the invitation had lifelong consequences for all.

Kate Keller returned to Tuscumbia soon after the commencement, but Helen and Annie remained in Boston through the summer—though Perkins was closed—staying first with Anagnos, then with newly made friends outside of town, and then in the town of Brewster on Cape Cod with Sophia Hopkins, a widow who had been a housemother at Perkins and to whom Annie was very close. Annie and Helen came back to Perkins for school in September and October, and then returned to Tuscumbia for the remainder of the year.[44]

Between 1888 and 1892, Helen and Annie traveled frequently between Boston and Tuscumbia, with periodic attendance at Perkins during the autumn and winter months. Helen's education now became even more visible to the world, largely through her own childish but precocious letters written with an assistive wooden frame that enabled her to write legibly in a "square hand," or box-shaped print, and through articles about her that Anagnos published which included her letters. Helen's animated personality and ability to describe her own feelings and experiences in her writings aroused empathy not only for herself but for other people with disabilities as well. This was still a time when able-bodied people viewed people with disabilities, and especially those who were blind, as "woefully afflicted" and pitiable. The only previous well-known example of an educated deafblind child was Laura Bridgman, but she did not have Helen's charm and intellectual talents and she lived permanently within the walls of Perkins. Helen was shifting views by showing that her disabilities did not make her different from other children.[45] She was a *cause célèbre.*

Anagnos reveled in the new "face" of Perkins. The September 1888 edition of the school's annual report included his description of Helen's attendance at the commencement exercises earlier in June. Like Reverend Hale, and indeed the entire audience, Anagnos had been captivated:

The reading exercise was supplemented by the introduction of that second Laura Bridgman, Helen Keller, eight years old, from Alabama,—a child of remarkable talent, whose rapid progress in the acquisition of knowledge and the command of language during the year and a half that she has been under the wise, affectionate and patient training of Miss Anna M. Sullivan, one of the most gifted and accomplished graduates of our institution, has been simply marvelous. On this occasion she read with the left hand, rapidly and easily, a little story from the raised type, telling it at the same time with her right hand through the finger alphabet to her teacher, who interpreted it to the amazed and delighted audience. The ways of the child were so attractive and so unaffected, she was so happy and enthusiastic in the acquisition of each new thought or image, so eager to learn more, almost acting the whole story out with an electric play of gestures and of features, an unconscious eloquence of the whole body, that she seemed inspired. There was a grace and fascination in her every movement. Life and the knowledge of new things, new thoughts, new people, seemed an insatiable delight to her. Her mental activity is untiring. Throughout the livelong day she seeks, she learns, and she enjoys. And her nature is most affectionate; she remembers and loves every one who has taken friendly notice of her, showing the most devoted fondness for her teachers and her nearest friends. Of course the whole audience were moved to deepest sympathy, and wholly captivated by so rare a child.

Certainly Perkins cultivated broader newspaper coverage of Helen's story. The Perkins annual report, published each September, included press articles from the year before that had been helpful to the school's cause. The 1888 report included almost thirty pages about Helen and her teacher, including details of her educational progress and the observation that she enjoyed "primping" and dressing up.[46]

The fascination with Helen extended well beyond Boston. In September 1889, the *New York Times* was one of dozens of newspapers across the country that published articles extolling her intellectual virtues.[47] But Annie remained scornful of the media attention, observing, "Indeed, I am heartily glad that I don't know all that is being said and written about Helen and myself. Nearly every mail brings some absurd statement, printed or written. The truth is not wonderful enough to suit the newspapers, so they enlarge upon it and invent ridiculous embellishments. One paper has Helen demonstrating problems in geometry by means of her playing blocks. I expect to hear next that she has written a treatise on the origin and future of the planets!"[48]

Anagnos vehemently defended his releases of information to the media—releases that would continue to be used strategically to benefit Perkins over the years. In one letter to Annie, he devoted multiple pages to his argument, writing that "the eagerness of the public to learn something of Helen's case is perfectly natural. Indeed, it is as it should be. It would be abominably inhuman if it were otherwise." Further, he believed, "the admiration and earnestness with which people follow Helen's progress are creditable to their intelligence and do honor to our civilization."[49]

Annie's lamentations about the voraciousness of the news media made a friendship with Ed Chamberlin all the more unlikely. But by the early 1890s, a unique friendship had been forged between them that would only grow stronger as future events unfolded.

CHAPTER THREE

The Move to Red Farm

By all accounts, a visit to the Chamberlin home brought guests into a vibrant family and social milieu. Several times during Helen's first winter in the North in 1889–1890, she and Annie visited the family, and Helen described the household as "a jolly place."[1] While it appears Ed and Ida were always renters and never again purchased a house after moving east from Chicago, wherever they resided their home was a gathering place for literary friends, and they earned a well-deserved reputation for warm and often spontaneous hospitality.[2]

But the Chamberlins' was also a refuge, especially for Helen and Annie. For Helen, it was a family home in which she could play and enjoy a normal childhood, away from her studies and the whirl of social events required of her.[3] It is easy to imagine that the Chamberlins provided family for Annie as well, the family she had perhaps always dreamed of, with a kind and nurturing father, a capable and caring mother, happy children, and the tantalizing prospect of brilliant guests at any moment. This was also a family that included an adopted child, a feature that must have resonated with Annie and bespoke a singular warmth and inclusiveness.

It was at the Chamberlins' during one of her first winters in the North that Helen, the child of the South who had never experienced a snowfall, became acquainted with what she called "the treasures of the snow." She was visiting one day when "chill air portended a snowstorm":

We rushed out-of-doors to feel the first tiny flakes descending. Hour by hour the flakes dropped silently, softly from their airy height to the earth, and the country become more and more level. A snowy night closed upon the world, and in the morning one could scarcely recognize a feature of the landscape. . . . In the evening a wind from the northeast sprang up, and the flakes rushed hither and thither in a furious melee. Around the great fire we sat and told merry tales, and frolicked, and quite forgot that we were in the midst of a desolate solitude, shut in from all communication with the outside world. But during the night the fury of the wind increased to such a degree that it thrilled us with a vague terror. The rafters creaked and strained, and the branches of the trees surrounding the house rattled and beat against the windows, as the winds rioted up and down the country.

On the third day after the beginning of the storm the snow ceased. The sun broke through the clouds and shone upon a vast, undulating white plain. High mounds, pyramids heaped in fantastic shapes, and impenetrable drifts lay scattered in every direction.

So dazzling was the light, it penetrated even the darkness that veils my eyes.[4]

Outdoors the next morning, Helen was introduced to tobogganing. She and the Chamberlin children, along with Annie, climbed on their toboggan at the top of a steep hill, were given a shove by one of the adults, and went flying. She later described how "plunging through drifts, leaping hollows, swooping down upon the lake, we would shoot across its gleaming surface to the opposite bank." Although Ed and others who had remained at the top of the hill worried that she had been frightened, Helen rolled off the toboggan into the snow, laughing, pulled off her soggy mittens, and spelled to Annie, "Let's do it again!" Helen called the experience "exhilarating madness!"[5]

As bright and convivial as the early Boston years were for the Chamberlin family, in 1890 they became shrouded in darkness. Thirteen-year-old Charley, a brilliant student, talented artist and writer, "the star of his generation," born with what Ed described as the same spirit as his late brother Everett, suddenly began to experience headaches for which there would be no cure.

Years later, Ed wrote of this bleak time, relating how "one night he walked with me to the spot in the lane at Medford where we commanded a view of the Fells, in which we so often rambled together. My arm over his shoulder, and his arm about my body, as we had so often walked, he repeated a verse that had come into his head: "Oh! Hollow my grave in the mountains wild!" and he said quite passionately, "Good-bye woods!"[6]

In the week that followed, Ida took Charley to Vermont on her own while Ed remained behind in Boston, perhaps not thinking that the situation was so dire. Ed later wrote, "He went away. I saw him alive no more. In a week, on the seventh day of June 1890, at the age of thirteen years, six months, and seven days, he died. My 'hyacinthine boy,' our new torchbearer, was gone, and I mourned and mourned on and on."[7]

Somehow the family pulled itself up from the depths of grief. Not long after Charley's death, perhaps seeking escape from painful memories and a return to a quieter, more pastoral life, the Chamberlins began renting the sprawling Red Farm property, located about thirty miles southwest from the *Transcript*'s Boston office on Washington Street. Late in 1890, the railroad had been extended out to Wrentham, and now its citizens could board a passenger train and commute to work in the city, while city residents could ride out to vacation at the resort lakes in the area. Prominent people began moving out to the country.[8]

Ed became a commuter—though he probably only returned home on weekends as it would have been too long a train ride for a daily commute. He kept an apartment in town at 76 Huntington Avenue, near a train stop and his offices at both the *Transcript* and *Youth's Companion*.[9]

Even as the Chamberlins grieved Charley's death, Helen and Annie retreated to Red Farm at every opportunity. They were not alone: a seemingly never-ending whirl of guests visited the household. Perhaps the presence of company provided a needed distraction for Ed and Ida and their children; perhaps just the prospect of guests could help keep the black curtain of grief from descending over the household.

On the expansive grounds of Red Farm, large gatherings could be held for the Chamberlins' circle of literary and artistic friends. Massive and even historic trees, one of them a huge oak, provided an elegant and sheltering canopy. From the writings of Helen and other guests, one can imagine summer evenings as Ida and Ed circulated easily among their visitors, some famous and well-known, others whose stars were ascending. It would not have been a stuffy crowd of socialites but an eclectic group of liberal intellectuals considered brilliant and *avant-garde* for the times.

Early summer would have provided perfect weather for the crowd of creative personalities to sprawl in conversation groups on blankets spread on the grass under the huge tree canopy. Guests could also perch on the posts and stone steps of the front porch, saunter to the dock below the property, or even take turns in the family canoes on the lake.

Helen's memories and descriptions of her time at Red Farm always included the esteemed Reverend Edward Everett Hale, her friend and distant relative. It is not certain how often he was in attendance, but the memory of his presence and influence was profound for her. A central and connective element of the Red Farm circle, and indeed all of New England culture at the time, Hale was a national leader in the Unitarian movement, a denomination that was essentially "a liberal reaction to the Calvinism (Congregationalism) of the New England Puritans [and] particularly the latter's rigidly uncompromising, from the Unitarians' point of view, doctrines of original sin, predestination, and eternal damnation."[10]

In 1890, he was nearing seventy and renowned for his kindness and optimistic spirit. It would later be written that "probably no man in America aroused and stimulated so many minds as Hale, and his personal popularity was unbounded."[11] Further, he was a voluminous contributor to newspapers and magazines and described as "having raised the tone of American life for half a century." His personal motto, "To look forward and not back, to look out and not in, and to lend a hand," became the mantra of many intellectual and philanthropic men and women of the time.[12]

Hale was part-minister/part-journalist, and his sympathies were closely aligned with Ed's. Although twenty years older than Ed, he had been deeply interested in the antislavery movement and was author of the nationally renowned and Union-strengthening story "The Man without a Country," first published in 1863. Hale's reassuring and optimistic presence must have been a comfort to the Chamberlins. And the two men likely had much to talk about at any gathering, with shared interests in liberal theology, abolitionism, social reform, and, most especially, a love for the White Mountains of New Hampshire.[13]

Helen also described other guests who were key contributors to gatherings at Red Farm:

A pleasant memory to dwell upon is the happy days when I left my studies in Boston and ran away to the home of Mr. Chamberlin, "Red Farm," Wrentham, Massachusetts. As the readers of the "Transcript" know, Mr. Chamberlin is wise in the ways of streams and woods and the wild life of the country. It was he who initiated me into the mysteries of trees and wild flowers, the stone walls and green pastures of New England.

The companionship of his children was precious to me, and I was stimulated by the bright atmosphere which his guests created. People of many professions and talents foregathered at "Red Farm," among whom were Mary Wilkins, the quiet, shy woman whose books are so filled with the tragedy and pathos, the comedy and rural beauty of the villages of New England, and Mr. Bradford Torrey, whose talk about birds made their songs and habits an unfailing source of joy in my silent world. Richard Hovey made me long to roam up and down the world with the open-hearted children of the sea. There was Bliss Carmen, the Canadian, big, shy, gentle, whose songs of the Out-doors have ever lent music to my steps as I walk back and forth, round my garden or in woodland paths.[14]

Bradford Torrey, the ornithologist and naturalist, spent many days and evenings at Red Farm and on nature excursions with Ed. Ed's friend, author Mary Wilkins, was a frequent visitor and also well known at the time. She was widely read and addressed feminist issues and women's roles in many of her stories. Mark Twain would later describe her as "a lady of high literary distinction; she is nobly gifted, [and] she has the ear of the nation."[15]

Perhaps the Red Farm guests congregated in groups linked by common pursuits, with the writers, reformers, and social activists finding one another, or the artists gathering to share studio travails or patron stories. The nature writers might have convened their own circle or taken guests off on bird-watching excursions.

Among the guests, Helen and Annie would have stood out. In her twenties, Annie was young and more sparkling than usual in this social setting, with Helen on her arm. Annie would have to describe the scene and conversations as quickly as possible through fingerspelling into Helen's palm to satisfy the girl's constant need for information. Occasional respite probably came from Ed and his family members, or other guests, as they took Helen in arm and escorted her to some new experience or personage. A responsible six-year-old, Beth Chamberlin could also have been counted on as a companion for Helen.

The remembrances of those who knew the family suggest that Ida was a capable homemaker and hostess—perhaps serving a well-loved blueberry cake with lemon sauce, fresh seasonal fruit, or fashionable bites on her sprigged china plates.[16] Candlelight flickered, illuminating faces and smiles. With the laughter of her children and guests; the song of a flute, violin, or other instrument; and bits of quiet conversation reaching her ears from time to time from among other murmurings and voices, Ida would have been at her best and most fulfilled as a hostess, wife, and mother. And she could briefly forget a profound absence.

For Ed, the gatherings were essential as well: for a brief second in time he could think of something other than the family's bright spark that had been extinguished too soon.

CHAPTER FOUR

Ed Chamberlin Steps In, 1892

One can imagine an icy afternoon at the end of February 1892 as Ed pulled closer the woolen sweater he wore to stave off the drafts seeping through the windows of his study whenever a gust of wind rattled past. He worried constantly he would have another episode of the asthma that haunted him. Sunlight reflected off the snowdrifts outside, illuminating the stacks of submissions on his desk not yet reviewed or edited for *Youth's Companion.* He was only forty years old, not an old man, but his chest and shoulders often felt so heavy that he wondered how he could summon the energy to go on.

The head of the household at Red Farm was weary and more thought-burdened than usual. The family was still reeling from the death of thirteen-year-old Charley, eighteen months earlier. It seemed that nothing could lessen the pain of this overwhelming loss. Often Ed tried to distract himself with his work. Sometimes it was effective, more often not. Ed and Ida's surviving children—Helen, Philip, Beth, and Corda—felt the burden each day of their own and their parents' shattered hearts.

On this day, Ed's chest felt even tighter as he pondered a situation that concerned him deeply: the young Helen Keller, whom he had come to know quite well, was embroiled in a sudden and disturbing scandal. What was now being called the "Frost King Affair" had unfolded over the previous two months. Helen was accused of plagiarism for writing a story called "The Frost King" that was strikingly similar to a children's book published in 1889 by an author named Margaret Canby and called *Birdie and the Frost Fairies.*

Helen had sent her Frost King story as a "birthday gift" to Michael Anagnos in late 1891. He was so delighted that he published it immediately in the *Mentor,* Perkins's alumni magazine.

Helen's story was then also published in the early January edition of the *Goodson Gazette,* a weekly publication of the Virginia Institution for the Education of the Deaf, Dumb and Blind in Staunton, Virginia.[1]

But a week later, a reader of the *Goodson Gazette* brought in a copy of Canby's book to the editor, protesting the similarities of Helen's work to *Birdie and the Frost Fairies.* In its next issue, on January 16, the *Gazette* ran the stories side by side, and the parallels were in fact startling—they appeared to be alike almost word for word. The editor added the following comment to the exposure: "*The Goodson Gazette* does not blame little Helen Keller for the attempt at fraud, far from it. She is not to blame. She has merely done what she was told to do. The blame for the fraud rests not upon her, but upon whoever knowingly attempted to palm off the Frost King as her composition and there the blame will lie."[2] The terrible accusation reached Michael Anagnos at Perkins and "brought chaos" and embarrassment to the organization.[3]

On January 30, the news reached Helen and Annie in Alabama. Both were understandably upset. In her personal journal that day, Helen described her heart as "full of tears."[4] She claimed to have no recollection of having been read the Canby story, and Annie swore she also had never heard of it nor read it to Helen. For weeks, the pair was under intense scrutiny as Anagnos investigated. Other newspapers quickly picked up the story, and Helen and Annie suffered through public embarrassment and accusations.

Annie and friends scrambled for an explanation. Some supposed that a person other than Annie, perhaps her friend Sophia Hopkins, whom they frequently visited in Brewster, had read Canby's book to Helen while Annie was away. With Helen's memory for detail, perhaps she had retained it and then created a story that she thought was out of her own head.

The uproar had not subsided a month later as Ed considered the situation and the negative publicity for Helen and Annie. He especially worried that it would have a harmful effect on Helen's growing confidence in her abilities. He himself could not believe the pair would deliberately deceive. Driven by his desire to lend whatever assistance he could to Annie and Helen, Ed decided on a plan. He felt compelled to channel the literary resources at his disposal, and he would make a request of Annie, one that could possibly help the pair out of their current difficulty.

Despite having been a mentor to Annie and benevolent figure to Helen, Anagnos was suspicious that Annie had in fact originally read the *Frost Fairies* story to Helen and was now lying about her role. There was precedent for his mistrust: in May 1890, just a year and a half earlier, while Anagnos was abroad, Annie had agreed to an interview with a reporter from the *Boston Daily Journal.* In the resulting article, she did not credit Perkins for her success with Helen, declaring that she was not, nor had she ever been, under Perkins's employ, implying that all credit for Helen's success was due to Annie's teaching alone. The article incensed several influential trustees of Perkins, and Annie had to work to mend the relationship through a formal letter of apology to the board—a board that included Frank Sanborn, who had originally rescued her from the Tewksbury Almshouse. In her letter, she asserted that she had tried to correct the tone of the article before publication, "but the writer did not keep his word." She wrote to the board:

I consider myself wholly at fault for having seen a reporter at all. . . . There it would appear that to me alone is due all the credit of Helen's education; whereas the truth is that the advantages she has had at the Institution during the past year have done more to develop and broaden her mind than any training I could have given her in years alone. Much as Helen is indebted to the Institution, I am much more so, for as you know, I was educated there; and since Helen has been in my charge I have been encouraged constantly by its director, Mr. Anagnos, and without the help of my Institution friends the work would have seemed an impossibility to me. It was farthest from my mind to speak lightly of my great education to my own school, and I beg that though you blame me for indiscretion you will not blame me for ingratitude.[5]

The muttering and grumbling among the board members abated, but the offense had been registered.

Michael Anagnos had much to lose if Helen was deemed a fraud in public opinion. He was a man of great integrity and stature in the United States and abroad, easily the most famous Greek American of the time.[6] Moreover, he had used Helen's charm, gifts, and intellect, and her teacher's success as a graduate of Perkins, to garner fame and support for the school around the world. He had made the rounds of royal houses of Europe with her story on an 1890–1891 tour, reportedly bringing one queen to tears. Humiliation for Perkins would be of a global scale; this was a publicity crisis that had to be addressed quickly. Many in the world still believed that people who were blind and deaf were uneducable. Others viewed them simply as "good working hands" who could learn vocational skills, but refused to provide them with any real education.[7] "Ableist" attitudes and discrimination abounded.[8] The educational work Perkins had been doing so successfully to combat these attitudes toward the blind and deafblind was at risk of being called fraudulent.

Now, Anagnos displayed a side Helen had not seen before. She later recalled that "Mr. Anagnos, who loved me tenderly, thinking that he had been deceived, turned a deaf ear to the pleadings of love and innocence. He believed, or at least suspected, that Miss Sullivan and I had deliberately stolen the bright thoughts of another and imposed them on him to win his admiration."[9]

As part of his handling of the matter, Anagnos convened an "investigation committee" to hear and decide the truth.[10] The inquisition that followed sometime in March 1892 traumatized Helen, who wrote later:

I was brought before a court of investigation composed of the teachers and officers of the Institution, and Miss Sullivan was asked to leave me. Then I was questioned and cross-questioned [by an interpreter] with what seemed to me a determination on the part of my judges to force me to acknowledge that I remembered having had "The Frost Fairies" read to me. I felt in every question the doubt and suspicion that was in their minds. . . . The blood pressed about my thumping heart, and I could scarcely speak, except in monosyllables. Even the consciousness that it was only a dreadful mistake did not lessen my suffering, and when at last I was allowed to leave the room, I was dazed and did not notice my teacher's caresses, or the tender words of my friends, who said I was a brave little girl and they were proud of me.[11]

Eleven-year-old Helen ended the day in a desperate state of distress. It would be many years before she revealed her feelings: "As I lay in my bed that night, I wept as I hope few children have wept. I felt so cold, I imagined I should die before morning, and the thought comforted me. I think if this sorrow had come to me when I was older, it would have broken my spirit beyond repairing."[12]

Years later, Anagnos made a statement that at the time of the "Frost King matter," he believed Helen was innocent. The court of investigation consisted of eight people, four blind and four seeing persons. After Helen's testimony, four of them, Anagnos recounted, thought she knew Canby's story had been read to her, while the others disagreed. Anagnos stated that he cast his vote with those who were favorable to Helen.[13]

Helen, however, recalled,

Whichever side he may have cast his vote, when I went into the room where Mr. Anagnos had so often held me on his knee, and forgetting his many cares, had shared in my frolics, and found there persons who seemed to doubt me, I felt there was something hostile and menacing in the very atmosphere, and subsequent events have borne out this impression. I never even knew the names of the members of the "court" who did not speak to me. I was too excited to notice anything, too frightened to ask questions. Indeed, I scarcely knew what I was saying, or what was being said to me.[14]

It was an experience that would affect Helen for decades, if not her entire life.

The Frost King situation also garnered serious concern from Alexander Graham Bell. He had played a guiding role in Helen's life with his introduction of the Keller family to Michael Anagnos at Perkins, as well as through subsequent visits and letters. Now, he became even more involved and would bring official resources to bear.

Scottish by birth, Bell was in his mid-forties. He had been fascinated by speech and hearing mechanics since childhood, and as a young man trained as a teacher of the deaf in London. In 1870, he immigrated to Ontario, Canada, with his parents. He moved to the Boston area soon after and began teaching at the Boston School for the Deaf. While there, the inventive Bell also conducted experiments with devices that could measure and convey sounds. He began working with a young machinist named Thomas Watson in 1875 and received the first patent for the voice transmitting apparatus that would become the telephone in March 1876. One of his students at the School for the Deaf was a young girl named Mabel Hubbard who had lost her hearing at the age of six due to scarlet fever. Over a number of years, Bell courted the much younger Mabel. They married in 1877 when Bell was thirty and she was nineteen.[15]

On March 10, 1892, Bell wrote a letter to his wife. He had been visited that morning by his Boston-based assistant, Annie Pratt, who apprised him of the Frost King plagiarism accusations. In his letter, Bell summarized her visit, reported on the situation, and laid out his own plan for addressing it:

Mrs. Pratt appeared while we were at breakfast in my parlor. She told us all that had been discovered about Helen Keller and the origin of the "Frost King" story. Helen and her teacher seem to have been treated in a most unjust and outrageous manner by Mr. Anagnos—who seems to have failed to grasp the importance of the Frost King incident and seems to suspect either Miss Sullivan or her dear little pupil—of an untruth.

I see clearly that a full investigation of the incident will throw light on this manner in which Helen has acquired her marvelous knowledge of language—and do much good. The child is quite incapable of falsehood about the matter—and her teacher never saw the book which undoubtedly suggested the story. I intend to come out strongly upon the subject soon. Will spend Sunday at Brewster Mass. with Helen and her teacher—so as to complete my investigation. I can then be of much assistance to Miss Sullivan.[16]

In 1890, two years before the Frost King affair, Bell had established the Volta Bureau for the Deaf in Washington, DC, using a portion of the Volta Prize awarded to him by the French government for his invention of the telephone. The bureau's purpose was "for the increase and diffusion of knowledge relating to the deaf," and the esteemed and kindly John Hitz was appointed superintendent. Hitz had previously served as Swiss consul to the United States, having succeeded his father in that position. Through the work of the Volta Bureau, he and Bell became key national opinion leaders in matters related to the deaf.[17]

Following his conversation with Helen and Annie, Bell assigned the sixty-four-year-old Hitz to further investigate the situation. A close relationship between Hitz and the pair would develop during the process of his inquiry.

Despite their ongoing fascination with Helen, newspapers across the country proved themselves fickle in their affection. Society still could barely accept that a deafblind child could learn and communicate with such proficiency—much less create publishable stories on her own—and the media fomented this ableist doubt. After the exposure of the similarities of the Frost King piece to Canby's story, Helen's precocious abilities and her teacher's methods—and honesty—were met with suspicion. The affair was avidly publicized.

But Ed Chamberlin was not a typical newsman and harbored no such prejudices. For some time, he, along with other *Transcript* writers, had been writing frequent and flattering articles about Helen and Annie and Perkins. In one of his columns in April 1891, Ed told of a recent visit to the Kindergarten for the Blind at Perkins, where Oliver Wendell Holmes, Phillips Brooks, and Julia Ward Howe, widow of Samuel Gridley, "hobnobbed" with Helen Keller and others in attendance. He also wrote about three other captivating deafblind children at the Kindergarten: a girl named Edith Thomas, originally from Massachusetts; a younger girl from Texas named Willie Elizabeth Robin; and a newly arrived little boy from Pennsylvania named Tommy Stringer. Tommy had lived in impoverished and severe circumstances in hospitals and almshouses since contracting spinal meningitis as an infant, and

Helen had been instrumental in raising funds to bring the feeble, five-year-old child to Perkins.

Ed wrote movingly of the sight at the Kindergarten of Helen carrying little Tommy on her hip. He described her as "born in a world of total darkness and silence" from which she had been led "into one which was not so dark and silent." Knowing that there were "still others back in the dark world from whence she came," Helen was reaching back and leading them out as well. Ed saw this especially in what she was doing for Tommy.[18]

In January 1892, Ed had written a column about a visit between Helen and Brooks during which their conversation about God and spirituality was discussed at length. Now, the *Transcript* began publishing almost monthly articles about Helen, blindness, and Perkins. These articles were probably features of the paper's department of "Divers Good Causes" in which "reformatory causes" were helped through "charitable agitation." This charitable emphasis was a priority of the current editor, E. H. Clement.[19]

Unwittingly, the *Transcript* had perhaps also bred skepticism of Helen's talents through its overly effusive slant. For example, the paper wrote in December that the "wonderful child of eleven years is simply one of the most brilliant girls who have lived upon the earth. Small wonder that Mr. Anagnos says he is willing to challenge the country to show us a girl in her latest teens of quicker thought, readier tact, clearer command of language or a stronger flame of genuine imagination than this girl who will not reach her teens for more than a year." The article also mentioned that "a story Helen wrote and sent to Mr. Anagnos for a birthday gift shows her imagination in its glowing power and adaptation beyond any futile words of praise."[20]

While other Boston dailies covered the Frost King scandal, the *Transcript* seems to have avoided any comment on the matter. Instead, the paper focused on receptions and events at the Kindergarten where Helen was present and advocated for the education of other blind or deafblind children. The *Transcript* also promoted a tea to be hosted by Helen on May 24.

But Ed also had influence far beyond the reach of the *Transcript* and was ready to mobilize it: in early March 1892, he spoke with

Annie and asked if Helen would be willing to write an original account, a "sketch," of her education for publication in the *Youth's Companion.* His intent was to allow her the opportunity to write in her own voice and from her own experience something only she could write—no matter how childlike it might be—and that would not be vulnerable to accusations and suspicion.[21]

Several weeks later, probably aware of Bell's concurrent investigation into the Frost King matter, for he was attuned to most of what occurred involving Helen and Annie, Ed followed his earlier request for the sketch with a letter to Annie on *Youth's Companion* letterhead:

My dear Miss Sullivan:

I hope you and Helen are favorably considering the proposition for her to write a little account of her instruction for the YOUTH'S COMPANION. *It has occurred to me that you might regard the matter as more of a task than it really is. You know me, I do not want a long story—a short one would be better—but we would want to have it in Helen's own handwriting. Do you think it need take very much of her time? The more informal and unstudied the narrative, the better-suited it would be to the purpose. Helen would be well paid for it; I know very well that she is not mercenary, but know that she is very generous, and would find an excellent use for the money.*

Sincerely yours, J. E. Chamberlin[22]

Although Annie's response to Ed's letter is not preserved, she encouraged Helen to write the sketch. But despite his personal urgency in hoping to sway public opinion through publication of Helen's "little account," delaying events would cause it to be almost two years before the plan was realized.

Meanwhile, John Hitz and Annie Pratt quickly compiled a report of their investigation into the affair, gathering statements from Bell, Sullivan, and others. These became part of a lengthy article that comprised the April 1892 issue of the *American Annals of the Deaf.* In addition to the statements, the report featured a copy of a letter from Canby to Sullivan. Canby began the letter by writing, "I hope you will be able to make [Helen] understand that I am glad she enjoyed my story." Since learning more about Helen as the affair unfolded, Canby stated, "I do not see how anyone could be so unkind as to call it plagiarism; [Helen's story] is a wonderful feat of memory and stands alone as doubtless much of her work will in the future." Canby asked Annie to "give [Helen] my warm love, and tell her not to feel troubled any more. No one shall be allowed to think she did anything wrong; and some day she will write a great beautiful story or poem that will make many people happy."[23]

Helen and Annie's supporters continued to try to rally favorable opinion. In May, Hitz published still another article about Helen the "Wonder-child" and her teacher in Edward Everett Hale's progressive magazine *Lend a Hand*, attempting to add to the stream of positive articles about the pair and the innovative instructional techniques Annie was using.[24]

Others in Boston were kind as well: when Helen and Annie visited a local grade school, a lengthy description of her visit was featured in the June issue of the youth-oriented *St. Nicholas* magazine. A "reception was held for her later in the day, and many people from town came in to see her."[25]

Also in May, very likely as an emotional balm for the humiliation of the Frost King affair, Helen decided to use her celebrity to raise funds for other blind children by giving a tea in aid of the Kindergarten for the Blind at Perkins. Helen felt deeply about the importance of the Kindergarten program. The Kindergarten was distinct from Perkins's original school program, which Helen had attended and which had been established for children ages nine to nineteen. Howe's methods were successful and groundbreaking with those older students, but the need for a program for younger blind children had been identified. Thus, Anagnos founded the Kindergarten in April 1887 in Jamaica Plain, a neighborhood in Boston, with ten students, the first program for younger blind children in the country.

Tickets to Helen Keller's fundraising tea sold for a dollar apiece, with all proceeds to go to the Kindergarten.[26] With help from the *Transcript* in publicizing the event, the response was so positive that the original location had to be changed to accommodate all the guests.

The *Boston Daily Advertiser* called the May 29 event a "highlight" of the social season and printed an article describing "tables laden with gay blossoms and bonbons" and "ladies all in pretty light tinted gowns." Many guests were listed by name, and the piece noted that Oliver Wendell Holmes "talked with Helen for some time."[27]

Ed, as the Listener, wrote after the event that "all Boston was at Helen Keller's feet yesterday afternoon." Guests waited in line a long time "in the crush" to greet her. Helen's face wore a "rapt and somewhat exciting expression, as all the people passed in review before her, but that she was in perfect master of herself was shown by her quick recognition of her friends as they grasped her hands, and her special word for each acquaintance." He was captivated by Helen's ability to recognize people by their handshake, noting,

It is a high sort of presence of mind that enables one who is "receiving" to say the proper word in the case of every person in a great crowd. The power to recognize an acquaintance by a mere grasp of the hand seems a wonderful thing to us who have learned to depend entirely on our eyes, and it must seem scarcely less so to the blind who learn to depend on their ears. But we simply do not know what a vast deal of differentiation there is in hand-grasps. To Helen herself, as it was with Laura Bridgman, probably it is hard to understand how people can regard it as wonderful. Helen's gift of always saying the proper thing and making exactly the proper inquiries is probably much more wonderful.[28]

Years later, Helen would recollect the fundraising event fondly with Ed, saying, "Not quite twelve years old, I felt round me and the blind children the great protecting arms of the City of Kind Hearts. The tea brought more than two thousand dollars for the blind children."[29] Two thousand dollars raised for the Kindergarten in 1892 would have constituted an incredible success—comparable to over fifty thousand dollars in modern terms.[30]

The positive publicity and the success of Helen's fundraiser pleased her but could not completely dispel the dark shadow of the plagiarism accusations, nor could the efforts of friends and family to cheer her up. Helen and Annie did not remain in Boston for the June commencement at Perkins; Helen would not be showcased this year. Soon after the May tea, they took the train to Tuscumbia for what they assumed would be just the summer months.

The tracks behind the pair had barely cooled when Ed wrote to Anagnos on June 8, 1892. Despite Helen and Annie's now-strained relations with the man, Ed wrote a long letter that deepened his own connection with Anagnos. The two men had known each other since before 1888.[31] Ed had taught himself Greek earlier in his life and asked Anagnos to bring back Greek newspapers when he traveled to Greece so that he might practice his reading.

In his letter, Ed thanked Anagnos for tickets to see the recent Perkins commencement exercises; Ida had been too ill to attend, so Ed gave his seats to friends and instead stood and observed the event from the wings of the auditorium. He enthused that "every successive witnessing of such an exhibition strengthens the admiration I feel for you, dear friend, and the sense of gratitude as a human being for the great work you are doing."

Ed then asked Anagnos if he could engage a piano tuner from among the students at Perkins to come to his house to tune the family's piano before a picnic to be held at their home on June 17. Piano tuning was one of the vocational skills that blind students at Perkins were taught, and they were often employed around the region for that work.

Ed also requested Anagnos's permission to announce that Helen might be writing an article for *Youth's Companion.* He appears to have respectfully viewed Anagnos as the gatekeeper for all information related to Helen.

Finally, Ed closed the same letter by relating that he had spent Decoration Day—a holiday that later came to be called "Memorial Day"—at the home of mutual friends in Metuchen and "heard there many cordial words about you." He hoped that Anagnos would be in attendance at the Chamberlins' upcoming annual Bunker Hill Day picnic, and closed the letter, "Ever sincerely yours."[32]

Newspapers other than just the *Transcript* also reported Ed's comings and goings at the time. According to the *Boston Daily Globe,* in June he attended a gathering of "disciples" of the recently deceased poet Walt Whitman on the verandah of William Sloane Kennedy's "idyllic home at Belmont." Kennedy was a journalist, biographer, and literary critic who had been an intimate friend of Whitman.[33] "Mr. J. E. Chamberlin of *Youth's Companion*" was second only to the Honorable Frank B. Sanborn, Annie's benefactor, on the list of dignitaries in attendance, a list that included a former Massachusetts senator and congressman, writers, editors, poets, social reformers, and the retired head of the Boston Public Library. Many of this group had been longtime devotees of Whitman, and Ed had written to the great poet personally in 1889 describing how their "reading club" had "for a good while celebrated you here and elsewhere."[34]

Sanborn had known Whitman personally, and on the verandah that day "talked most interestingly about his acquaintance with Whitman, and related the incidents of his visit at Concord some years ago, when he was [Ralph Waldo] Emerson's guest."[35]

Ed likely took the opportunity at the Belmont gathering—if it was needed—to defend Helen and Annie to Sanborn. For his part, Ed knew the sixty-year-old Sanborn as a bold and self-directed man of "marked energy, individuality, earnestness, and ability" and would have done his utmost to channel that energy and influence, within the Perkins constellation and beyond, on Helen's behalf.[36]

Also in June, in a further attempt to deflect attention from the Frost King scandal, Alexander Graham Bell published an article about Helen's education in the *Silent Educator*. Ever fascinated by Annie's teaching techniques, he wrote that

She employed the manual alphabet exclusively as a means of communication up to the period when Helen was taught to speak. She adopted the principle of talking to Helen just as she would to a seeing and hearing child, spelling into her hands the words and sentences she would have spoken to her if she could have heard, in spite of the fact that at first much of the language was unintelligible to the child. She did not pick and choose her words, but by frequent repetition of complete sentences containing ordinary idiomatic expressions, she sought to impress the language upon the child's memory and thus lead her gradually to imitate it.[37]

Bell was and would remain one of the definitive scientific authorities on matters related to the deaf, and he now more actively communicated his belief that Annie Sullivan was an innovative and brilliant teacher.

Despite the encouraging efforts of others, once home in Tuscumbia, alone in her dark and silent world, Helen contemplated the haunting experience of the past few months. The summer and early fall would be difficult for Helen, her teacher, and her family.

On November 5, Annie wrote to John Hitz, who by then had become a confidant and father figure to both herself and Helen. She was very concerned about Helen:

My dear Mr. Hitz:

... We went to our lovely retreat in the mountains early in July and stayed there until the middle of September. I was very glad to get in the country for a while and do nothing until all incentive to keep up was gone, then I collapsed, I think that word describes my condition during the first part of the summer. I think I wrote you after we got home, that Helen was very complaining. The excitement of the last few weeks in Boston had overtaxed her strength; but we thought the pure mountain air and perfect quiet would soon restore her health and spirit. But the days past [sic] *and we failed to see any change in her. She remained pale and listless—taking very little interest in her surroundings. Even her books were neglected. She would sit in the same place for hours without speaking and in every way was so unlike her own bright self that a great anxiety took possession of my heart. Her mother and I watched her helplessly. There seemed to be nothing we could do but wait for a change, and waiting is so hard. Then there were other trials, misunderstandings which I cannot explain here [involving Helen's physical maturation and the onset of painful menses] which made my summer peculiarly unpleasant, and my Helen's sunny smile and sweet companionship were sadly missed. Do you wonder that I had no heart for letter-writing? Had I written to you, Mon Pere, my letters would have been full of trouble and vexation of spirit.*

Out of the fullness of the heart I would have written and said things that I should regret now.... Since our return to town Helen has seemed better—more interested and cheerful. I have endeavored to keep her as quiet and free from excitement as possible.[38]

The trials of the year and the change in Helen's personality alarmed all concerned. Annie went on:

We all feel it will be best for her not to resume her regular studies for at least a year. But you have no idea how difficult it is to keep her quiet. She becomes restless and depressed if she does not have something to do. Indeed we seem to have a difficult problem upon our hands. She has two or three lessons, irregularly, just to relieve the monotony. She has written a very few letters on her typewriter recently and they have been full of the old sweetness and joy. She says, in one of them "God has hidden the sad days. I know not where—I only know that he has sent these bright, beautiful Autumn days in place of them." These words filled my heart with a new, glad hope. Surely a change for the better has come![39]

Annie further believed it would be profitable for Helen to communicate with Margaret Canby, who had been so gracious and forgiving about the similarities to her story, but Helen showed no interest in doing so. Annie wrote that she had "tried several times to persuade her to write; but without success. She seems to shrink from any reference to the sad experience with which that kind lady's name is connected. I wish I knew what I ought to do about it. It seems almost as if Helen ought to be made to write a proper acknowledgement of Miss Canby's generous treatment and yet, I do not think she would value such a letter. She would value only a spontaneous expression of the child's love. Can you advise me in this matter?"[40]

Helen later told of her own feelings during this difficult time, writing in her autobiography, "I was still excessively scrupulous about everything I wrote. The thought that what I wrote might not be absolutely my own tormented me." She further acknowledged,

It was with the hope of restoring my self-confidence that [Annie] persuaded me to write for the Youth's Companion *a brief account*

of my life. I was then twelve years old. As I look back on my struggle to write that little story, it seems to me that I must have had a prophetic vision of the good that would come of the undertaking, or I should surely have failed. I wrote timidly, fearfully, but resolutely, urged on by my teacher, who knew that if I persevered, I should find my mental foothold again and get a grip on my faculties.[41]

Helen's completed sketch—fifteen typewritten pages—was sent by Annie directly to Ed with a request that he show it to Anagnos. Annie noted in a subsequent letter to Anagnos that she had "sent the sketch to the *Companion* as soon as it was finished, but I do not know that they will accept it."[42]

In spite of Helen's statement that she had been convinced by Annie to write, Annie wrote that she had not encouraged the undertaking:

I knew that she would not find writing about herself an easy task, and I strongly advised her not to bother with the sketch, as she calls it, but she would not rest until it was begun and finished. Her object in writing has been to get money for Christmas and when she brought me her manuscript to read, I had not the heart to tell her that I did not think the COMPANION *would accept it. But I am very sure it is too long, and I fear too elaborate to answer Mr. Chamberlin's idea of a simple account of her education.*

Still, Annie found Helen's effort and the end product to be heartening, writing to Anagnos—whose approval and affection she still sought—that "in my opinion, it is the most touching and the most beautiful thing she has ever written."[43]

CHAPTER FIVE

Helen's Story

Although he had not yet received Helen's sketch, Ed was alerted to its imminent arrival by a note from her in early December 1892. He responded immediately with a long and familiar letter on December 13. His tone was gently instructive, paternal, and respectful. He had heard she was not well, which concerned him. He wrote,

My dear Helen:

I have received your most pleasant and interesting little note; and while I am waiting for the manuscript, which is not yet at hand, I will drop you a line to tell you how glad I am to hear from you, and to thank you for taking such pains to write us the article. I am eager to receive it, and have no doubt it will be in at the next mail; letters come more quickly than bulky parcels.

What a great pleasure to hear from you and to hear that you feel well again! We have all had you very much in our thoughts all summer, and have been thinking of you resting and gaining strength. Next to having your dear self where we can see you, it is pleasantant [sic] *to think of you growing stronger and better at your home. So many inquiries as I have heard for you! Only the other day Annie Alden [wife of the editor of HARPER'S MAGAZINE] wrote to me asking about you and now I shall send her your letter as soon as Mrs. Chamberlin and the children have seen it, but she will have to send me back the letter, for I shall always keep it.*

Ed provided charming updates on Beth and Corda, his children closest in age to Helen and probably the ones most involved with her during visits to Red Farm. Ed spoke of Beth, who always seemed to have a special connection with Helen, saying, "I know some one who will read every word of your letter herself with great interest—it is my little Beth, who has got to be a great scholar, and reads so much poetry and history and geography that we have to stop her."

He then described the charming personality of three-year-old Corda: "Little Corda is not quite old enough [to be a great scholar] yet, but she's awfully sweet for her age. She speaks of you sometimes, though I fear your face has grown a little cloudy in her memory. But if she could see you again, she would love you as affectionately as ever." Just that morning, Ed reported, he had heard her say, "I'm ever and ever drinking water this morning. I'm sirfty and sirfty!" Later, in hindsight, Corda's seemingly innocent words would prove haunting.

Ed stepped gingerly around the topic of Perkins and Michael Anagnos, commenting, "I have not seen Mr. Anagnos for quite a while; he came to see me one day not long since, but I was out, and I have been too busy and too much occupied at home to go to South Boston. Did you know that they had made me a member of the corporation, or something of that sort of the Perkins Institution? I think it is merely an honorary office, as there are no duties connected with it, apparently, but I am sure that it is a very honorable office; any service, even a merely nominal one, connected with the Perkins Institution would be honorable."

He then told Helen about Ida's recent poor health: "I am sorry to say that Mrs. Chamberlin has not been at all well since last summer. She does not go out at all now, and she is so poorly that I do not go out either, except to go to my office to work. But we are not alarmed concerning her. If she were here she would send you a great, great deal of love—and so would all the children."

As would become his custom in writing to Helen, Ed could not resist a little literary instruction and shared a poem in "Olde English" that he thought Helen would enjoy. He then lamented his office-bound life in the cold North and sent along a brief greeting for Annie:

I wish I had a chance to go to Tuscumbia! You know how I love the South, and how cold weather is the bane of my life, and hot weather—lots and lots of it—is so much strength and nourishment to me. It is funny how some people are—seem to be—misplaced in this world—I am by temperament meant for the South, but I spend all my life in the cold north; I am meant to be a farmer, and I grub away all my days in an office; but not all my days, either, for I get out a good deal, and have a great many things to make me happy. However, I wish Boston had been built in Alabama!

Please give Miss Sullivan my most cordial regards. I hope she is very well (Perhaps you needn't mind telling her that we are all very happy that Cleveland is elected—you can do as you like about that!).

He then closed the letter:

I have scarcely left myself time and room to tell you how much astonished and pleased I am about your proficiency in type-writing. I will write you again when the manuscript arrives—which I thank you again, so cordially, for writing for the COMPANION.

We all hope to see you again before long. Much health and happiness to you, dear Helen![1]

Meanwhile, Michael Anagnos was working to regain Annie's favor. Theirs was a complicated relationship: she was his protégé, Perkins's most famous graduate at the time, and he was fond of her. For her part, Annie owed Anagnos a great deal: he had been responsible for taking her in as a student at Perkins in 1880, he had tolerated her rocky adjustment to the program, and then he had watched her flourish as a student and teacher. They were intimates in many ways, and despite what could be called his betrayal over the Frost King affair, she who had no family and few friends in the world still needed his friendship and affection. She could not blithely cast him out of her life.

One cannot help but wonder how Helen reconciled her own feelings of betrayal by Anagnos with Annie's efforts to maintain favor with him—if indeed she knew about them.

From his Boston perch, Anagnos continued to be interested in anything Helen did or produced. He had heard about the completion of the sketch and so "promptly got in touch with *The Companion.*" He then preempted Ed's announcement and reported to Annie that "Helen's article was received with great pleasure at the office of *Youth's Companion.* Mr. Ford [the editor] has decided to send Helen one hundred dollars for it. This pleased good Mr. Chamberlin very much."[2]

In the year 1892, one hundred dollars was a large sum of money to be paid to a twelve-year-old child.[3] The news of the payment must have created considerable excitement in the Keller household.

As always, the news media remained fascinated by Helen. When she failed to return to Perkins for the school year after her "dark" summer, reports surfaced of her overwork and poor health. On December 19, Helen wrote in her own defense to John Hitz from Tuscumbia, where she and Annie remained:

My dear Mr. Hitz:

I hardly know how to begin a letter to you, it has been such a long time since your kind letter reached me, and there is so much I would like to write if I could. You must have wondered why your letter has not had an answer, and perhaps you have thought Teacher and me very naughty indeed. If so, you will be very sorry when I tell you something. Teacher's eyes have been hurting her so that she could not write to any one, and I have been trying to fulfill a promise which I made last summer.

Helen of course meant the piece for the *Companion.* She found it hard to write about herself but went on,

I sent the sketch to the Companion as soon as it was finished; but I do not know that they will accept it. Since then, I have not been well, and I have been obliged to keep very quiet, and rest; but to-day I am better, and to-morrow I shall be well again, I hope.

The reports which you have read in the papers about me are not true at all. We received the Silent Worker [publication] which you sent, and I wrote right away to the editor to tell him that [the article about me] was a mistake. Sometimes I am not well; but I am not a "wreck," and there is nothing "distressing" about my condition.

I enjoyed your dear letter so much! I am always delighted when any one writes me a beautiful thought which I can treasure in my memory forever. It is because my books are full of the riches of which

Mr. Ruskin speaks, that I love them so dearly. I did not realize, until I began to write the sketch for the Companion, what precious companions books have been to me, and how blessed even my life has been; and now I am happier than ever because I do realize the happiness that has come to me. I hope you will write to me as often as you can. Teacher and I are always delighted to hear from you. I want to write to Mr. Bell, and send him my picture. I supposed he has been too busy to write to his little friend. I often think of the pleasant times we had all together in Boston last spring.

Lovingly your little friend, Helen Keller[4]

Later in December, Ed sent payment for the sketch to Helen in Tuscumbia with a brief note. He again expressed concern for her health and wellbeing and encouraged her not to work too hard:

Dear Helen:

By the order of Mr. Ford, the Editor and Proprietor of the YOUTH'S COMPANION, *I enclose to you a check for $100.00 (one hundred dollars) in payment for the article which you sent to the paper. It was, as you will therefore understand, duly received and appreciated. To me, personally, it was a delightful and interesting article; it is a credit to you and also to your teacher, for if you had not been well taught you could not have written such an article, could you? But go on, my dear girl—not trying to learn too much of books, for that may weary you too much—but taking in more and more of the goodness and beauty of this world. Merry Christmas and happy New Year to you, dear Helen, and to Miss Sullivan and all those about you!*[5]

A few months later, on March 2, 1893, a most welcome baby boy, Raymond, was born to Ida and Ed, thirty-nine and forty-two years old, respectively. Ida's "ill health," which Ed had reported to Helen in December, was likely due to her pregnancy. In the 1890s, women's pregnancies were not often discussed. Ed would have especially avoided the topic in a conversation with a young girl like Helen.

Ed later said of Raymond's birth, "On a night when the world was full of dazzling light of the moon on deep wastes of snow in early March, another boy was born in our house, whom we called Raymond, reviving an old family name. Here, once more, was surely a child of beauty, though a different spirit seemed to breathe from his face and form."[6]

The happiness of the family was short-lived, however, as tragically, on April 6, their daughter Corda, whose sweet spirit Ed had earlier described in a letter to Helen, died at the age of four. Within three short years, the family had lost their second son, Charley, and their youngest daughter. It is plausible that as Raymond came into the world, his older sister Corda lay dying elsewhere in the house at Red Farm. By coincidence, when Ed had quoted Corda as saying she was "sirfty and sirfty" and "ever and ever drinking water today," he was perhaps unwittingly describing the sudden onset of the extreme and unquenchable thirst of juvenile diabetes. There was no treatment for the disease at the time, and if she did have diabetes, Corda would have endured a torturous descent toward inevitable death over those four months. It would be almost thirty more years before the cause of the disease was understood and treatment became possible. The Chamberlin family could have only watched helplessly as their little girl suffered through a painful, lingering struggle and then finally slipped away.[7] There is no further mention of Corda anywhere in preserved letters nor in the written family genealogy and history, not even among the writings of later family members.

It was a loss too devastating to ever mention again.

Somehow, once again, the family summoned strength and carried on. Only a month after Corda's passing, Ed was back at his desk, working to get Helen's sketch published. He wrote to Annie on May 6 regarding photographs to accompany the piece, noting his "great pleasure in having seen her recently." He added an important closing to the letter:

Sometimes I fear that in our interest in Helen, some of her friends fail to express the great sympathy that they must feel with you personally. It is one of the greatest of Helen's blessings that she has fallen into your hands! The world will surely not forget you, who have endowed Helen with so much of your own thought and feeling and gentleness, and give her your devotion, a lesson in love that is better than any other lesson that she has ever received.

Faithfully yours: J. E. Chamberlin[8]

This would prove to be a defining exchange. Ed was one of the few figures of the time to express his profound respect for Annie, his belief in her place in history, and her absolute necessity in Helen's life. Even before the accusations and suspicions of the Frost King debacle, Annie had craved personal and professional reassurance. She felt that need even more deeply now. Ed's statement was highly significant for her and bound her closely to him.

Ed had become Annie's firm ally. He understood and appreciated the complex, temperamental, and often difficult Annie Sullivan. That aspect would perhaps shape the future of the friendship he shared with Helen more than any other.

Throughout the remainder of 1893, Helen made numerous public appearances, including participation in the groundbreaking for the Volta Bureau's new building in Washington in May and serving as commencement speaker for Perkins in June.[9]

That same month, Annie wrote to John Hitz regarding studio photographs of Helen taken to accompany the *Youth's Companion* sketch. She asked for various photos to be sent to friends, including one to Anagnos, "from me with my compliments."[10]

Helen's sketch appeared in the January 4, 1894, issue of *Youth's Companion* and was called "My Story." A preface note under the title and author's name declared, "Written wholly without help of any sort by a deaf and blind girl twelve years old, and printed without change." In a touching and intimate style, Helen described her earliest memories of a world that went dark and silent after a sudden and unexplained illness at the age of nineteen months. Helen had only dim memories of life as a seeing and hearing child:

Of course my recollections of my early childhood are very indistinct. I have confused memories of long summer days filled with light, and the voices of birds singing in the clear sunshine. . . . But the brightest summer has winter behind it. In the cold, dreary month of February, when I was nineteen months old, I had a serious illness.

I still have confused memories of that illness. My mother sat beside my little bed and tried to soothe my feverish moans, while in her troubled heart she prayed: "Father in Heaven, spare my baby's life!" But the fever grew and flamed in my eyes, and for several days my kind physician thought I would die.

But early one morning the fever left me as mysteriously and unexpectedly as it had come, and I fell into a quiet sleep. Then my parents knew I would live, and they were very happy. They did not know for some time after my recovery that the cruel fever had taken my sight and hearing; taken all the light and music and gladness out of my little life. . . .

I was too young to realize what had happened. When I awoke and found that all was dark and still, I suppose I thought it was night, and I must have wondered why day was so long in coming. Gradually, however, I got used to the silence and darkness that surrounded me, and forgot that it had ever been day.

I forgot everything that had been, except my mother's tender love. Soon even my childish voice was stilled, because I had ceased to hear any sound.[11]

The Keller family was anguished by the outcome of Helen's illness. The toddler's once sweet personality was replaced by one full of anger and frustration; here now was a child who clung to her mother's dress as she went about her household duties, and whose hands "felt every object and observed every motion, and in this way learned a great many things," but unable to express her own thoughts and desires verbally, she began to have frequent and violent temper tantrums, even once toppling her infant sister from her cradle. Fortunately, sister Mildred was caught by her mother before hitting the floor.[12] Helen herself later called the frequency of these outbursts "daily, sometimes hourly."[13]

Helen described her first meeting in 1887 with Annie Sullivan, the woman she would come to call "Teacher":

I was standing on the porch when Teacher arrived. I had been waiting there ever since my mother kissed me and went to the station to meet the strange lady. I can imagine it all now. There

I stood, clinging to the lattice of the porch, wistfully waiting for I knew not what.

The last rays of the setting sun fell upon my hair and softly kissed my upturned face. Suddenly, I felt approaching footsteps; they came nearer; I stretched out my little hand eagerly, someone took it, and in another instant I was in my Teacher's arms. I felt her face and hands curiously, and let her kiss me, while feelings that I cannot describe entered my heart.

We could not speak to each other; I could not ask her why she had come. Yet I am sure I felt, in a vague, bewildered way that something beautiful was going to happen to me. I knew the strange lady loved me, and that her love would make my life sweet and good and happy.[14]

In April, the realization that Annie was spelling letters that formed words into her hand "startled" Helen's soul, and by May Helen had learned to read books in braille. She continued in her sketch: "I read my first story on May Day, and ever since books and I have been loving friends and inseparable companions. They have made a bright world of thought and beauty all around me. They have been my faithful teacher in all that is good and beautiful. Their pages have carried me back to ancient times, and shown me Egypt, Greece, Rome! They have introduced me to kings, heroes, and gods, and they have revealed to me great thoughts, great deeds."[15]

Helen's sketch ends with an expression of gratitude and sweetness impossible for readers to resist: "I will end here this little story of my childhood. I am spending the winter at my home in the lovely south, the land of sunshine and flowers, surrounded by all that makes life sweet and natural; loving parents, a precious baby brother, a tender little sister and the dearest teacher in the world. My life is full of happiness. Every day brings me some new joy, some fresh token of love from distant friends, until in the fullness of my glad heart, I cry: 'Love is everything! And God is Love!'"[16]

The public's response to "My Story" was immediate and positive. An outpouring of letters began to arrive in Tuscumbia for Helen. She wrote to Reverend Edward Hale that "the publication of my little story in *The Youth's Companion* has brought me a large number of letters,—last week I received sixty-one!—and besides replying to some of those letters, I have many lessons to learn."[17]

In February 1894, Ed wrote to Annie, in response to a request from her to print a plea for readers not to send letters to Helen:

My dear Miss Sullivan:

I received your note of January 29 and at once did what I could to comply with your suggestions, but I found that your letter had come about a week too late. . . .

A notice was prepared [asking that letters not be sent to Helen] and put in type, and will appear in the current number of THE COMPANION. *Mr. Stanwood tells me that if [only] my request had come a week sooner. . . . I do, indeed, fear that you will have more letters. It is a strange world; I shall never understand why so many people will write importuning letters to famous people. I do not know a single person who has written a book or many articles or poems who is not thus written to. . . . Happy for Helen, and hard for* YOU *that she cannot see and read these missives!*

With the business nature of his correspondence completed, Ed went on to explain his lack of communication during the preceding months. The family was struggling:

It was very pleasant to hear from you, though I should greatly have liked to hear how YOU *are. I trust your duties are not wearing nervously on you. When may we see you again here? Please give to Helen the dear love of myself and all my family. We have had some illness at home this winter,—I myself had to run away in the fall for a month from asthma and nervous exhaustion—but I am all right again now and hard at work.*

*Our baby, our little Raymond, is eleven months old now, and a very vigorous and jolly fellow—*A GREAT COMFORT. *[Our oldest daughter] Helen is well along with her second year in the Institute of Technology.*

I am very sorry that I couldn't do what you asked. My best wishes are always with you and Helen.[18]

The trauma of the past year for the Chamberlins had caught up with Ed, and he had to run away in the fall for a month "due to nervous exhaustion."[19] Perhaps he retreated to the mountains of Vermont, away from all thoughts of work and deadlines; possibly he stayed in East Corinth—long a favorite vacation spot—where his son Charley had spent his last days and near where Ed had family. But he was now back at work.

The publication of Helen's sketch was met with great acclaim in the press, as well as with readers. Among other critiques, the *Illustrated American* commented, "Her sketch is beautifully composed, a distinctly fine quality of literary skill." "My Story" effectively launched Helen on a writing career.[20] Although it took almost two years to accomplish, the publication of the sketch helped further dispel the dark cloud of suspicion the Frost King affair had fostered. Ed had offered a lifeline to Helen and Annie, and they would not forget it.

But Helen's lack of mention of Perkins irritated the attention-seeking Anagnos and led to the end of their already tenuous friendship.[21] In his mind, it further confirmed that he could not trust Annie, and that she would not credit the school for Helen's success nor advance Perkins in the public eye.

In 1906, after Anagnos's death, Helen wrote bitterly of the demise of the relationship:

It was after 1893, after we had ceased to avail ourselves of the hospitality of the Perkins Institution, that Mr. Anagnos proved untrue to the friendship between us. It was then that he began, not in written statements but by word of mouth, to impugn our integrity. . . . And after we, of our own will and contrary to Mr. Anagnos's wish had left the Institution finally, he declared and continued to declare to one person and another his opinion that we were one or both guilty. Once at the Kindergarten for the Blind in the presence of several friends, one of whom reported the matter direct to us and demanded explanation. He did not deny that he had said that thing, but reported that my teacher had taught me to deceive. . . . That was the wrong Mr. Anagnos did my teacher. That was the untruth he told of me.[22]

While Annie and Helen spurned Anagnos, Ed maintained his loyalty to the man, saying many years later, "I know he was terribly shaken up by the Frost King episode, and if he cooled toward Annie it was because he had a fear that her zeal for Helen had a tendency to exaggerate her personality and ability. I think he was wrong in feeling thus. But I believe he always had a sincere affection and high regard for Annie. I never lost my own confidence in and affection for Anagnos."[23]

Ed Chamberlin tried his best to see and understand all sides of the situation.

PART II

CHAPTER SIX

Away and Back to Boston, 1894–1896

On June 27, 1894, Helen turned fourteen. Throughout the remainder of 1893 and the first part of 1894, she and Annie had lived primarily at the Keller home in Tuscumbia. Travel opportunities had arisen, however: Helen and Annie were guests of Alexander and Mabel Bell in the spring of 1893, and toured Niagara Falls with Dr. Bell in April. Later that summer, once again with Bell, they attended the World's Fair in Chicago.[1]

During that same time, they occasionally visited Robinswood, the countryside estate of philanthropist William Wade, in Hulton, Pennsylvania. Wade was an extraordinarily generous man who had taken an early interest in Helen, having read about her in *St. Nicholas* magazine in 1889. Soon after, he sent her a mastiff puppy and other gifts of braille books and educational materials. During her stays at Robinswood, he provided a tutor to instruct Helen in Latin, arithmetic, and poetry.[2] The visits provided welcome respite for the pair and assisted Annie with Helen's schooling. Wade was a benefactor to many other deafblind individuals as well, "furnishing them individually with books, bicycles, vacations, and other luxuries to 'alleviate their loneliness.'"[3]

But even as the Frost King scandal calmed in the public eye, other concerns arose. As Helen grew and her intellectual abilities became apparent, family and friends recognized that she needed an appropriate setting in which to further her education. But all suitable schools required funds for tuition and board, and her family had few resources. American southerners were not the only ones struggling: the years 1893–1894 saw an economic crisis on a national and global scale.[4]

It was a challenging time to be looking for philanthropic support. Helen's education and Annie's salary only created further burdens on the already financially challenged Keller family. Annie reported to Anagnos in a letter that Arthur Keller had "taken custody of stock, checks, and the story money that Helen received from *The Youth's Companion*," most likely to help support the family.[5] Annie, who had known abject poverty in her childhood, was justifiably worried about Helen's financial future as well as her own.[6]

During these years, Helen and Annie had become more aligned with Bell and John Hitz than with Perkins and Michael Anagnos.[7] Bell was a tireless learner and a wealthy and influential man, having invented the telephone almost twenty years earlier. In the summer of 1894, he was in his late forties, physically and intellectually impressive, with a head of thick white hair, a full beard, and the girth of a man who lived well. He was constantly experimenting. In addition to his interest in the science of sound, Bell was also fascinated with the idea of flight and was conducting extensive experiments on flying machines and kites at his family's summer home in Nova Scotia.[8]

Helen always acknowledged Bell's formative role in her life, saying of the day she met him with her father in Washington, DC, in 1886, "that interview would be the door through which I should pass from darkness into light." Further, in a later letter to him, she wrote, "Even before my teacher came, you held out a hand to me in the dark. I have not forgotten how you followed step by step my teacher's efforts to free my mind, my life, my heart from the tyranny of circumstance. . . . When others who had little faith in the power of spirit to conquer blindness doubted and faltered, it was you who heartened us for the struggle."[9]

Probably through letters from Annie, Bell now learned of the Keller's financial constraints. In the spring and summer of 1894, he began soliciting supporters among Helen and Annie's friends in Boston.[10]

On July 20, Bell wrote to Captain Keller on the matter of Helen's education and financial support, saying, "I must apologize for not writing you on this regarding Helen, but I did not wish to make any suggestions until I had had an opportunity of talking with Helen herself and with Miss Sullivan. . . . I have had a long talk with Helen about herself so as to get her ideas concerning her own advancement. She expresses a strong desire to have her education continued in conjunction with seeing and hearing young ladies, and I think she is right." Based on Helen's wishes, Bell believed it important to send her to "the best private school for hearing and seeing young ladies" and advised her father to "consider first what may be best for Helen quite irrespective of expense." He believed "Helen's friends will be glad to co-operate with you in carrying out whatever plan you may deem best for her future."[11]

Bell also mentioned that a new school had been established in New York City and was demonstrating interest in Helen's matriculation. Helen's parents and Annie would end up choosing that school, the Wright-Humason School for the Deaf, for Helen. They were particularly attracted by its expertise in lip-reading and speech skills. Beginning in 1890, Helen had worked with Sarah Fuller of the Horace Mann School in Boston on her speech skills, as "the impulse to utter audible sounds had always been strong" in her, but even after intense instruction and practice, only those very close to her could understand her speech, and only with difficulty.[12] Helen desperately wanted to learn to speak and hoped Wright-Humason could help realize that dream.

The *New York Times* did not miss the opportunity to share the news of Helen's arrival, posting an article on January 6, 1895, with the headline, "A Bright Blind Girl: Helen Keller of Boston Comes to a School in New York." The article described Helen as "the pretty and remarkably intelligent blind, deaf-and-dumb girl of Boston," and noted that "her cheery words, sweet thoughts, and great enjoyment of life under conditions—the loss of sight, hearing, and until recently the power of speech—which would seem to many persons unbearable, have made her known all over the world."[13]

Helen attended the Wright-Humason School for the next two years, paid for by one of Bell's "friends," the wealthy Boston sugar magnate John P. "King John" Spaulding, who was a Perkins supporter who had met and befriended Helen and Annie during their early days in Boston. He was a legendarily generous benefactor whom Helen described as "one who made every one happy in a beautiful, unobtrusive way, [and] was most kind and tender to Miss Sullivan and me."[14]

While at Wright-Humason, though she "did not make the gains in speech that she had hoped," Helen learned the lip-reading method she relied on for the rest of her life with close friends, called the Tadoma Method: "She placed the index finger of her left hand on the speaker's lips, perpendicular to the lips, and her thumb on the speaker's throat.[15] She read the vibrations of the throat and the movement of the lips . . . to comprehend at least the majority of what was said. This left her right hand free to fingerspell quick exchanges with Annie or another companion."[16]

In April 1895, Helen took the opportunity to extend an olive branch to Anagnos back in Boston and wrote him of her efforts to learn "lip-reading and voice-training." She reflected on her "fond memories of when she was a little child and sat on his lap," though she "now sometimes felt that he would not want to hear from her."[17] Hurt feelings still lingered.

The positive publicity Helen's presence garnered for Wright-Humason was not lost on its principals, John D. Wright and Thomas A. Humason. They released monthly reports of Helen's progress throughout her attendance. But, though Wright-Humason provided an adequate educational setting for Helen, and she and Annie enjoyed New York's atmosphere and cultural opportunities, Annie soon began chafing at the instructional methods being used.

Sometime during the 1895–1896 school year, Annie, for whom letter writing was becoming increasingly difficult due to the strain it caused her eyes, wrote an unusually long and vehement letter to John Hitz regarding Helen's experience at Wright-Humason and the current trends in deaf education. In her letter, she gave insight into her own approach to teaching language to Helen: "Thank Heaven I didn't have to follow a curriculum when I began teaching Helen. I am convinced she wouldn't have learned language as easily as she did. . . . Helen learned language almost as unconsciously as the normal child."

At Wright-Humason, she wrote, learning "is made a lesson. The child sits in-doors, and for an hour the teacher endeavors more or less skillfully to engrave words upon his brain." Annie believed that "children learn language more quickly when they are free to move among objects that interest them. They absorb words and knowledge simultaneously. In the class-room they cease to be actors in the drama.... Passivity does not stimulate interest or mental energy. The child learns eagerly what he wants to know, and indifferently what you want him to know."

Annie attended all of Helen's classes with her to interpret lessons. She went on in her letter, "I have thought much about methods of teaching since I came here. The contrast between these children's plodding pursuit of knowledge and Helen's bounding joyousness makes me wonder. When I go into one of the class-rooms and see little children sitting demurely behind their small desks, while a teacher sits in front of them, holding an object in her hand for their inspection . . . I feel somehow as if they were chained to their seats, and forced to gaze intently at a giantess who made faces at them."

Annie was critical of what she had seen, observing, "I very seldom speak of what is in my mind. I do not think teachers are at all open-minded. To say that they do not welcome ideas which imply criticism of their methods is to put it mildly. I do not know if all teachers close their minds to the stupidities they practice. I have known only teachers of the blind and the deaf, and I pity them more than I blame them."

She summed up her feelings: "There isn't a doubt in my mind that schools force upon the young an abnormal life. The hours are too long, too many subjects are taught, too complicated methods are employed."

Annie hoped that Hitz would show her letter to Dr. Bell and have him use his influence to "impress upon the instructors of the deaf that what their pupils need is more out-of-door lessons—lessons about living things—trees and flowers and animals—things they love, and are curious about." She concluded, "The child happily interested in his work learns quickly and without conscious effort."[18]

John Hitz replied enthusiastically to Annie's letter: "Dr. Bell is so delighted with your criticism of educational methods in the schools for the deaf that he is desirous for you to prepare a paper (it need not be long) for the Convention on the subject."[19]

The American Association to Promote the Teaching of Speech to the Deaf Convention was to be held that summer and Helen and Annie would make plans to attend.

The time in New York was productive in terms of new friendships for Helen and Annie. In addition to their established Boston connections, Helen and Annie now developed important relationships with powerful New Yorkers. In reality, there was not a great deal of separation between the literary worlds of Boston and New York. Many Boston writers, editors, and publishers had important ties to New York—and vice versa—through constant collaboration and contact.

Two new and important New York friends were Laurence Hutton and his wife, Eleanor. Helen Keller scholar Kim Nielsen has noted that Laurence Hutton, much like Ed Chamberlin, was a significant, powerful figure in the American literary sphere, having served since 1886 as literary editor of *Harper's* magazine.[20] The Huttons met Helen and Annie in 1895 and "drew them into the active social world of their New York home," introducing them to philanthropists and business giants like the oil magnates John D. Rockefeller and Henry H. Rogers, as well as prominent literary figures such as Ed's friend William Dean Howells, editor of the *Atlantic Monthly,* and his close friend, Mark Twain—both frequent contributors to *Youth's Companion.*[21]

Eleanor Hutton became a close friend and advocate for Helen and Annie. A kind yet strong woman with significant business skills, she took an increasing role in managing their finances through the years, and Annie relied on her extensively for business advice. Helen later described her as "a true and tried friend" who was "ever encouraging," adding, "much that I hold sweetest, much that I hold most precious, I owe to her."[22]

As for Mark Twain, Helen would later tell of having felt the "twinkle of his eye" in his handshake when they first met.[23] Twain was fascinated by Helen and became her lifelong friend. He described himself as "in disbelief" of Helen's bright spirit and expressed "limitless admiration of the wonders [Annie] performed." He considered Helen to be "the most remarkable woman he had ever met in his life" and later advocated strenuously among his wealthy New York friends to support her education.[24] Although he had not known Helen during the Frost King affair, he described the accusations of plagiarism as "unspeakably funny and owlishly idiotic and grotesque." In a letter to Helen on the subject years later, he could barely contain his disgust, describing her accusers as "a gang of dull and hoary pirates piously setting themselves the task of disciplining and purifying a kitten that they think they've caught filching a chop!"[25]

The pair made numerous other New York friends, among them wealthy bankers and businessmen who would take a long-term interest in their welfare.

Although their time in the city was beneficial in many respects, plans to continue at Wright-Humason were under review by late in Helen's second year there. It is possible that Annie's disdain for Helen's educational experience at the school was not limited to letters she sent to John Hitz and Alexander Graham Bell. She was also increasingly worried about the future, with growing concern about finances. Helen and Annie's primary benefactor, "King John" Spaulding, had died suddenly in January 1896, which grieved them personally. While he had suggested he "would be providing for them in his will, that did not happen," to their additional great disappointment.[26] Helen wrote a poignant tribute to Spaulding that appeared in the *Boston Transcript* on January 17.[27]

Dr. Bell had already been trying to build support for Helen's education, but fundraising now began in earnest.[28] The Huttons, and in particular Eleanor, would be especially important in this endeavor. Collectively, after the second year at Wright-Humason, Helen, Annie, and her supporters decided that a school should be found in the Boston area that could better prepare her for Radcliffe College—for ever since Helen had visited Wellesley as a little girl, her dream had been to attend Radcliffe, Harvard's counterpart for women.[29]

Back in Boston, Ed Chamberlin remained a vocal advocate for the Perkins Kindergarten for the Blind. In many ways, after Helen left Perkins in 1892, Ed continued the philanthropic work she had cared about most, as demonstrated through her fundraising tea. Ed advocated for little Tommy Stringer's education and worked extensively to raise funds for the Kindergarten. Michael Anagnos favored Ed's newspaper, the *Boston Transcript*, with frequent reports and friendly visits to their offices. Between January and April 1895, a "*Transcript* fund for the benefit of the Kindergarten for the Blind" raised more than $5,000 for "immediate needs." The paper published fundraising progress on a weekly basis, with all donors publicly acknowledged. In a letter to the editor, one reader noted that Ed, as "a clear-sighted critic," was an esteemed and respected friend of the Kindergarten; if he said it was a worthwhile investment for the public, "so it must be."[30]

Once Helen and Annie left the Boston area, Perkins drew on the charms of their remaining three deafblind students for public appeals. Laura Bridgman had died in May 1889, and without Helen Keller as a student, Edith Thomas, Willie Robin, and Tommy Stringer became the new "faces" for the deafblind at Perkins. Their images, stories, and academic progress appeared frequently in newspapers across the country, and just like Helen, they became household names.

Along with his advocacy for the Perkins Kindergarten, Ed still worked as an editor at *Youth's Companion*. Under the ownership of Daniel Sharp Ford, the magazine had grown its circulation to almost half a million subscribers. It was now one of the most popular weekly family magazines in the country. Each issue was densely packed with adventure stories, anecdotes, poems, and historical articles. Since 1892, it had become widely known as "The Pledge of Allegiance" magazine, which added to its wholesome and patriotic image. The magazine continued to popularize both new and established writers. Since the early 1890s, the magazine had featured the poems of Emily Dickinson, who had died in 1874 but whose works were now being released for publication by her relatives and friends.[31]

Close to home, Ed's columns for the *Transcript* were cherished by his readership. In 1896, he published two small "companion" books that were compilations of his best work from the "Listener in the Town" and "Listener in the Country" columns.[32] Upon publication of the books, *The Critic* literary review described "a dinner given to the author" at the Revere House, one of the finest hotels in Boston at the time, "by a number of well-known literary men and women. Many who could not attend sent interesting letters of regret; for Mr. Chamberlin's graceful contributions to the *Evening Transcript* have won a wide circle of readers and admirers."[33] The *Boston Herald* wrote a feature about the event that listed twenty-six notable members of the literary community in attendance and commented that Reverend Edward Hale and W. D. Howells, the latter considered "the Dean of American Letters," were not able to attend but sent letters of congratulations that were read to those in attendance. Conspicuous among the attendees honoring Ed that night was his friend and admirer Mr. Michael Anagnos.[34]

Annie and Helen planned their return to Boston, with its range of memories and opportunities, spending the summer of 1896 searching for an appropriate school setting for Helen. In the meantime, they intended to spend the first three weeks of the summer at Red Farm. While there, Helen would turn sixteen.

Although it had been several years since Ed and Ida had last hosted the pair, with customary good cheer they welcomed Annie and Helen back to their household. Since the women's last visit, another Chamberlin family member had been added: a baby girl named Mary Eleanor, called "Dolly." The Chamberlins' eldest daughter Helen had graduated from MIT with a degree in architecture in 1896 and was working in the Boston area but likely still living at Red Farm.

Among other pleasures, Annie could anticipate that Ed would provide a ready and sympathetic ear to her lamentations about the state of education, with shared beliefs that education should occur as much as possible through direct experience, including outdoors. And he would be pleased with Helen's new speaking and lip-reading abilities.[35]

According to plan, Helen and Annie arrived for their vacation in early June. They were now back in Ed's "Listener" column territory. Helen delighted in his astute observations. The columns also pleased Annie, whose eyes allowed her only to see at a distance with opera glasses, and even then with great difficulty. But Helen and Annie could see all through Ed's vivid and picturesque writing and would follow his columns faithfully for more than thirty years.

As "The Listener in the Town," Ed wrote what he called "humanity studies" of the people inhabiting Boston and the cities and towns around it. The studies painted detailed and lively pictures in the mind of the reader. No social strata went unnoticed or unremarked upon; the columns were varied, surprising, entertaining, and highly anticipated. Ed enjoyed writing them, saying, "When I cannot walk in the real woods, I often walk in the forests of humanity,—in those withered, smoke-swept thickets of people that we call locally the South End, and the North End, and the Cove. They are not sweet, like other woods, and yet some rare flowers are found there—together with many sad, morbid fungus-growths."[36]

He explained his fascination with the human form: "Seen for the first or the last time, indeed, the human being is the most beautiful thing we know. . . . When I meet a great crowd, my eyes go over the faces as a swift reaper's sickle goes over a field, harvesting the beauty that has ripened there. I like the rude growth of the street, that has ripened under the sun and the storm, better too, than the hot-house plants of choicer stock; and I know that the crop that grows there I shall never exhaust."[37]

"The Listener" examined scenes that most readers saw every day. He created elegant contemplations of the most mundane aspects of daily life, which heightened his readers' sensitivity and illuminated the humanity and similarities in people—leaving a new, shared, and often amusing appreciation of the ordinary. Most of the studies were of women and men who did not know they were being observed, creating a somewhat voyeuristic experience for the reader. The reader was invited to observe and think and even judge along with him but could be ever confident that any judgment would be kind.

In a piece entitled "A Little World," Ed described the "slices of life" and social strata that one could observe by sitting at a vantage point opposite the facade of a city building. He wrote, "There is no better way of getting at a clever epitome of human life in this epoch than by taking possession of a window opposite the middle of the front of some big city building in which a variety of occupations is carried on,—somewhere well down town, where there are stores at the bottom of the building, offices higher up, and then small industries in the lofts at the top. It is astonishing to observe what a microcosm of the world, its aspirations and passions, its vices and its virtues, one has before him."[38]

Each "plate-glass" window captured a vignette: the merchant, the printer, and those conducting unknown commercial enterprise. Above ground, "we peep into the windows of the offices above the store. . . . This lawyer's office is eminently masculine in all its ways, from the flat, open table, upon which a big man, leaning far back in his swivel-chair comfortably disposes his large feet. . . . No *work* is ever done in this office; but we are reminded, by the earnest, tense expressions of this little group of men waiting there, that great things may be done in a moment, and fortunes decided by a word."[39]

Above the lawyer's office, "the women sewing in the large rooms . . . are women as much as you, but their lot is surely less agreeable. They do not use machines, these seamstresses; they are at work upon some mysterious commodity of trade which can be made with nothing but the hand; and they have been toiling there for months and years just as they are today." After offering peeks into other floors of offices, he summed up: "All sorts of people to make a world; and here they all are, scattered along the front of this six-story brick building in Tremont Street."[40]

In a more poignant vignette, Ed's benevolent heart clutched at the sight of a child of the streets, a "city child," whom he described in a column titled "The Victim":

Up and down [a] miserable court toddled a small human figure,—a little boy, who looked as if he might be three or four years old. He was half clad. His little face was grimy and weazened, and his bare legs bowed out wretchedly. . . . All at once another and much bigger boy—an evil-looking chap—rushed out of the door of one of the houses and made toward the little fellow, who cowered at once, the expression on his face changing to one of dreadful terror. There, as if fearing brutal fists, the crooked child stood in abjectness,—not a child, but a gnome, a being of the Under World, proclaimed a Victim in every line of his terrified face, in every unbeautiful curve of his little body, in every rag that clothed him. . . . He crouches still in my heart.[41]

The image painted by Ed's words would linger vividly in Helen's memory and be revisited in the future.

Although fascinated by cities and their inhabitants, Ed often needed to escape the rigor and hum for the country, where all was quiet and restorative and he could turn his attention to nature. In his "Listener in the Country" columns, Ed made the natural world accessible to all. He wrote often of mountains and sought their solace throughout his life, with "their great beauty and exceeding individuality," and to his mind, "a loveliness that nothing in nature could surpass."[42]

He extolled the pleasures to be found in rural places. He shared studies of birds, animals, seasons, and the folk of the countryside. The bird studies were detailed illuminations of the personalities of birds: stories of the woodcock, the "queer, uncouth water-bird who has taken to the land"; the screech-owl "whose cry, despite his ill name, is one of the sweetest sounds in nature"; and the musical and quirky whippoorwill who inhabited Ed's dooryard.[43]

Winter held a special fascination for Ed. Venturing out after an ice storm, he put on a pair of rubber boots and a mackintosh and started for the woods. He wrote,

The boots go grating through the shallow crust, and the walking is not particularly easy, but the splendor and wildness of the spectacle put all thought of the hard walking out of my mind. Crossing the field and descending into a ravine, the loosened icy fragments from the tall blades of grass rattle down after me like a hail-storm on a glass roof. Here is a clump of cedars, pitch pines, and white birches growing on the side of the hill, with a little extemporized pond at its base. . . . The surface of the pond is a clear, brilliant Nile-green, the ice and snow showing through the shallow water, and its surface seeming to gather the light from snow and clouds all about.[44]

In his "Lost in the Fells" narrative about the Middlesex Fells natural area outside of Boston, Ed suggested, "There are many people in Boston who complain of an inability to find any new and thoroughly distracting amusement. Why not go out and get lost in the Fells at nightfall, as I did the other night?"

He had originally gone out in search of a "certain jungle of wild trumpet honeysuckle" and found himself lost. His readers struggled alongside him as he traversed a succession of "rocky, briery ridges and dark ravines, the tops of ledgey knolls," and many paths and roads that "dissipated themselves in the woods." He blundered on, and his feet grew sore. He "dragged away tough branches from in front of his face until his hands and wrists were almost painfully scratched," and until he was discovered, "as it were, by a long glittering landscape of lights, stretching out beneath the hill-top to which a cart-path led his feet," he was quite scared. The return to the inhabited world was "an unwelcome grip." He wished that he had not been found.[45]

For her part, Ida Chamberlin wore with pride the mantle of wife of Joseph Edgar Chamberlin, the "Listener" of the *Boston Evening Transcript*. Certainly, details of the Chamberlin household were known throughout New England from Ed's writings. It was a personal, and very public, domestic transparency that required a confident wife.

Ida came to her role naturally, having spent her childhood immersed in the news world of Chicago as the daughter of an editor and then, after marriage at the age of sixteen, as the wife of a writer and editor. She was accustomed to being at the forefront of news and information. She had also grown up close to the affluent households of her aunts in Chicago and had known a lively, intellectual, and *au courant* social life. In Boston, Ed commuted into town, meeting luminaries with whom his work brought him into contact, and Ida was eager to meet those people as well.

Ida clearly loved to arrange gatherings at Red Farm, and she was a capable, energetic, and welcoming hostess. With her maternal nature and social graces, she charmed her frequent and numerous guests.

Helen and Annie's return to the area was cause for celebration. Helen reported in a July 15 letter to John Hitz, "We spent about three weeks in Boston, after leaving New York, and I need not tell you that we had a most delightful time. We visited our good friends, Mr. and Mrs. Chamberlin, at Wrentham, out in the country, where they have a lovely home. Their house stands near a charming lake where we went boating and canoeing, which was great fun. We also went in bathing several times."[46]

Ed was by this time a member of the St. Botolph's Club of Boston, a private club for eminent members of the arts and literary community, but there were also many other connective social groups and institutions that expanded the Chamberlin circle of friends even wider, including colleges, churches, and shared avocations. The boundaries of the Red Farm circle were fluid, and numerous men and women circulated in and out over the years. Many of the "members" of the circle were connected to the Chamberlins and to one another through Reverend Edward Everett Hale.

With Red Farm an easy train ride from the city, a colorful crowd of young and attractive intellectuals visited the household. These were people who made their living through words, music, and art, and they gathered at Red Farm, attracted to Ed for his gentle nature, progressive thinking, "encyclopedic knowledge," and love of language, and to Ida for her welcoming spirit and love of family, home, and music.[47]

For Helen, whose view of life and the world around her was shaped by the words spelled into her hand, time spent among the friends gathered by Ed and Ida was transformative. It was at Red Farm that the maturing Helen was nurtured in many ways. As she herself said, "What a wealth of thought Uncle Ed introduced me to in the talk of his friends who looked at things in a fresh way, so that the world grew young again with their new interpretation of it!"[48] The Red Farm circle provided unique and ideal interpreters of life for Helen and Annie.

Helen wrote to a friend that "the Chamberlins celebrated the 17th of June by giving a picnic to their literary friends. There were about forty persons present, all of whom were writers and publishers. Our friend, Mr. Alden, the editor of *Harper's* was there, and of course we enjoyed his society very much."[49]

The event celebrated Bunker Hill Day and was an annual tradition for the Chamberlins. Ida once described it to a friend as "the day [each year] when our friends congregate 'en masse.'"[50] The *Boston Herald* described the picnic in its July 4, 1896, edition and included a list of attendees, among them Helen and Annie.[51]

Red Farm was a safe place to be unusual or forward thinking. Annie's brashness and strong opinions neither shocked nor alienated Ed and Ida or their friends. In return, the influence of the Red Farm circle on Helen and Annie was significant. The frequent visitors inspired and nurtured, challenged and thrilled the pair. Helen later acknowledged to Ed the significance of these experiences at Red Farm:

When you included us in the circle of your charming hospitality, we entered the intellectual atmosphere of which Teacher had dreamed. Through you she enjoyed satisfying conversation with persons who had seen or traveled or done large things. Eagerly she drank with me the fresh, sweet waters of thought that flowed under the old linden in the yard at Red Farm. I remember how we sat in its shade, listened to the poems of Bliss Carman, Richard Hovey, Louise Guinney [sic], *Archibald Lampman, and heard the comments of you, Edward Everett Hale, Miss Nina Smith and Mary Wilkins. What wit, spontaneous humor, flashing criticisms and good-natured banter there were! We both have ever looked back upon those days as the richest and brightest experience of our lives.*[52]

Louise Imogen Guiney, whom Helen frequently mentioned, was a poet, author, and essayist. It is easy to see why she was so memorable: if Guiney was there, the party was going to be fun. One of Guiney's friends called her "the most vital and creative personal influence in the lives of all of us who gathered together at the time. She was equally at ease in intellectual debate and athletic contests. She loved fresh air, high winds, rowing and hiking, often with her pet St. Bernard dogs as companions."[53]

Perhaps most colorful of the crowd was Guiney's close friend Fred Holland Day, who often dressed flamboyantly and dramatically. Artistic and sensitive, he was the publisher, along with Herbert Copeland, of Ed's *Listener* books. The Copeland & Day firm was established in the later 1890s, financed by Day, whose father had made a fortune in leather manufacturing. With his financial resources, Day could pursue any enthusiasm he chose. After just a few years in publishing—during which Copeland & Day issued more than one hundred titles, "at least a quarter of them by authors associated with *Youth's Companion.*" Day devoted himself to photography. He was one of the first in the United States to advocate for photography as a fine art.[54]

From his home in Norwood, Day made several photographic expeditions to the area around Red Farm and "produced a series of open-air studies, comprising both group and individual images."[55] One of these expeditions was captured in an informal photograph that depicts Louise Peabody Sargent and her children frolicking in the woods with the Chamberlins. The Sargent and Chamberlin children are dressed in fantastical costumes and playing antique musical instruments.

In reaction to one of the images from that excursion, Guiney wrote to Day that she regarded "a study of [Beth] Chamberlin lying on a leopard skin in the grass as particularly moving: your Wrentham photo is such a wonder, I haven't words for it. If you ever want a title for it for exhibition, please do call it, 'Papillon Dormant.' It gives the most lovely, moth-like effect in the world."[56] The photograph of Beth was later owned by the famed photographer Alfred Stieglitz and subsequently became part of the permanent collection of the Metropolitan Museum of Art in New York. In the image, Beth is posed semi-nude, covered by a sheer drape and lying on a leopard skin.

When not together, Day and Guiney corresponded almost daily, leaving behind a detailed record of their lives and their work.[57] By the turn of the century, Day would become one of the most influential photographers in the world, along with Gertrude Kasebier, Edward Steichen, and Stieglitz. Later, Day abandoned all photographic work, "took ill," and became confined to his bedroom, living out his life—though he welcomed visitors—in his large gabled home in Norwood, outside of Boston.[58] But between 1895 and 1898, he had seemingly boundless "creative energy and artistic imagination" and held an esteemed place in American photography.[59]

Ed and Ida were patrons of many of those who frequented Red Farm. In 1896, they commissioned the handsome young Uruguayan-born artist F. Luis Mora to create oil and pencil portraits of their children. Mora had studied at the School of the Museum of Fine Arts in Boston, finishing his schooling by the age of nineteen. In the summer of 1896, Mora had recently returned from Spain where he had coincidentally met and painted with the American impressionist painter William Merritt Chase in the El Museo del Prado in Madrid. He was now beginning his professional career back in the states as a portraitist—a career that would lead to important commissions and widespread recognition.[60]

Charles Waddell Chesnutt, an African American author and political activist, described one visit to Red Farm: "Yesterday evening I went out to Wrentham with my friend Mr. Chamberlin of the *Boston Transcript* and stayed all night. They meant to invite our girls to visit them during Easter, but the lady [Ida] was taken down with the grippe yesterday and received me in her bedroom, for she insisted on my coming up. Lovely people."[61]

As the summer of 1896 began, the Chamberlins could celebrate: the family was healthy and thriving, Helen and Annie were back in their midst, and there were intellectuals and progressive thinkers to be entertained. Ed had recently published his *Listener* books and had future works in cultivation.

Just as he had been introduced to the joys of nature during his own childhood in Wisconsin with his father, older brothers, and friends, Ed and his coterie introduced Helen and Annie to the natural world around them at Red Farm. There, Helen lived in the full embrace of the out-of-doors. All experiences were made available to her: boating, hiking, swimming, walking, cycling, and horseback riding. Although the Chamberlins made accommodations when necessary, their goal was always to enable Helen and Annie to live the limitless, active lives they themselves enjoyed.

For Helen and Annie, Red Farm was the retreat—the idyll—they both needed and craved. Helen described her enjoyment of times at Red Farm in a later letter to Ida: "We can never forget the happy days we spent with you, nor all your many kindnesses to us. Oh, how often I think of the jolly times I had at Wrentham, rowing and canoeing and sleeping in a tent! Often . . . I think of the nights when the radiant moon and stars peeped in at our tent-door. How fresh, and lovely and cool the mornings were!"[62]

Red Farm and its residents and guests were ideal narrators for Helen. Without the senses of sight and hearing, Helen's hand was "her window to the world." As she herself said, all of her knowledge and understanding of her surroundings was poured into her hand: "My hand is to me what your hearing and sight together are in you. In large measure, we travel the same highways, read the same books, speak the same language, yet our experiences are different. All my comings and goings turn on the hand as on a pivot."[63]

Helen wrote often of things she "saw," and of course this was only figurative. However, Annie and Helen's companions tried to describe her surroundings so clearly that Helen was able to describe the visual world as if she had seen everything through her own eyes. Helen's friend Nella Braddy Henney noted much later in Helen's life that people were aroused to the work of "seeing" for Helen and became their best selves in her presence: "All who come near her are affected. No one is quite himself. People mount to levels they had not thought themselves capable of reaching. Gifted and ungifted alike bring her the best they have and, remembering her lost eyes, look at the world for her as well as for themselves and describe from the passing show what they think will most increase her knowledge and pleasure, receiving in turn new insights that startle them."[64]

Without sight or hearing, the senses of touch, smell, and taste became dominant for Helen and were finely cultivated. Helen once noted, "Remember that you, dependent on your sight, do not realize how many things are tangible. Every object is associated in my mind with tactual qualities which, combined in countless ways, give me a sense of power, of beauty, or of incongruity."[65] She elaborated,

Through the sense of touch I know the faces of friends, the illimitable variety of straight and curved lines, all surfaces, the exuberance of the soil, the delicate shapes of flowers, the noble forms of trees, and the range of mighty winds. Besides objects, surfaces, and atmospheric changes, I perceive countless vibrations. I derive much knowledge of everyday matter from the jars and jolts which are to be felt everywhere in the house.

Footsteps, I discover, vary tactually according to the age, sex, and the manners of the walker. It is impossible to mistake a child's patter for the tread of a grown person. The step of the young man, strong and free, differs from the heavy, sedate tread of the middle-aged, and from the step of the old man, whose feet drag along the floor, or beat it with slow, faltering accents. On a bare floor a girl walks with a rapid, elastic rhythm which is quite distinct from the graver step of the elderly woman.[66]

As essential as touch was, Helen called the sense of smell "the fallen angel." For her it was most important. "Smell is a potent wizard that transports us across a thousand miles and all the years we have lived." The odor of fruits recalled her southern home, "to my childish frolics in the peach orchard." As she considered the sense of smell and its importance to her, Helen recalled those examples from her times at Red Farm:

The faintest whiff from a meadow where the new-mown hay lies in the hot sun displaces the here and now. I am back again in the old red barn. My little friends and I are playing in the haymow. A huge mow it is, packed with crisp, sweet hay, from the top of which the smallest child can reach the straining rafters. In their stalls beneath are the farm animals. Here is Jerry, unresponsive, unbeautiful Jerry, crunching his oats like a true pessimist, resolved to find his feed not good—at least not so good as it ought to be. Again I touch Brownie, eager, grateful little Brownie, ready to leave the juiciest fodder for a pat, straining his beautiful, slender neck for a caress. Near by stands Lady Belle, with sweet, moist mouth, lazily extracting the sealed-up cordial from timothy and clover, and dreaming of June pastures and murmurous streams.

I know by smell the kind of house we enter. I have recognized an old-fashioned country house because it has several layers of odors, left by a succession of families, of plants, perfumes, and draperies.[67]

Eventually, Helen's schooling needed to resume, and so it was that while staying with the Chamberlins in June 1896, Annie "called on Mr. Arthur Gilman, Director of the Cambridge School for Young Ladies to ask if Helen might attend during the upcoming school year, in order to prepare for the Radcliffe entrance exams. Strategically, the Cambridge School would bring Helen and Annie closer to Radcliffe," as it was considered a preparatory school for the college and had "a reputation for having sent a larger number of students to the College than any other private school." Publications of the time reported that "strangers applying for admission must be introduced to the director, and give the names of previous schools. They are supposed to be willing to study and not to require petty rules of behavior. It is the intention . . . to cultivate in them the habits of application and the self-control requisite to true womanly character. They are taught that study is work, but that it is agreeable work."[68]

In his personal notes, Gilman later described his reaction at Annie's visit and request for Helen to attend his school: "I was astounded by the proposition and replied that I thought it was impractical. Miss Sullivan urged me not to decide until I had met Miss Keller. She gave me much information about her and agreed to bring her to me on the occasion of our [upcoming] closing exercises."[69] Subsequently, the pair attended closing exercises and Gilman noted there was "much interest" in Helen, which perhaps helped convince him to accept Helen as a student.[70]

Gilman continued in his later notes, "It was arranged that Miss Sullivan and Helen . . . should come at the end of September and occupy a room in one of the 'In School Residences,' as any two girls might, and that Helen should take her place in the classes and be treated in school and home as nearly as possible as any seeing and hearing girl of 15 or 16 is treated."[71]

The plan for Helen was in place for the upcoming year; Helen had found her school and her hoped-for path to Radcliffe.

After their stay at Red Farm in the early part of the summer, Helen and Annie spent the remainder of the season in Brewster with Annie's friend Sophia Hopkins. Annie also made a brief trip to Boston to discuss finances with Dr. Bell. He assured her that funds would be raised to pay for Helen's tuition at the Cambridge School.[72]

It was during this summer that Helen also matured in her spirituality. She had for many years consulted with Bishop Phillips

Brooks about God and Christianity, but she found what she called "spiritual puzzles" among his responses, and he had died of diphtheria in 1893.[73] John Hitz was an ardent follower of the religious teachings of Emanuel Swedenborg, founder of an open-minded and forward-looking Christian church that espoused a God of unconditional love—a doctrine that Helen now adopted. She was attracted to what she called Swedenborg's "genial, tolerant and liberal" teachings, which were consistent with what she had learned from her friend Bishop Brooks and the impulses of her own overflowing heart."[74]

Ed Chamberlin said later he believed her religious views to be closer to those of Unitarianism—the "Boston Religion," as it was dubbed—than to those of any other denomination.[75] Her newfound clarity of belief, with its accompanying freedom from the fear of death, would be helpful in the near future.

The summer had been pleasant and relaxing—and provided Helen and Annie with a well-deserved vacation. But on September 3, 1896, Annie wrote to John Hitz with terrible news: Helen's father had died. Annie related that "poor Helen is heart broken. Helen was frantic with grief and her one desire was to get to her mother."[76]

Annie immediately tried to arrange travel to Alabama but soon received an urgent telegram from Helen's mother telling them not to come, as she "thought it would be inadvisable and far from prudent for us to go south as it was the beginning of their sickliest season." Annie told Hitz that

This was another great blow to Helen and she is still inconsolable. I never dreamed there was the possibility of such great sorrow in the dear child's nature. She bears and has always borne her own terrible affliction so patiently and uncomplainingly that I am afraid I had come to feel that her peculiar limitations had dulled her emotional nature so that she did not feel as intensely as many. But I see that I was wrong and I am sorry. I thought she would at least be spared the acute mental suffering which our griefs so often bring with them.[77]

It is rather stunning that even after so many years together, Annie still assumed Helen would not feel grief deeply.

Further, it might seem strange to modern minds that Helen's mother would not have her daughter travel home for her own father's funeral. But as Annie herself noted, there seems to have been little understanding of Helen's interior world and emotional capacity, with no precedent for such grief in the teenager's life. In addition, prevailing attitudes that demonstrative grief was inappropriate and that children should be shielded from the realities of death may have influenced decisions.[78]

Although grief-stricken, Helen wrote to Ida Chamberlin on September 10 from Brewster. She began in an appreciative and cheery tone, most likely having written part of the letter before receiving the devastating news about her father. She and Annie had "had a quiet, restful summer" and she told of their many pleasures at the seaside. Helen then told Ida of the loss of her father: "I have lost my own dear father. Oh, Mrs. Chamberlin, it is very hard to think I shall not see him again for a long, long time! He was always such a good, loving father! But I know there is a kind purpose in this as in all sorrow. Only my tears, like a mist, prevent me from seeing God's beautiful purpose; but after a while the mist will lift, and I shall see that God knew best."

In what would become a frequent theme, Helen apologized for Annie's lack of letter writing due to her tired eyes. While only sixteen, Helen had already become the primary correspondent for the pair. She closed the letter by asking Ida to "please give our dear love to Mr. Chamberlin, and Miss Helen, and kiss Beth and Raymie for us."[79]

The passing of Helen's father left Kate Keller in an even more precarious financial situation, with four-year-old Phillips and ten-year-old Mildred still at home, and Helen and Annie far off in New England. In the future, she would of necessity rely increasingly on others to make decisions regarding Helen's wellbeing and future. But despite the distress and upheaval in the Keller family, Helen and Annie reported for classes at the Cambridge School on October 1, 1896.

CHAPTER SEVEN

The Cambridge School

Before school began in the fall of 1896, details of Helen's expected attendance had already been released to the news media, probably by Arthur Gilman. Although he would later deny it, Gilman was aware of the attention and celebrity she would bring to his program. In fact, a reporter later said he had been paid for publicity by Gilman.[1]

As for Helen, she would be going to school with seeing and hearing girls—in contrast to her Perkins and Wright-Humason experiences. She was eager to attend, writing that

at the Cambridge School, for the first time in my life, I enjoyed the companionship of seeing and hearing girls of my own age. I lived with several others in one of the pleasant houses connected with the school . . . and we all had the advantage of home life. I joined them in many of their games, even blind man's buff [sic] *and frolics in the snow; I took long walks with them; we discussed our studies and read aloud the things that interested us. Some of the girls learned to speak to me, so that Miss Sullivan did not have to repeat their conversation.*[2]

Fortunately, for the time being at least, their financial concerns had been relieved, as under the direction of the capable Eleanor Hutton in New York, and with the support of a wide array of wealthy friends, an education fund had been raised.[3]

But what hadn't been worked out in early discussions with Gilman was what the presence of Annie Sullivan would bring to the situation. Of necessity, Annie accompanied Helen to all her classes, for with the exception of the German teacher and Gilman, none of the other teachers at the school knew the manual alphabet, and there were few books available in braille.[4]

In 1896, the Cambridge School had just completed its tenth year, enrolling approximately one hundred pupils. Arthur Gilman and his wife, Stella, had established the school "to give to girls and young women thorough and well-ordered instruction."[5] As an energetic social innovator, Stella Gilman believed in higher education for women. She previously had "induced her husband to make in 1877 a plan for the systematic instruction of women by the professors of Harvard College." Through his subsequent "instigation," what was originally known as the "Harvard Annex for Women" was established in 1879 and later became Radcliffe College. He served as the first regent.[6]

In the late 1880s, Stella Gilman had also wished to conduct a small class in her home for the instruction of her own younger children. When others became interested in the class, "Mr. Gilman took it up, establishing the Cambridge School, with himself as its director."[7]

Arthur Gilman was a recognized writer on history and family genealogy. In 1896, nearing sixty years of age, he was selected to write a history of the city of Cambridge by a committee of the city government and citizens. In the history, he described the Cambridge School academic program and its "essential" residence arrangement: "The teachers are supreme in their own departments under the director, who is not a teacher himself. Out of the schoolroom the girls are under the charge of four experienced ladies, two in each residence. Their duty is to 'make a home' for the pupils, and they study how to bring this about with as much pains as do the teachers their own part. Thus the social and home life of the students as well as their actual school life is developed at the same time in all legitimate ways."[8]

Gilman described the curriculum at the Cambridge School as embracing "all that is needed either to fit a young lady to enter college, if she is destined to do so, or to send her home the possessor of a finished education." Further, he wrote, "high ideas of womanliness are constantly held before the pupil, and the cultivation of the social graces and courtesies of family life is ever insisted upon."[9]

Gilman wrote that the school "purposely" had no instructors living in the residences, so that the pupils and teachers would be separate and "come fresh together at the beginning of the school day." He acknowledged that "the plan is an expensive one to carry out," but his own faith that it was "best for the young woman" gave him great confidence in it, and experience in carrying it on "has shown its advantages."[10] He considered himself an expert in the education of young women. But Annie Sullivan's presence with Helen at all times would appear to be contrary to the school's ideal that no instructors live in the student residences.

Gilman was impressed by Helen, and in particular her devotion to study, writing to a friend that "the avidity with which Helen read whatever was placed within her range kept her always ahead of the respective lessons. School-girls sometimes study as though it were a 'task,' as indeed our fathers called it, but Helen never. With her a new text-book was a fresh and delightful field for investigation. Difficulties were merely new heights to be scaled. The exhilaration of overcoming obstacles kept this school-girl as much interested as another might be in achieving a conquest in a game of golf or tennis."[11]

He wrote to another friend that "Helen is the liveliest and happiest girl in the world yet!"[12] Gilman also believed he was providing her with a sanctuary from the outside world, telling Eleanor Hutton, "She is a person of mark wherever she goes. When I took her to Boston the other day to meet her mother, it was almost impossible for her to walk through the station without being surrounded by interested persons, who under their breath called her by name or made sympathetic remarks about her. She cannot even pass though our quiet streets without being observed, and what she does is telegraphed to the remotest portions of the country, and distorted at that." He concluded, "Every one who comes in contact with Helen is put under a spell."[13] And Gilman too was captivated.

Not far into the school year, Helen began harboring hopes that her sister, Mildred, might also be able to attend the Cambridge School. Having developed a new and stronger relationship during two recent visits, including one to Red Farm in June, Helen now said she missed her "inexpressibly." When Helen and Annie made a decision not to return to Tuscumbia for the Christmas holidays and Helen's mother instead came north with her son and daughter, "everyone had fallen in love with Mildred."[14]

Mildred was only eleven years old, but her poise, charm, and southern manners were evident and probably exemplified the "high ideas of womanliness" that Gilman so esteemed. To Helen's surprise, after the holidays, Gilman wrote to her at Wrentham and offered Mildred the opportunity to attend school with Helen.[15] Kate Keller agreed to send Mildred for the spring semester, doubtless grateful that her tuition was to be paid by the same wealthy benefactors who were supporting Helen's education. And Helen was elated.

Soon after Helen's initial enrollment, Gilman began writing "accounts of her education" for magazines, journals, and annals of national deaf and blind organizations.[16] He quickly came to be considered an expert by other practitioners and was flattered by the attention. In early April 1897, the *Transcript* printed an article written by Gilman called "Helen Keller's Studies." In the months during which she had been at his school, he wrote that he had been impressed by Helen's "breadth and keenness of perception, a vividness of imagination, and an intense desire for knowledge." He spoke of his and Annie's mutual goal of preparing Helen for Harvard's examinations and concluded the article: "What is coming I know not, but this I know, that Miss Sullivan and I have in our keeping the highest interests of the sweetest and most spiritual young woman that Providence ever brought into this school—one who treats me as a daughter would, and one upon whom I look with an affection like that of a father."[17]

He also became an arbiter of information about, and access to, Helen. Thomas Humason, cofounder of Helen's former school in New York, became a regular correspondent, as did William Wade, Helen's benefactor in Pennsylvania, along with other leaders of schools for the deaf and blind across the United States and Canada. Eleanor Hutton in New York sought Gilman's advice on how to raise funds for Helen's education. In describing Helen's program of study to others, he spoke of Annie's "indispensability and dedication" in class and after-class study, all the while interpreting to Helen "with infinite patience."[18]

By late spring 1897, however, trouble was brewing and Gilman's relationship with Annie had soured. One could see it beginning to percolate in Gilman's rather urgent April 26 letter to her in which he declared, "It has come to me emphatically that we must have some explicit understanding in reference to the management of Helen, and I would like it if you could come to see me Monday afternoon so that we may consult about it."

It is not clear what the instigating circumstances were, but Gilman went on unexpectedly to discuss "exploitation" of Helen:

I have said in public and in private that it is your wish and mine that Helen should lead the life of a normal girl of her age, and that she should not be "exploited" in public. I cannot stultify myself by permitting things to be done which seemed to have my approval or at least my consent which are contrary to my expressed statements.

I know that you approve what I write as thoroughly as I do. You can no more allow yourself to appear in a false light before the public than I can. Helen and her interests suffer if we do so appear.

In order that I may carry out the plan that I understand you to ask me to carry out, I must be placed in a position to do it. You and Mrs. Keller are able to give me the directions that will be sufficient for the purpose. In case you do this, I am willing to carry Helen's education to any point that may be desired. The present arrangement is loose.

It has been my intention to do the work that you asked me to do, and to do it in the way that you wished me to do it; nothing else has been in my mind. The interests of Helen are my only criterion, and ever shall be.

Please let me see you. Four o'clock would be a good hour, but I will meet your convenience.[19]

Annie's response to the letter is unknown, and the content or result of a meeting—if one occurred—is likewise uncertain, but a serious disagreement was developing.[20]

Helen seemed unaware of any controversy and later wrote that she "took . . . preliminary examinations for Radcliffe from the 29th of June to the 3rd of July in 1897. . . . Mr. Gilman read all the papers to me by means of the manual alphabet. Mr. Gilman sent my written work to the examiners with a certificate that I, candidate No. 233, had written the papers."[21]

Despite the rising tensions, Helen finished out her first year with great success: she passed the Radcliffe preliminary exams in elementary and advanced German, French, Latin, English, and Greek and Roman history. Final entrance exams to Radcliffe in additional subject areas would be taken after the next academic year.

The 1896–1897 school year ended and Mildred returned home to Alabama for the summer. Helen and Annie, however, were eager to retreat to Red Farm. On July 9, Helen wrote to her mother that she and Annie had been there since early July, having received "a loving welcome, as they always did," and had celebrated Helen's seventeenth birthday—belatedly, as she was studying for her exams on her actual birthday, June 27—with "an angel cake lighted prettily with seventeen candles." Helen told her mother that "Mrs. Chamberlin's loving, motherly ways remind me of you and make me feel a part of this sweet, friendly home life, which I find so seldom these days."[22]

That same day, Helen also wrote happily to John Hitz that she and Annie were in Wrentham "in the quiet country where all is beautiful and free from strife and anxiety, and where my thoughts turn lovingly to my friends. And you dear Mr. Hitz, are very near to my thoughts. I am thinking how dearly I love you and how happy you have always made me and my heart goes out to you in love and gratitude."

Helen added, "Teacher and I are going to spend the summer at Wrentham, Mass. with our friends the Chamberlins. I think you remember Mr. Chamberlin, the 'Listener' in the Boston Transcript. They are dear, kind people. They seem to have but one thought, and that is to make sunshine in the lives of other people and ourselves a part of their sweet household."[23]

In both letters, Helen also shared news of her academic successes and wrote of her debt of gratitude to Annie, saying, "I consider my crown of success is the happiness and pleasure that my victory has brought dear Teacher. Indeed, I feel that the success is hers more than mine; for she is my constant inspiration."

Helen closed her letter to Hitz by talking about the beauty of Red Farm and their plan: "I do wish you could be with us and enjoy the quiet rural life! How you would enjoy the lovely lake, the pine woods and the delicious green fields! Surely it would fill your heart with gladness to sit under the trees and watch the golden moonrise over the calm lake. But Teacher and I are going to be quite idle this summer. We are going to study a little together every day."[24]

That spring, Ed Chamberlin had offered up his own views on Helen and her education in his "Listener" column. The campaign to raise funds for her schooling and future was underway at full speed, and Ed could use his pen to garner support. He wrote,

The movement to obtain a sort of public endowment for Helen Keller is a peculiar and most interesting thing. Public subscriptions for men and women, who have done a great deal in the world, and have possibly served their fellow-beings with ungrudging service of poetry or art, so faithfully that they have been unable to provide for their own old age, are well enough known; but a public subscription to equip a young girl with a fortune appears to be a new thing.

Helen Keller's education is an experiment that the world has an interest in. It is not so much that she is a phenomenon, a genius—for as she grows older it does not appear that her intellectual gifts are superior to those of many girls her age—but that the peculiar powers of sympathy and soul perception, as it were, which enable her to see across the gloom that envelops her, make her education a thing of psychological interest to the rest of mankind. These powers, to some of those who know her best, often appear to exist not so much in spite of her blindness and deafness as on account of them. It is as if the deprivation of these senses had intensified the inner sense of which we are all, in this age, so keenly endeavoring to obtain an understanding of the meaning and uses.

One feels, when engaged in conversation with Helen Keller, as if one were in closer communication with the soul itself than one had ever been before. Though intellectually Helen Keller is merely strong rather than extraordinary, it is apparent that sympathetically she would be gifted above the ordinary, even if she possessed all her senses; and if, as the Listener has already surmised, her deprivation of the two most important senses has increased rather than lessened the sympathetic and psychic sense in her. . . .

Helen Keller, through the misfortune of her total blindness and deafness, had opened to her this other, and in some respects finer, way of seeing and hearing all in one: and her naturally fine sympathetic

gifts were developed in a way of her own along this path, strange and strangely interesting to us.

Perhaps the strangest part of the matter is that her mind is apparently susceptible of a conventional "education" without the loss of this fine soul quality. . . . Her education should be encouraged by her friends, not with the hope that any prodigious harvest of intellectual works is to be reaped for the world as the result of it, but with the assurance that the spiritual enlightenment which her development may afford will be of real value.[25]

Ed spoke for Helen out of deep affection. He saw her as a complete human being, not a young woman with deficits or disabilities. As Helen would later write, "His attitude toward my limitations was noble. He looked beyond them to my soul dowered with imagination and the desire to know."[26]

When Ed said that Helen's education should be encouraged, to him this meant much more than an education accomplished or achieved in a book-lined library or classroom. Her education as he would define it meant exposure to the world, to nature, to contemporary thought, to history, to art, to music, to people, to every experience available. And Red Farm provided all of those opportunities.

While friends worked to raise funds, Helen and Annie spent the entire summer with the Chamberlins. By all reports it was quiet and restful, and the affection that Helen and Annie felt for the family deepened.

As the 1897–1898 school year approached, Helen looked back with pleasure on the summer. She wrote for Annie from Wrentham to Annie Pratt, Bell's assistant, on September 23 that Annie had especially enjoyed helping Ed and spending time with him outdoors on the farm and in the surrounding countryside:

My naughty teacher is so busy helping Mr. Chamberlin with the harvesting, riding horseback and hunting wild grapes that I'm afraid she is forgetting her manners! But I know she intended answering your kind letter immediately that you might have felt the pleasure it gave her; but the pleasant weather and some other things have interrupted her; so that the fine intention has faded, yet leaving a sweet thought behind. . . .

Our school begins on Friday. . . .

I have had a delightfully restful summer, and I am now looking forward eagerly to my books and studies. No doubt I shall find it rather difficult at first to discipline my thoughts to regular study again. Nevertheless, I feel sure that this happy, idle summer with Nature has greatly intensified my love of what is intellectual and beautiful; and I long to be at work, gathering in the rich harvest of thought and wisdom which the [?] and Wise and Good have shown in the thoughtfields of Life.

So opens the new school year, I greet it with a smile, believing that before it closes I shall see many bright anticipations fulfilled.[27]

She also wrote to Gilman, "missing him sadly" and describing her reading and outdoor activities of the summer.[28]

But a school year that began with so much optimism and excitement on the part of Helen would deteriorate rapidly. The impending crisis drew all of Helen and Annie's influential friends into the "fray"—the Chamberlins, Alexander Graham Bell, John Hitz, Annie Pratt, Lucy Derby Fuller, and Eleanor Hutton.[29]

But perhaps no one would play a larger role than Ed Chamberlin.

CHAPTER EIGHT

The Gilman Affair

On the morning of December 9, 1897, Ed dressed quickly and hurried toward the depot and train to Cambridge. He had received a telegram from Annie in the early hours that said simply, "We need you."[1] As he rushed forward, Ed could not have foreseen what lay ahead that day.

From Helen's later report, the situation unfolded as follows: though she had been optimistic before the start of school, the classes she was in were large and she could not be given special instruction by the teachers. This obligated Annie to read to Helen all of the textbooks and to interpret for the instructors. A braille writer was procured to help her with algebra and geometry and to solve problems in physics, but "every study had its obstacles."[2]

It appears that, out of frustration with these challenges, Helen had several emotional outbursts that she later regretted because they were "used against" Annie by others. She wrote that

just before the books came, Mr. Gilman had begun to remonstrate with Miss Sullivan on the ground that I was working too hard, and in spite of my earnest protestations, he reduced the number of my recitations. At the beginning we had agreed that I should, if necessary, take five years to prepare for college, but at the end of the first year the success of my examinations showed . . . that I could without too much effort complete my preparation in two years more. Mr. Gilman at first agreed to this; but when my tasks had become somewhat perplexing, he insisted that I was overworked, and that I should remain at his school three years longer. I did not like his plan, for I wished to enter college with my class.[3]

On November 17, Helen did not feel well and did not go to school. According to Helen, "although Miss Sullivan knew that my indisposition was not serious, yet Mr. Gilman, on hearing of it, declared that I was breaking down and made changes in my studies which would have rendered it impossible for me to take my final examinations with my class."[4]

When Annie protested Gilman's changes to Helen's schedule, he took her response as a direct challenge to his authority. He began sending letters to Helen's supporters beyond the school walls, suggesting that Helen's health was precarious, that she was being driven too hard by Annie, and that the two should be separated.

In an October 22, 1897, letter to Eleanor Hutton, Gilman wrote that "Miss Sullivan has changed her mind in regard to the length of Helen's preparatory course. You know she asked me to lengthen it last year. She has now asked me to *shorten* it, so that she can finish in one year after this. . . . The new arrangement will give her two very busy years—perhaps harder than the first one. This I am sorry for and I hope Miss Sullivan will change her mind." He stated that he "did not care to press" his views, but he thought that "Helen's comfort, and especially her health, ought to be the only basis for judgments," as "we all wish to keep her in the best health."[5]

Additional letters from Gilman to Hutton followed. Sometime later, in an undated letter, knowing the Chamberlins saw Helen and Annie on a regular basis, Hutton sought Ed's advice, telling him,

Mr. Gilman has been writing me letters lately which have worried me considerably—he thinks Helen Keller is very much over-worked, and is afraid that if this pressure is not taken off she will break down. Miss Sullivan writes that Helen is very well—Now at this distance it is very puzzling to tell which of Helen's teachers is right. So I write to ask you what you thought of Helen's physical condition when you last saw her? And did you think Miss Sullivan seemed less patient with her? Or in any way irritable? I fear, that in Miss Sullivan's zeal she may overtax Helen—and it would be a very disastrous thing to do.

Hutton was consulting Ed because she was "raising the money which pays for her education," and as such she felt "more or less responsible for the dispensing of it—Helen is already such a wonderful creature that it seems a pity to force her in any way. She is bound to develop into something wonderful. Will you kindly write me how she and Miss Sullivan impressed you during their recent visit—and oblige."[6]

Ed and Ida both responded to Hutton, disputing Gilman's perceptions. A second letter from Hutton to both Ed and Ida followed on December 1, 1897, thanking them for their "kind letters." They had told her "exactly what she wanted to know about Helen." She shared that their "accounts of Helen entirely contradict Mr. Gilman's statements." Gilman had written her, "My medical advisor told me last night that if Miss Sullivan were allowed to [persist] in her plans, Helen would collapse, and that it would not be like a breaking down of a normal child from which a recovery could be expected." Gilman also reported that "Miss Sullivan talks of taking Helen to another school, but, of course her freedom of leaving here is not absolute and besides Mrs. Keller will have to be brought to agree with her first."

Hutton went on, noting,

I don't understand this statement as Miss Sullivan has the right to change the school provided those who are paying for Helen's education agree. . . . The money is all sent to me—and Mr. Hutton pays the school bills—without this money—Helen would not go to Mr. Gilman's school. It is a splendid advertisement for him having Helen as a pupil—I agree with you in the matter of higher education for Helen—but after all, it is what SHE *most desires and it would be cruel to deny her any wish so near to her heart.*

Ed had long advocated that Helen be encouraged to go to college, and Eleanor Hutton was in agreement. She hoped to get to Boston soon and said she would make plans to visit with Arthur Gilman and try to sort out the situation between him and Annie. She noted that she would "hope to see for myself how matters have been adjusted—it is quite evident that Mr. Gilman and Miss Sullivan disagree—he says in his last note to me that 'I would discharge any teacher in this school who treated a pupil as Miss Sullivan treats Helen often in class—she loses her temper, her former patience is gone.'"

The work of raising funds for Helen's education was ongoing. Hutton wrote that "we have now about $20,000 on hand, but no one has responded lately." She was finding it difficult to raise the additional $30,000 toward the goal of $50,000 to cover Helen's education over the long term and also living expenses for her and Annie. Never temperate in her opinions, Annie had alienated prominent Bostonians. Hutton's letter continued, "Miss Sullivan seems to have antagonized people—She has a great deal of false pride, and has been an hindrance to me in raising the money I have as she has objected to any publicity—on the plea that they were not paupers! As I understand it, they neither of them have any money."[7]

Meanwhile, Gilman had become ever more convinced that Annie Sullivan was detrimental to Helen's wellbeing, and he now actively sought to separate the two, and to gain control of Helen, even guardianship if possible. William Wade was apparently not fond of Annie Sullivan either, believing that "any proficient teacher of the deaf-blind could have educated an intelligent child like Helen" and later claiming that he was the first to suggest to Gilman that Helen and Annie be separated.[8] As Gilman's relationship with Annie deteriorated through the fall of 1897, he gained determination from correspondents such as Wade. He also wrote confidentially to Sophia Hopkins, Alexander Graham Bell, Eleanor Hutton, and others about Helen's "condition." A few positive responses gave Gilman all he needed to begin pressuring Kate Keller to support a plan to separate Helen from Annie.

Annie and Mrs. Keller even exchanged letters on the matter, with Keller writing to Annie on November 28. She was stern: though she expressed gratitude to Annie for her "drudgery" on Helen's behalf, in a rambling letter she agreed with Gilman that the workload was too challenging. It "distressed her to differ with" Annie on any matters relating to Helen, but she was sure Gilman was "sincerely interested in Helen and a wise and kind friend" to Annie. She was also sure that his opinion that Helen was working too hard must be valid.[9]

Annie must have felt the sands of support under her feet shifting seismically: it was clear that Keller was being swayed against her.

The crisis reached a head on December 8 when Gilman summoned Annie to his office. They exchanged angry words regarding what was best for Helen and who would have authority over her education and care. Gilman produced a telegram that Keller had sent after his campaign of letters to her, agreeing that Annie and Helen should be separated based on what he had told her.

Annie was understandably distraught. She left Gilman's office, spoke quickly with Helen and Mildred, and then left in a distressed emotional state. She "fled to the closest refuge, the nearby Beacon Street home of a longtime friend with whom she often corresponded, Lucy Derby Fuller, and her husband, the Reverend S. Richard Fuller."[10] The Fullers were also friends of Reverend Edward Hale, and Annie must have known they would embrace her in a moment of desperation.

With no other source of livelihood other than Helen's care and education, Annie's very existence was threatened. Later Annie would say that she had even contemplated suicide that night, having considered throwing herself into the Charles River in her darkest moments.[11]

Gilman had prepared, but not yet sent, a packet of letters to Keller that was shocking in its scope and audacity. He exploited the recent loss of Helen's father and sought to establish himself as a benevolent father figure. With himself as her "father," manager of her affairs, and instructor, Annie would no longer be needed. The packet included three letters for Keller to sign—letters Gilman may have shown Annie during the meeting in his office—that gave him full122 responsibility for Helen and Mildred, as well as one that "directed Annie to submit all of Helen's books, money, and property to Gilman." Keller would "thus be in control of her daughters through Mr. Gilman," and Annie would have no further responsibilities.[12]

In one of the unsent letters, Gilman told Keller that

you have given me your confidence and I appreciate it fully. Dear Helen shall be a sacred trust. Most of all, I wish to have everything that I do for her to be OPEN *and* SEEN, *so that no one can think that there is anything underhanded. I could not for a moment think of undertaking to receive the money that comes for Helen, and to pay it out, without rendering an explicit account of it with vouchers. You do not know, but I do, that money is being sent to Helen in varying sums, of which nobody is informed, and it is spent without any statement to anyone.*

Then, in a remarkably condescending statement for a man who was guiding the education of modern and highly intelligent young women, Gilman wrote, "Of course, a woman knows nothing of accounts . . . and the importance of them has probably never occurred to Miss S." Gilman assured Keller that the "unanimous opinion" of the Cambridge School teachers "was that Helen's present difficulty is that her Teacher is behind her in knowledge, and is constantly irritated with her."

He added a postscript regarding future communications between Keller and himself, saying, "I suggest that if you have any special message to send to Helen, you put the letter in a cover addressed to me, and not to her. Then I shall get it and read it to her."

Other enclosures in the packet included a letter to be sent to Mildred that Keller was to copy in her own handwriting, which directed her daughter to "go to Mr. Gilman for advice, and to do what he wishes you to do. He will represent me, and I shall tell him from time to time what I wish for Helen and you. In doing this I am carrying out the wishes that your dear father would have expressed, were he here, for he told me what he desired, especially for Helen."[13]

Another letter for Annie in the same packet, which Keller was to copy and sign, directed that Helen be placed fully in Gilman's care. Annie was to give him all of Helen's property and money and to "allow him to manage the whole as he would the property of one of his daughters." Gilman would receive all of Helen's future income and render to Keller "accounts of everything that he pays out." The letter ended with appreciation to Annie for "the labor that you have given in the care of Helen in the past."[14]

It is uncertain whether Gilman shared the contents of the packet with Annie. It is more likely that he simply described the three letters and told her of his intentions to send them.

What Arthur Gilman did not comprehend was that Kate Keller no longer had much say in decisions related to Helen's wellbeing. Helen was essentially being raised by a committee of prominent men and women friends and philanthropists in Boston, Washington, and New York who were guided primarily by the desires of Annie Sullivan.[15]

And there was fight left in Annie. The next morning, on December 9, she sent telegrams of distress to Keller and to a few friends whom she knew she could call on in a crisis: Alexander Graham Bell, Ed Chamberlin, and Annie Pratt.[16] Annie's hosts, the Fullers, also wrote hastily and urgently to Eleanor Hutton.

Annie went back to the Cambridge School and demanded to see Helen, but Gilman denied her access. A standoff of several hours ensued during which Annie refused to leave "except by force."[17] Finally, Gilman allowed Annie to see Helen with a housekeeper chaperone.[18] Helen and Mildred were both upset and crying. After a brief conversation with the girls, Annie returned to the Fullers to regroup and plan her next steps.

Ed arrived at the school that morning and met with Gilman. He listened patiently to Gilman's side of the story. He was then allowed to see Helen and Mildred at Howells House, nearly hysterical victims in the drama that was unfolding around them.[19] "Seeing the dangerous state Helen was in," Ed went immediately to Gilman and obtained consent to take the girls to Red Farm, a logical place of refuge.[20]

"Rightly or wrongly," Ed wrote many years later, "I had become convinced that Gilman intended to use Mrs. Keller's authority to separate Helen from Annie."[21]

Ed gathered Helen and her sister, collected Annie from the Fullers, and escorted all three to Wrentham. Desiring to know Helen's true feelings in the matter—the only ones that he believed should be of concern to anyone, and wanting to give her a chance to speak her mind—Ed took Helen alone into his study and told her it might soon be incumbent on her to decide whether she would stay with Annie or go away from her with her mother. In response, Helen told him, "Uncle Ed, if I have to decide between my mother and Teacher, I will stay with Teacher."[22]

Ed would later say simply, "This decided me as to my own sympathies in the case."[23] All his subsequent actions and advocacy would be guided by Helen's statement.

That same day, Eleanor Hutton penned a letter to Gilman strongly protesting any separation of Helen and Annie. Further, she explained, the financial support for the pair was contingent on them staying together. In the event of their separation, the funds would revert to the original donors, primarily John D. Rockefeller and Henry Rogers.[24]

Mrs. Keller had by now received the same "we need you" telegram from Annie and made arrangements to come at once to Boston. Arriving on December 10, she first visited with Sophia Hopkins in Brewster and was due to arrive at the Cambridge School on the afternoon of December 11. Just before Keller's anticipated arrival, Gilman responded to Hutton's most recent letter:

Your letter of the 9th is received. Mrs. Keller has written to me that Capt. Keller wished before he died to remove Helen from her teacher, and that she herself felt that she should never have allowed her authority to lapse. I have told her that if she wished me to be of service to her in any way, I would serve her, but that I should not perform any acts on my personal responsibility. Of course I cannot separate Helen and Miss Sullivan, nor can I have any part in such separation unless, indeed, the mother assumes her personal guardianship.

My position is this, that the mother has a right to her child, and that some one ought to sustain her. My advisers tell me that on account of my own delicate health it is my duty to undertake nothing further for Helen, and that is my personal preference, and has been since the late erratic doings of Miss S. Your letter shall be brought to Mrs. Keller's attention on her arrival here. I asked her to come and she writes that I may expect her this afternoon.[25]

Gilman was making an obvious attempt to save face, even suggesting that Keller's trip north was his idea, not hers. He also now said he could not "separate Helen and Miss Sullivan," contradicting his own actions to this point.

Keller arrived at the Cambridge School and expected to see her daughters and Annie. After meeting briefly with Gilman and learning that her children were with the Chamberlins, she took the train to Wrentham and was reunited with the trio, all of whom appeared to be in perfect health, although very upset.[26] Keller now recognized her error, saying later, "I really did not realize at the moment what a cruel thing I was doing, in giving Gilman the authority to separate the two." She elaborated,

Very soon the injustice of it overcame me and I had already decided to come to Boston when Miss Sullivan's telegram "we need you," brought me on the first train. I found that Mr. Gilman had made a cruel use of the authority I had given him to distress my children and Miss Sullivan, after ten years of service. I certainly never dreamed of Miss Sullivan being forced away from Helen. I could not but feel on my arrival in Wrentham that I had been made to endure most unnecessary and uncalled for distress. Helen is in perfect physical condition and if she shows any evidence of nervous prostration or over-work, I cannot discover it.[27]

By now, many of their friends outside of Boston knew that Annie and Helen were at Red Farm. The next few weeks would see a flurry of letters to and from the household. Hastily penned, the letters frequently crossed in the mail, as the players sorted out what was happening, the facts were gathered, and decisions were made.

One can imagine that the Chamberlins kept a close watch on the Red Farm mailbox.

For one, Lucy Fuller wrote to Annie that "we are in readiness to come to you at any moment if it be needed—but I do hope that Mrs. Keller is with you and that all is well. . . . I have no words to tell you how it outrages my sense of justice and right that either of you two should be subjected to this for a moment—and that Helen should have this unnecessary suffering is a piece of barbarity on the part of those who have caused it."

She noted that the editor of the *Transcript* had heard the news, and "if it comes to the worst pass the paper will call the wrath of the world down on the heads of those who would try to kill this child—but that is not to be—and the misery of a newspaper contriving is not to be—for I am sure Helen will guide her mother's heart." She had sent a letter received from Ed "to Mrs. Hutton to keep her informed—and I would write a long letter to Mr. Bell if I knew where to reach him. I sent Mrs. Hutton 20 pages yesterday. It seems to be all I can do."[28]

Lucy Fuller followed the above letter with another several days later. Now that the pair was safe at Red Farm, she weighed in on what she thought the future should bring for them. She acknowledged that "Mr. Chamberlin's note of yesterday brought with it a sense of profound relief."[29]

A day later, Fuller wrote again to Annie. Emotions remained high. She was "full of interest to know how things are with you—three letters from Mrs. Hutton came this morning with various brochures—copies of which had been sent to Mr. Chamberlin also." She believed Gilman "has made the great blunder of his life! . . . Let us hear all we can whenever we can."[30]

Ed and Ida were now providing a home for Annie and Helen. While Annie was still in charge, Ed and Ida were seen as critically important in the process of any decision-making regarding Helen and Annie's future. In her letter, Fuller continued, "Will you ask Mr. Chamberlin if he will not dine with us on Saturday night at quarter of seven—we want so much to see him under our roof. Are you and Helen feeling well and how is Mrs. Keller?"[31]

On December 16, Annie went back to the Cambridge School alone and packed up her own, Helen's, and Mildred's belongings. They would not return.

The friends of Helen and Annie were in high gear. Suggestions for what should happen next abounded. Of course, Dr. Alexander Graham Bell in Washington needed to be apprised of the situation, Lucy Fuller had reminded Annie in one of her letters.[32]

Gilman wrote to Ed on December 17 that it was evident that many people were "under misapprehensions." He supposed that Ed "would like to know the truth, and I shall take pleasure in having a confidential talk with you tomorrow [at the school], where we can have uninterrupted quiet, if you wish." A handwritten postscript added, "I have no statements for the public."[33]

On December 18, Ed wrote to Gilman that he would "very much like to talk with you about this whole matter" but had imperative engagements that would not allow it at the moment. He would make an "effort to escape that afternoon if possible and would certainly try to see him." He said he felt he should have responded to Gilman earlier that week with regards to Helen and Mildred, since Gilman had put the girls in his care, but "as Mrs. Keller has been with us since last Monday, and the children have been consequently under her charge," Ed felt he could no longer answer for them. He related that Kate Keller was still at his house and would remain there over Christmas. Ed concluded, "She has not informed me of her intentions regarding Helen," though he had heard her say "she intends to take Mildred back to Alabama."[34]

Eleanor Hutton shared a financial update with Ed on December 19: the donor Henry Rogers felt "that any money which he contributes [to the fund] is for Miss Sullivan *& Helen jointly* and that it is a matter much to be regretted that any question of separating them could have arisen." She would "oppose Helen's returning to Mr. Gilman's school, and should not feel justified in giving any money entrusted to my care for such a purpose."

She was collecting copies of all correspondence and letters concerning Helen and Annie—documenting any decisions that were being made and why—for presentation to the fund committee. She added a postscript: "P.S. Did I tell you that a rich friend of mine promised to send Helen to Vassar—& pay all their expenses! Miss Sullivan refused this offer."[35] Vassar was not Helen's goal, and Annie was not inclined to pursue any opportunity to attend there, even with the offer of full subsidy.

Even in the face of vocal opposition, Gilman persisted in his quest to separate Annie from Helen. Apparently he had now abandoned his earlier efforts to save face. He wrote to Ed on December 24, 1897:

I regretted that you were not able to see me on Saturday. The extraordinary case that we were to discuss grows more remarkable as I hear of the past. I trust that you will be able to call and have a quiet chat next week on my return to Cambridge.

It is more evident that Helen should be separated from her Teacher, as Mr. Wade and Mrs. Keller suggested.

I am refraining from seeing any who are contributing to the success of the Fund, for I am unwilling that it should be thought that I interfere with that. Miss Sullivan should be rewarded for her work, of course, but any arrangement binding her to Helen for life would be a disaster for Helen. If the friends of Helen who have seen her Teacher as a guest or visitor or in her agreeable social guise, only knew her as those do who have worked with her, there would be a revulsion of sentiments. No fund would be raised to bind the two together for life.

I expect to see Mrs. Keller as she said that I should, at some time next week. I want to see you also, my dear sir.[36]

More than two weeks had passed since the dreadful night on which Annie fled the Cambridge School. In a long, summary document titled "A Terrible Extreme," transcribed and typed by Ed, Helen told of her experience with Gilman. On the night of December 8, she reported that "Mr. Gilman came in and asked for me. Oh, I do not know how I ever could have borne to see him! His very manner, pleasant and unchanged as it was, rendered it most fearful." He was one of the few staff at the Cambridge School who was skilled in the manual alphabet, and he communicated that he wanted Helen and her sister "to come with him to his house for the night." Helen went on: "He said he had received a telegram from my mother, requesting him to take charge of me, and he tried to persuade me to go. He said he would care for me as if I were his own daughter. . . . But of course I did not believe him: I could not think that my mother would ever allow anything of that kind to happen. I said I would not go, and after much talking to no purpose, he went away."

The next day Gilman again came to see Helen "for a few minutes" and told her that her father, before his death, had wished for Helen and her teacher to be separated. Helen said, "The shock almost stunned me. But I retorted that if my dear father had understood the whole matter, and known how dearly I loved and cherished my teacher, he would never have entertained a thought of separating us."

She concluded the document,

My teacher and I have been plunged together into this misery: we have struggled together through a maze of falsehood and injustice: and we have landed together on the firm, safe stand of Right and Justice. Nevertheless, I feel that I ought to make a statement of our sorrow: so that all my friends may know the real truth, and understand that my dear, faithful teacher has never deserved the cruel things that Mr. Gilman has said about her. But, if Mr. Gilman had dreamed how much I loved my teacher, I do not believe he would have dared to do the things he did.[37]

Eleanor Hutton wrote once again to Ed, cautioning that "nothing should be printed in the paper as it could only be harmful."[38]

John Hitz soon arrived at Red Farm to sort through the events that had transpired and make an assessment of the situation for Bell, who was dealing at the time with the death of a family member and unavailable to travel.

Hitz conducted interviews with all of the involved parties and submitted his detailed report to the Bells on December 27. As in the Frost King situation, during which Bell had "set matters aright before an intelligent public, when the character of Helen and her teacher were wrongly assailed," this report sought to do the same. Hitz wrote that "the deep and eternal interest you have jointly taken in Helen A. Keller and your consistent recognition of all important personal relations existing between her and her faithful teacher and friend, Miss A. M. Sullivan, . . . prompts me to place before you, briefly, as clear a statement of the recent occurrences at the Cambridge School, as an impartial, personal inquiry into the matter, enables me to give."

Most significantly, Hitz reported that "Mrs. Keller upon learning from her two children, and Miss Sullivan, the truth in regard to all that had taken place, in turn, showed herself highly incensed at the manner in which she had been written to by Mrs. Hopkins, Mr. Wade, and Mr. Gilman. She expressed her appreciation of all Mr.

Gilman had done for her children during the previous school term, but in a very emphatic manner, let it be understood, that she had been cruelly misled, and that any attempt made to separate Helen from her teacher, Miss Sullivan, met with her unqualified condemnation."

Evidently, according to Hitz, "Mr. Gilman asserted to Mrs. Keller, he had concluded from her letters that it was Major Keller's expressed wish, previous to his death, that her separation from Helen should be effected, and this Mr. Gilman even stated to Helen's little sister, Mildred, to have really been the case. This assumption on the part of Mr. Gilman, Mrs. Keller declares utterly at fault; that she had written nothing that could reasonably have given that impression." To presume to speak for the deceased Mr. Keller was considered particularly heinous. Mrs. Keller had given Mr. Gilman guardianship over Helen "in total ignorance of the real facts in the case."

Hitz went on, describing Gilman's disrespect for Helen's feelings, reporting that "Mr. Gilman, in what might be termed an underhanded manner, by letter and otherwise, not only sought to undermine the good opinion which Miss Sullivan enjoyed among her friends, but actually proceeded to enforce a separation of Helen, from her friend, and faithful teacher, totally regardless of Helen's feelings in the matter."

Finally, the report concluded, "To my mind, it would seem in summing up this whole matter, that Mr. Gilman . . . sought by disreputable means to displace Miss Sullivan from her well earned and legitimate place as dearest friend and teacher of Helen, in order that (as he alleged), the Cambridge School might claim the exclusive credit of her higher education."[39]

Hitz gave a draft of his report to Ed for approval before submitting it to Bell and asked that Ed make any changes he saw fit.[40] After Ed's review, the report was sent to Bell, and Hitz subsequently relayed Bell's reaction to Ed: "Dr. Bell said very little after reading Helen's statement but what he did say was emphatic in Helen and Miss Annie's favor." Hitz further noted that "should Helen's statement ever have to be put before the public, [it] would as effectually dispose of Mr. Gilman's future career as an educator as if the plague had visited him." Hitz wrote that he would rely on Ed to counter any publicity Gilman might seek, "the wording and time to publish . . . must be left to you who are best qualified to do the right and wise thing."[41]

The letter culminated with the request that Ed remember Hitz "affectionately to every member of your family and tell Mrs. Chamberlin that in speaking to you I feel always as if I were speaking to her too."[42]

Gilman clung tenaciously to his opinion that Annie should not remain as Helen's teacher. Over the holidays, he met in New York with administrators of the Wright-Humason School and gathered support for his position. On January 3, 1898, he wrote to Bell, saying that he did not "favor any plan that binds Helen to Miss S. for life," and if "Bell had met with the Wright-Humason administrators, he was sure he would agree."[43]

Gilman assured Bell, "My interest in Helen is stronger than I can tell you, and you may well understand that no slight 'misunderstanding' would have led me to risk the continuance of my direction of her education. On the other hand, I do not wish to harm her teacher, and therefore I do not make any accusation against her, further than may be implied in saying that she has proved this year, to use the language of the manual of this school, 'not a harmonious member of the household.'"[44]

Bell responded directly to Gilman's letter. He expressed surprise that he had not known that "anything but cordial and pleasant relations existed between Miss Sullivan and the teachers of the Wright-Humason School." If he could not "be of service" in repairing the relationship between Gilman and Annie, then Bell "would rather not hear anything further concerning the matter." He concluded with the statement that he "would rather remain in ignorance of the details—unless in your judgment or hers I can be of aid in bringing you together again."[45] Alexander Graham Bell had a gracious but definitive ability to put a person in his place.

Ed continued to serve as intermediary. He wrote to Gilman on January 4. On Helen's behalf, he thanked Gilman for forwarding books for her that had been sent to the Cambridge School. Ed noted that the future address for any mail or gifts for Helen and Annie would be Wrentham, in his care.[46]

Although all parties had weighed in, John Hitz had made a summary report, and ostensibly the matter had begun to quiet, Gilman still felt obliged to attempt to improve his position and continued to write to Ed and others.[47]

Meanwhile, Eleanor Hutton visited Red Farm on January 4 and gathered facts, statements, and artifacts, writing to Ed a week later with further questions. She believed that Gilman and others had ignored Helen's feelings entirely. She added that she planned to make another visit to Wrentham in the near future.[48]

Annie provided a fatigued update on the matter to John Hitz on January 14. She and Helen were resting comfortably at Red Farm and recovering from the crisis:

My dear Mr. Hitz:—

Have patience with me if I have not answered your affectionate and touching letter. Even now I cannot answer it. I can only thank you for it. Mrs. Keller and Mildred have returned to Tuscumbia, leaving me in full charge of Helen and with full authority to do what seems best to me in regard to her studies.

I have decided to stay in Wrentham the rest of the year, where Helen can have plenty of exercise and fresh air. I shall continue her preparation for college with the assistance of tutors. So much is settled. Mrs. Hutton is in Boston doing all she can to straighten the dreadful tangle into which we have been dragged by this ill-advised and unrighteous warfare. I think Mr. Gilman has met his Waterloo, but alas, he cannot suffer alone. He has caused us all to suffer with him most cruelly.

Helen is still very nervous and that is one of the reasons why I have decided to spend the winter in the country. You will be sorry to hear that the newspapers, in spite of all our efforts to keep the whole thing quiet, have at last got hold of the story. The HERALD *had a very poor, though friendly account yesterday morning. The* TRANSCRIPT *following in the evening with a clear concise statement of the affair, from beginning to end, or rather to present time, I doubt if the end has come yet. Mr. Chamberlin will send you copies of the papers when he goes to town tomorrow. Mrs. Hutton and indeed all of our friends seem to expect a reply from Mr. Gilman. We do not know of course, what form it will take, probably he will make Mrs. Keller responsible for the separation, if so we would like to have her Statement to use if necessary.*

Will you kindly send a copy to Mr. Chamberlin? Then, too, what Mr. Bell says has great weight with people. Every one knows that he has been deeply interested in Helen ever since I began to teach her; and they also know that his familiarity with the education of the deaf, makes him a competent judge of results. Can we have a copy of his letter? Not for publication but simply to show certain people. Helen had a dear kind letter from Mrs. Bell the other day which comforted us both inexpressibly. Will you give them our love when you see them. Mr. Bell shall never regret his confidence if Helen and I are spared to complete the work we have begun. Something tells me, and it is not vanity either, that the day will come when the friends who have stood by us in the days of persecution, will be proud they did so. We will see.

You will be glad to know that Dean Irwin of Radcliffe is assisting me in the selection of tutors. I had a long talk with her the other day and she agrees with me that it will be quite possible for Helen to take her finals in June of 1899.

We all wish you every happiness and the fulfillment of every longing in the year which is just beginning.

Yours, Annie Sullivan[49]

Although tired, Annie was calm and clear in her letter. The support of Dean Agnes Irwin of Radcliffe in the choice of tutors was reassuring. Subsequently, Annie and supporters engaged Merton Keith, a teacher who could prepare Helen for her Radcliffe examinations. He came to Red Farm once a week for three-hour sessions. Kate and Mildred Keller had returned to Alabama, having deemed a move to the North impractical once early emotions abated.

Letters from supporters and detractors of both Annie and Gilman continued to circulate. Annie was "an unfit person to be Helen's guardian" wrote a friend of Gilman named George Hodges. In his letter, he cited Michael Anagnos as saying, "Miss Sullivan had no regard for the truth."[50] His disparaging statement regarding Annie was a reminder that even six years later, the suspicions of the Frost King affair still festered and doubters remained. This present crisis generated even more fuel for Annie's opponents, like William Wade, who was corresponding sympathetically with Gilman from Pittsburgh. Gilman would receive letters from various heads of schools around the country for months.[51] And anger would simmer for years.

But the additional input fell soundlessly on the ears of friends and proponents who had already formed their opinions; the pair would not be separated. Helen was Annie's life's work.

As historians have noted, Annie had powerful reasons for wanting Helen to maintain a rigorous pace of study and prove she could keep up academically with her seeing and hearing peers at the Cambridge School: if Helen were to graduate in three years, Annie's "claims about Helen's exceptional abilities would be validated," and her methods verified.[52] Still insecure and wounded from the Frost King experience, Annie needed this validation deeply.

Helen would later say that the Cambridge School experience led to a profound loss of trust on her part: "I have found that I cannot always put my hand in another's with a trustful spirit. This terrible experience has made a woman of me. My childhood has slipped away with its simple unreasoning trust in human goodness, and its dreamy unconsciousness of the evil there is in the world. I know now that men can be false and wicked, even while they are kind."[53]

CHAPTER NINE

"The Happiest Months"

For the residents at Red Farm, the long ordeal wound down to an everyday quietude of study and play. The *Transcript* provided a calming, even benign explanation of the reasons for Helen's withdrawal from the Cambridge School on January 13, 1898. After laying out vaguely the sequence of events, in the article Helen defended her teacher, writing that "Miss Sullivan's judgment had been flung aside as of no value; and I knew, too, that she had taken the best care of me for nearly eleven years, and that no harm had come to me while I was with her. She had worked all those long years to make my life sweet and happy. I had never overworked in my whole life, and she had." The piece ended with the news that Radcliffe dean Agnes Irwin "was making arrangements for Helen's further studies under private tutors," which would make it "practicable for Helen to complete her preparation in time to take her final examinations for entrance to Radcliffe in June 1899."[1]

As Annie reported to John Hitz, she and Helen planned to stay in Wrentham through the remainder of the school year. In fact, they would stay there through the summer as well. The move to full-time residence at Red Farm represented not only the resolution of a painful chapter but also an important evolution in their friendship with the Chamberlins. Through constant, day-to-day contact, they would now come to know one another deeply. "Aunt Ida" and "Uncle Ed" were Helen and Annie's chosen Boston family.

In early January, Helen wrote to Annie Pratt that she and Annie were "well and as happy as circumstances permit." She was impatient to resume her work, worrying that she would lose "precious time." She was trying to forget the "cruel suffering" that Arthur Gilman had caused. It had been a terrible experience, "unlike anything which had ever happened" to her before, and she regretted that "a woman cannot forget as easily as a child."[2]

The household at Red Farm buzzed with the energy of its two new residents. Ida's strong maternal instincts now came to the fore. Having lost her own mother when she was five years old, Ida understood loss and longing: Helen's longing for a home and Annie's longing for a family. Ida created an exceptional and welcoming home for the pair, now seventeen and thirty-one respectively. She was an accomplished and capable homemaker, and she loved both Helen and Annie. In the absence of Mildred, Helen formed a stronger relationship with twelve-year-old Beth, writing to a friend, "Mr. Chamberlin's little girl, Beth, is a sweet child, and fills in some degree the great vacancy Mildred's going left in my life."[3] And five-year-old Raymie and three-year-old Dolly were always eager for Helen's attention.

In early February, Helen wrote to John Hitz, apologizing for Annie's lack of communication and sharing their plans:

I think Teacher told you in her last letter something about the happy turn our affairs have taken. We are going to stay here for the rest of the year. I am so glad, for I feel sure that it will be the best thing for us both. I shall keep her out of doors as much as possible, and make her take plenty of exercise and have a real good time. Mr. Keith, my new tutor, came here two weeks ago, and we began work at once. He said he thought it would be an easy matter for him to fit me, so that I could take my finals in 1899. Isn't that lovely? I cannot tell you how very happy I am to be at work once more! I study Greek, Geometry, and Algebra, and I shall probably take Physics and Latin very soon.

She wrote of a recent blizzard and the tobogganing that resulted from it. Just as she had loved "the treasures of the snow" as a child, her delight was still evident:

Last week, we had a tremendous blizzard. It snowed furiously for two whole days and we were literally snow-bound. The snow piled itself above the fences, and up in our piazza, and entirely filled the yard. Phil [Chamberlin] was obliged to work his way to the village on foot Tuesday and brought back the thrilling news that no trains had been through all that day! Nor had there been any telegrams or telephone messages or letters! I don't believe an army could have cut off our communications with the neighboring towns more completely than the storm did. But now we are having great fun sleighing, coasting and rolling down the hills. The coasting is especially fine just now for there are a great many "thank-you ma'am" hollows. Our little sleigh looks like a kangaroo as it goes springing and bouncing along! . . .

So you see, dear friend, how well and happy and hopeful we are.[4]

In a similar tone, at the end of February, Helen wrote to Eleanor Hutton, telling her, "I resumed my studies soon after your departure [in early January], and in a very little while we were working as merrily as if the dreadful experience of a month ago had been but a dream. I cannot tell you how much I enjoy the country. It is so fresh, and peaceful and free!"[5]

As springtime arrived, Helen enthused in her journal on March 11:

This has been a perfectly wonderful day! Teacher and I took a little drive this morning, and the air was so fresh I wanted to breathe it all in. I could never have enough of it! It was full of fragrant messages of coming spring. I could feel a throb of joy in every breeze as it came dancing across the fields. Teacher said the very trees seemed to tremble with expectancy. Even old Jerry,—Uncle Ed's horse that is usually UN PEU PARADEUX*—felt the glad influence and trotted away gaily, he would hardly wait for us to get into the carriage if we jumped out for any purpose.*[6]

A month later, she wrote reassuringly to Hutton of her studies: "I find I get on faster, and do better work with Mr. Keith than I did in the classes at the Cambridge School, and I think it was well that I gave up that kind of work. At any rate, I have not been idle since I left school; I have accomplished more, and been happier than I could have been there."[7]

While Helen was nearly euphoric, Annie was seen by other residents at Red Farm through the lens of day-to-day contact, and her tendencies to pessimism and depression became apparent. Now that others were also able to help with Helen, Annie was released somewhat from full-time responsibility for her and, with idle time for the first time in many years, had time for reflection. Helen later described Annie's moods: "When I could observe her more closely, I learned that her moods changed continually. . . . Teacher . . . suffered, though not long, from a melancholy which bred a wretched incapacity to respond even to the kindest approaches of her intimate friends. She would fly from them to the woods, or if she was near the water, she would conceal herself for hours under a boat on the shore. But then she would come back to her friends asking forgiveness."[8]

Even those who knew her well found Annie "perplexing." Helen shared that "Teacher's many-colored temperament, to which frayed nerves were an incessant aggravation, puzzled simple folk, and even the wise did not always chart the currents of her nature rightly. Only genuine affection enabled the best of friends to decipher some of the lights and shadows of her character."[9]

But under Ed and Ida's care, Annie blossomed, and according to Helen, "the melancholy which had oppressed her slackened its hold." Helen wrote that Annie "used to say that those eight months were among the happiest periods of her life. It was the first time since she had been with me that she had tasted genuine liberty." Helen continued, "Relieved that my life was natural, Teacher relaxed in an intelligent, affectionate atmosphere where she knew she was appreciated." Moreover, "She was surrounded by simplicity, pure kindness, and a wholesome rural environment. By spring she had shaken herself from a many-year load of frustrations and regained her old spontaneity. . . . As May approached, she felt intensely, joyously alive."[10]

Wrentham provided far-ranging opportunities for the vigorous outdoor pursuits that Helen and Annie loved. Perhaps for the first time in Annie's life she could relax and enjoy the natural beauty around her. She learned to swim and became an expert swimmer. She had loved horses since her childhood and became "most skillful in the equestrian art."[11]

According to Helen, Annie approached each day with a "renewed energy": "She was forever seeking an outlet for her restlessness. She believed in going somewhere often and seeing something new. . . . She went out of her way so that [Helen] might meet young people and have unusual experiences, thus introducing a constant element of change into my environment."[12]

As always, Red Farm offered other entertainments as well. Through association with Ed and his friends, Helen and Annie's "education in literary ways" was expanded and now included introduction to the works of Walt Whitman, whose poetry Annie had "resisted" since her Perkins days "out of prudery," according to Helen. She added, "All kinds of people visited Red Farm. . . . In their society Teacher was lifted up like a bird in air. Their stimulating talk electrified her and multiplied her thoughts as showers do flowers."[13]

Annie responded to the boisterous household and rich cultural life created by the circle of friends circulating in and out of the Chamberlins' house, and made her own contributions to the atmosphere, as Helen later wrote: "Over and over I heard people say that Annie Sullivan was a fascinating woman and that there was an irresistible sparkle in her repartee. At times, like other young women, she played clever pranks on some of the young men who flirted with her. . . . She was ever eager to listen to ideas, and it was a new world that opened to her."[14]

From Helen's perspective, "this was the nearest [Annie] had come to self-possession." She related that

The sparkle of Teacher's inventive spirit was infectious, filling our days with exciting adventures—in some of which I could participate—diving and swimming on the top of the water or under (I tied a long rope round my waist, with one end fastened to the shore or to the boat, so that I could move freely), canoe races at the conclusion of which we young people tipped one another over, water polo, lantern parties among the firs and pines, and long rambles around the lake or investigations of the many ponds that shone like bewitching eyes in the Wrentham landscape.[15]

Annie's relationship with Helen now changed as well, and Helen recounted that "the future was uncertain, but her doubts concerning me were lessening, and her grasp upon life was growing firmer. Her powers and executive ability were expanding, and she ceased to treat me as a child, she did not command me any more."[16]

Even while Helen and Annie sheltered and savored life at Red Farm, events near and far intruded on their bliss. In April 1898, the United States became involved in the Spanish American War in Cuba. Forty-six-year-old Ed signed on as a traveling war correspondent for the *Transcript* and *New York Evening Post.* He spent the next few months abroad to witness and report on the war. Helen would later write, "That summer we were all lonely; for the master of the house was far away in Cuba."[17]

The carefree spring mood was further interrupted when Annie's trachoma worsened. The eye infection that had plagued her in childhood and been untreated for years had caused serious damage. Repeated trachoma infections could lead to blindness. Immigrants arriving at Ellis Island had their eyelids peeled back to determine if they were suffering from the disease, and if so were denied entry to the United States. In modern times, a course of antibiotic treatment and careful hygiene generally cures the disease.[18] The damage to Annie's eyes could not be reversed, but rest could relieve some of the blurring and pain she experienced.

Helen was very young when she first realized Annie had serious vision challenges, but it was not until years later that Helen understood Annie had overtaxed her own sight to read on subjects connected to pedagogy, to gain self-improvement, and to educate Helen. So strong was her drive for Helen to succeed that, as Helen wrote, Annie "almost quenched her vision to read her way to the treasures she sought."[19]

The presence of a tutor at Red Farm, as well as others who could read to Helen, partially relieved Annie and enabled her to rest somewhat. But even with that relief, her vision problems were worsening.

Ida was concerned about Annie's eyes, and began to take a more assertive role in both Helen's and Annie's day-to-day lives. She cared deeply about the two young women and knew them better than almost anyone. On June 10, 1898, she wrote to John Hitz and invited him for a visit.

She shared the first part of the note with Annie, but she continued confidentially to John Hitz regarding her grave concern for Annie's eyes, which a doctor had said would require an operation:

"There is something for me to say to you that is not for her," she began. Now a close witness to Annie's propensity to dark moods, Ida believed Annie would potentially commit suicide rather than face surgery or blindness. Ida told Hitz, "She is in a desperate frame of mind about her eyes. While in N.Y., Dr. Derby made a thorough examination and his verdict has frightened her almost to desperation. He said that unless her eyes were operated upon that she must lose her sight; that the eyes were in a most aggravated state, even saying more emphatic things than I shall repeat. . . . The result is that she has given up hope and *has* flatly refused to see any one here."

Ida tried to be respectful of Annie's position on the matter but could not stand by silently. She told Hitz, "I have remonstrated with her but she says, 'Dr. Derby . . . has told me the truth, I *will not* be operated upon so there is nothing but blindness ahead, and then death, for I will not live blind.' I know her so well now that I know this is no idle threat, nor could I blame her for feeling so about it."

Without Annie's knowledge, Ida was searching for options. She went on in her letter:

Yesterday I went in town to see her own doctor hoping to get his help in the matter. He is ill, has given up his practice and as his trouble is rheumatism, in the hands now, he is not likely to ever do anything again. Anyway what is done for Annie must be done AT ONCE. *There is no time to be lost. Her sight has failed noticeably since the winter and within the last week symptoms have come which I recognize and fills me with alarm. She told another person who told me, that she could not have any treatment because of the terrible expense.*

Ida, therefore, sought Hitz's help. Ida knew Annie must be handled carefully. She pleaded,

Do you not think Dr. Bell or some of the rich men who are interested, would rather pay such bills than that the poor girl should be blind? I do. What I advise, and please trust me, for I know my girl and know that she is to be treated tactfully, is that you consult Dr. Bell, now or after you have been here, as to what had best be done. She is not to be commanded but you and I, I am sure are the only ones who really LOVE *Annie Sullivan and if we cannot* PERSUADE, *no one can* MAKE *her do what she should now. She has got to be saved from herself if possible. Please know that I am not easily frightened, and that I say it, it is absolutely necessary for you to come here as soon as possible. I should like to know when I can come and meet you and have a talk with you before she sees you. It absolutely rests with you and me what becomes of her now. You surely know me well enough to know that I would not meddle in this if I did not feel that a crisis is on us through her agony, and God only knows the outcome.*

Apparently Annie had not written to Mrs. Hutton for financial help and Ida added, "I dare not write for Mrs. Hutton's aid or advice in this matter, for I know she would try to use authority and that would fail in this, and perhaps injure our chances with Annie." Ida closed the letter with the request that Hitz "do come soon if possible."[20]

Meanwhile, Annie tried to downplay the seriousness of her eye problems. It seemed understandable, given that in other ways she was enjoying life so thoroughly. It must have felt unfair to be so afflicted at such an otherwise contented time.

Not long after Ida's letter was mailed to Hitz, on June 19, Edward Everett Hale visited a friend in Wrentham and stopped by Red Farm, after which he reported to his assistant:

It was a charming day at Wrentham. I went over to the Chamberlin's where Helen Keller and Annie Sullivan were staying. They spend the summer there. It would have made you happy to see the joy with which they welcomed me. It was as if I had been a brother just home from sea. Miss Sullivan has had some anxiety about her eyes, but she made light of it, saying that all the doctors said was that she needed rest. Helen is deep in her GREEK *and is even enthusiastic about it. As for the place, it is perfectly beautiful. We went to see an old oak tree. 800 years old.*[21]

Helen continued to enjoy life in the country, noting gleefully in her journal on the first of July:

What a cool, breezy day it has been! And the children and I have been like kittens all day—never stopping our play a minute. This morning we rambled off to the woods. No, rather, we skipped along the road helter-skelter, as the peas do on the piazza sometimes when I don't shell them properly. We tried to push each other off the path every chance we had, and once when we were crossing a field, the children ran with me plump into a pile of hay! Away we went rolling over and over with Buff jumping on us and barking in high glee. When we got to the woods, we tried to make our way through a balsam fir thicket, and we were kept busy falling down and disentangling ourselves from briers and small trees. But we did come out of the tangle, all sweet with the smell of the firs we had rubbed up against, and as happy as bobolinks! I have never laughed so much as I did then. I seem to laugh more all the time here at Red Farm, and I get happier and happier.[22]

She wrote to Hitz a few days later, reporting that "in spite of its terrible heat, I am enjoying my vacation very much. I row almost every day all round the lake, which is a great pleasure to me, for I love to be out on the water."[23] Annie had sought some sort of therapy for her eyes, and at least from Helen's viewpoint, she was better.

And while Annie struggled with her vision problems, she also had worries about the future. Helen was poised to go on to college or some form of employment—but all was still uncertain. Annie was either to accompany her toward those goals or form goals of her own. Later letters and materials reveal that Ida had many conversations with both Helen and Annie about their life hopes and plans.[24]

Meanwhile, Ed was in Cuba. He would later count his time there as one of the most significant periods of his life. Although the war was brief, lasting only ten weeks, it led to "rancorous" debate over expansionism.[25] The Listener for the *Transcript* brought the same watchful, detached approach to his observations of the war, and his telling of events was counter to that of most of his media peers and colleagues.

Ed did not glorify war. He expressed his views in an article sent from Cuba for the June 1898 edition of the *Public Forum,* concluding his article with an admonition to those who would be warmongers: "The war can hardly be ended without enormously extending the range of the direct influence of the United States. This extension will call for the immediate settlement of the question of the Isthmian Canal. It can scarcely be settled otherwise than in a way to aggrandize the republic. Aggrandizement will lead to aggrandizement."[26]

Upon his return in late July, Ed shared his experiences in an August 8 "Listener" column titled "Reflections on Cuba and Spanish-American War," and in other articles published in *Youth's Companion* and several New York newspapers and national reviews.[27]

He had been stricken while away with a debilitating illness called "Cuban Fever," probably malarial fever, which delayed his return. His journey home had been a "long nightmare." While ill, he had "ceaselessly dreamed" himself home but had twice been denied reentry into his country and "put ashore on a quarantine island." The experience made his eventual return to the "jolly household" a "dizzy unreality."[28]

Ed's honest war reporting set him apart from other journalists. He spoke of a "disorganized military campaign, disease that ravaged the soldiers and civilians, of few doctors, and even when there were doctors, no safe place to establish a hospital." But despite the disasters, there were positives: "one could easily find things not to admire in this campaign; one could find nothing but matter for admiration in the bearing of the soldiers."[29]

Always considering Helen's broader education, on returning from Cuba Ed talked seriously with her about humankind and war. She wrote of one such conversation in her journal in August, quoting him as saying, "There are some kinds of success not admirable. He has talked about Caesar and Napoleon. I had supposed they were benefactors because they were praised and extolled to the skies in everything I read about them. But he said they became famous by killing great numbers of their fellowmen, ruining their lands, and spreading misery and hatred everywhere. He went on to say that whatever good they accomplished was small compared with the evil they did and the suffering they caused."[30]

Ed challenged Helen to "think more systematically and critically," and he respected her thoughts as she expressed them. Later, he wrote in an article published in the *Ladies' Home Journal* that "Helen is an unconquerable liberal in her ideas. She inclines to take the side of the people in all matters which they make their concern. She is instinctively philanthropical and benevolent. Her notions in sociological matters are pretty nearly the direct opposite of those of Miss Sullivan, who is extremely conservative."[31]

Helen's enjoyment of the summer in Wrentham continued into early September, when she wrote to a friend:

I am out of doors all the time, rowing, swimming, riding and doing a multitude of other pleasant things. This morning I rode over twelve miles on my tandem! I rode on a rough road and fell off three or four times, and am now awfully lame! But the weather and scenery were so beautiful, and it was such fun to go scooting over the smoother part of the road, I didn't mind the mishaps in the least. I have really learned to swim and dive—after a fashion! I can swim a little under water, and do almost anything I like, without fear of getting drowned! . . . It is almost no effort for me to row around the lake, no matter how heavy the load may be. So you can well imagine how strong and brown I am.[32]

Helen would also write of that summer, "Here the long, sunny days were mine and all thoughts of work and college and the noisy city were thrust into the background. In Wrentham we caught echoes of what was happening in the world—war, alliance, social conflict. . . . But we little heeded these things. These things would pass away; here were lakes and woods and broad daisy-starred fields and sweet-breathed meadows, and they shall endure forever."[33] For Helen especially, the months at Red Farm had indeed been the happiest.

Figure 1. Helen Keller reading a braille book, probably photographed in the late 1880s, around the time she met Joseph Edgar Chamberlin in Boston. She has short, curly hair and wears a long-sleeved, lacy white dress and black boots. She sits on a high-backed, upholstered chair with her feet on an ottoman and a large book open on her lap. Her right arm rests on a table next to her. A vase and framed photo are on the table. Courtesy of the American Foundation for the Blind, Helen Keller Archive.

Figure 2. Helen Keller and her teacher, Annie Sullivan, in 1895, when Helen was fifteen years old. Helen has short, curly, dark hair and is wearing a light colored blouse. She stands in front of Annie, facing sideways, with her head resting on Annie's shoulder. Behind her, Annie is facing the camera, but looking slightly away. She has dark, curly hair styled in a loose bun on top of her head. She wears a white dress with ribbon embellishment on the front. Courtesy of the American Foundation for the Blind, Helen Keller Archive.

Figure 3. Ida Atwood Chamberlin as a young woman, possibly taken around the time of her marriage in Chicago in 1873. She has long, light brown hair, pulled back in an elegant style. She wears a white jacket with embroidered trim over a white ruffled blouse, with a black ribbon tied at her neck. She also wears several necklaces. Photograph by Copelin Photographers, Chicago. Courtesy of the Chamberlin family.

Figure 4. Ed Chamberlin as a young man in Chicago in 1875, two years after marrying Ida Atwood. He was twenty-four years old at the time and working for the *Chicago Times.* He has short, brown hair, neatly combed and parted on the side, and has a mustache. He wears a suit with wide lapels over a white shirt with a black bow tie at the neck. Photograph by Mosher's, Wabash Avenue, Chicago. Courtesy of Peter Boshco.

Figure 5. Ed Chamberlin and his daughter Beth in July, 1889. He is crouching, with leaves and flowers strewn on the ground around him. He wears light colored clothing and a hat. His arm is around three-year-old Beth, who is standing at his side. He looks down at a flower in his hand. Beth is looking directly at the camera. She has dark hair and wears a broad-brimmed hat and an embroidered jumper over a white blouse. Courtesy of Peter Boshco.

Figure 6. Ed Chamberlin in a studio portrait, taken in approximately 1898. At this time, he was "The Listener" columnist for the *Boston Transcript* and an editor at *Youth's Companion* magazine. He wears a business suit, a white shirt, and a tie. He has a receding hairline and a mustache and wears glasses. He is seated at an angle on a wooden chair, looking away from the camera with a contemplative expression on his face. Courtesy of Peter Boshco.

Figure 7. Helen Keller as a young woman in 1901, around the time she enrolled at Radcliffe. She is seated indoors on an elegant wicker chair with large potted plants on either side of her. Her hair is pulled back in a bun, and she wears a white, high-necked dress with long sleeves. She is seated at an angle and is looking down at something in her hand. Courtesy of the American Foundation for the Blind, Helen Keller Archive.

Figure 8. Red Farm, overlooking King Philip's Pond, Wrentham, Massachusetts, as it appeared in the early 1900s. In a black and white photograph, a large farmhouse with dark siding and many windows sits on a hill above a steep bank that leads down to the lake. A small boat can be seen at the water's edge. Courtesy of the Murray Family.

CHAPTER TEN

Radcliffe Aspirations

Late in the summer of 1898, Annie and Helen made the decision to take an apartment of their own in Boston, to be closer to the tutor, Merton Keith, and to continue preparing for the Radcliffe entrance exams that would be required at the end of the next school year. Perhaps there were altogether too many distractions at Red Farm.

In October they secured an apartment at 12 Newbury Street. Keith now gave Helen lessons "five times a week, in periods of about an hour. He explained each time what Helen did not understand in the previous lesson, assigned new work, and took home with him the Greek exercises which Helen had written during the week on her Hammond typewriter [which could be set to type in different languages], corrected them fully, and returned them."[1] Annie assisted Helen with interpretation and homework.

Once in the city, though, Helen's thoughts often turned to Red Farm. In late October she wrote to Eleanor Hutton, "I wish the Wrentham woods were round the corner! You will think I'm pining away for my beloved Wrentham, which is true in one sense and not in another. I do miss Red Farm and the dear ones there dreadfully; but I am not unhappy. I have Teacher and my books."[2]

In early December, Helen sent an update on their activities to John Hitz. She wrote of Annie, "Poor thing, her eyes trouble her a good deal. We have just been over to Chelsea, and Aunt Polly [Annie Pratt] seemed quite anxious about them." Of her studies, Helen noted, "My work goes merrily on, but we miss the beautiful, free country life more and more. Indeed, it seems sometimes as if I should never overcome my intense longing to throw my books aside, and run away from the city, and just frolic with the dear children at Red Farm in the snow. But, when we are tired or discouraged and want to think of some quiet, beautiful restful spot, we think of the blue hills, the lovely lake and the charming road at Wrentham, and we feel refreshed."

Helen and Annie were making plans for the holidays. In her letter, Helen added, "Now we have a little plan for Christmas. It is possible that we may go South for the holidays, but we are hoping that Mother and Mildred and Phillips will be able to come up here for a little visit. It would not cost any more than for Teacher and me to go to Alabama, and it would be a nice change for poor Mother. If they do come, we shall all go out to Wrentham. I am anxiously waiting for Mother's decision."[3]

While Helen and Annie weighed whether to go to Alabama or Wrentham, John Hitz invited them to spend Christmas with him in Washington. On December 22, Helen wrote to him, saying,

We are going to spend the holidays with the Chamberlins. Teacher left the decision with me, and I thought I should like to go to Wrentham better than anywhere else; for I could be out-of-doors there, and frolic with the children in the snow. Of course, I know it seems ungracious not to accept your loving invitation and perhaps I am selfish, but really, dear friend, I thought it would be best for Teacher to be in the country too. She seems tired and nervous, and I want her to be quiet. She says, "Wouldn't it be lovely if Mr. Hitz would come to Wrentham also," and so it would. Why not use the money which you were going to send us to come to Washington, and take a little trip yourself? Nothing would delight Mrs. Chamberlin so much as to have you make her a visit. She thinks a great deal of "dear Mr. Hitz."[4]

In spite of Helen's invitation to come to the Chamberlins', Hitz had other obligations and did not visit over the holidays. On January 7, 1899, Helen wrote that she had received his "dear" letter while she was at Wrentham, and told him of recent events:

We had a happy Christmas at Red Farm, though we should have thought it more like Christmas if dear mother, Mildred, and Phillips had been there to share its pleasures with us.

Our Christmas Eve we all hung up our stockings before the mantelpiece and found them simply crammed with gifts in the morning. We first watched the happy children as they opened their bundles and danced round in wild delight with their new treasures. Santa

Claus had been very generous indeed, and had given them so many lovely toys they could hardly play at all! You know what a very military fellow Raymie is. He was made thoroughly happy with a real campaign hat, a toy warship, a cannon and a little army; so you can easily picture to yourself the joy of the little ones, especially as you have seen it in the faces of the children to whom you carry your gifts yourself as dear Santa Claus! What delighted me most among many presents was a beautiful rubber plant from my own dear Teacher. I also received two books, "Paul of Virginia" and "A Dog of Flanders." Have you read either of them?

We stayed with the Chamberlins two weeks longer than we at first intended because I had a very bad cold. But we did a good deal in the Eclogues of "Virgil the Aeneid" [sic] *and the "Iliad," so I don't think I am far behind in my work. Although we had plenty of snow, yet I could not play in it much to my sorrow, but I romped with Raymie and Dolly, and told them their stories. Bless you, they ask me to tell them the same tale from five to twenty-four times! Do you not think they pay me a great compliment?*

Now we are back in our own little quarters, and trying to get all our "thank yous" off before Monday comes upon us, so I must say goodbye.[5]

Helen resumed her studies, but Annie's eyes were bothersome. On February 3, Helen was worried and wrote again to John Hitz:

I really dread going to college next year on her account. I cannot bear the thought of the constant and terrible strain upon her poor eyes, which I fear will come with our new studies. How I wish we could slip away, and live in the peaceful country for a year, at least, away from every one we know, and just be happy and free from care and anxiety! We could find a little house and make our nest there, and do just as we please. We wouldn't let anybody except you and mother into our secret. You could come to see us once in a while, but no one else would know our hiding place. Perhaps her eyes would there get well and we would be quite ready for any amount of college work. But alas, we have not the means of carrying out this plan, so I suppose we must keep on until I take my "finals" in June. If you have any advice do not hesitate to give it, we should be happy if we could find a way out of this sad dilemma.[6]

Helen's worries about Annie's eyes were reiterated in a March 5 letter to Hutton, in which she said that "teacher's eyes are no better." Helen further expressed her distress that Annie was "sacrificing her sight for me." She wrote that she felt as if she ought to "give up the idea of going to college altogether: for not all the knowledge in the world could make me happy, if obtained at such a cost." She wished for Hutton to "persuade Teacher to take a rest, and have her eyes treated," as Annie would not listen to Helen.[7]

Even as Helen continued to prepare for her Radcliffe examinations, by April she was already thinking ahead to summer in Wrentham and making preparations. Although she was usually spared the details of finances, she began plotting out arrangements for cottage rental as a vacation for Annie by soliciting donations from wealthy friends, such as Hutton and Bell. She wrote another letter to John Hitz on April 11 with the news that her family would be coming to Wrentham for the summer, with their travel expenses and cottage rental largely paid by friends. She hoped that the presence of her family would relieve Annie somewhat, but she told Hitz that other financial assistance might still be needed: "We may have to call upon you, dear friend, to help us before we get through. Teacher thinks that perhaps, if you tell Mr. Bell of the plan, he will do something towards making it successful. Of course you must not say anything about it if he is occupied with other things. You know, Mrs. Bell has helped us in many ways, and we hate the idea of being regarded as a pair of 'Oliver Twists.'" Helen hoped that Hitz might also come for the summer; there would be room for him at the Chamberlins' while Helen and her family summered at a nearby cottage.

She continued in her letter, telling Hitz, "We have just returned from Wrentham where we have been spending our Easter holidays. We have enjoyed our visit very much. Every day I took a long walk with Bettie [Beth], and . . . I found the woods full of life. At every step we startled a partridge, or a whole flock of blackbirds, and robins and bluebirds filled the air with joyous song. We even saw two or three butterflies. Spring always comes with a glad surprise, does it not?" But Helen was concerned about Annie and what the coming months would bring as they prepared for final examinations: "Now Teacher is somewhat rested, but she has so much to do before June that I really feel alarmed. However, I think that happy thoughts of the coming summer will make the 'home stretch' easier for us both."[8]

Later in April, Helen again updated Hitz regarding their summer plans:

Teacher was pleased to receive your letter, and as delighted as I am to know that you were really coming to spend a month with us. We told Mrs. Chamberlin of your plan and she exclaimed, "Why, of course he shall stay with us," so you may be sure of a cordial welcome at Red Farm and enjoy yourself to the full, as you did last summer. I shall of course be there many times every day, so we shall see each other a great deal, and enjoy many a piece of outing together. Teacher has already hired a cottage for mother, and everything will be ready when she comes. I wrote to her, telling her that we thought she had better start about the twenty-fifth of June. We believe that we have now all the money needed, and we are looking forward to the most delightful summer imaginable for every body concerned, and ourselves especially.

A postscript discussed the possibility of Annie teaching another child—possibly to earn extra money. This never happened, and perhaps the point was only raised to reinforce the need for financial support.[9]

Helen and Annie were living in Cambridge but spending every opportunity at Red Farm. Meanwhile, the *Transcript* continued its frequent coverage of the work of Perkins and the Kindergarten for the Blind.

But time was passing, and Ed now lent his voice to Helen's cause for a national audience in an article entitled "Helen Keller as She Really Is" in the spring 1899 issue of *Ladies' Home Journal*. His advocacy was needed now: Helen was almost nineteen and wanted to continue her education at Radcliffe, if possible. There were biases about this deafblind young woman that needed to be overcome—some lingering from the Frost King affair, possibly, but also from the ableist prejudice that someone who could not hear or see could not succeed in the larger world—and Ed was uniquely positioned to speak for not only her talents but also her normalcy.

Short excerpts from the lengthy *Ladies' Home Journal* article appeared in newspapers and publications across the country. In the article, Ed wrote, "Helen Keller is as normal a young person, in the respect of her ordinary likes and dislikes, as any one you would be apt to meet in a day's journey." He felt that

she certainly comes nearer to being completely good than any other person whom I have ever known. She is unable to frame deceit. Nevertheless, she loves dearly to play practical jokes of an innocent sort; but they are generally very melancholy failures through her total inaptitude for any form of guile. She is extremely fond of outdoor romping and yearns for adventures by sea and land. She struggles—of course with a guide, for if she is left entirely alone out-of-doors she simply stands stock still or sits down on the ground until rescued—with great joy up the steepest hills and through the densest thickets. To be "lost" in our little woods with only a child for a guide is an intense delight to her. She revels in rough handling and friendly "scraps." She is a strong and healthy girl and feels the need for exercise.

He noted further that "she eats heartily, but has a somewhat—that is, an extremely sensitive—palate. Any taste which is but faintly perceived by other people seems to be strongly marked to her. The number of articles of diet which 'she does not like' is alarming, but there always remains a good variety of things, mostly plain and nutritious articles, to meet the demands of her appetite."

Ed also spoke about the keenness of Helen's sense of touch, relating the story of how during the previous summer, when "Helen was taking her exercise by walking up and down the veranda," and he was seated in a chair by the door, "a little child, barely a year old but able to walk freely, came walking lightly out upon the veranda. Helen stopped at once, and coming up to me and touching my lips asked 'Is Marion here?'" Ed answered, 'Yes." He continued,

"Helen smiled and said, I thought I felt a soft sound." Likewise, she was able to "hear" the sounds of a piano by holding her hands against it when it was being played. She was adept at recognizing people she had met before by the touch of their hand, which Ed was convinced was done by Helen's recognition of "the slight individual or characteristic movement or movements of each person."

For all of her abilities, however, Ed was quick to emphasize that they were "unquestionably developed from a merely normal foundation." There was nothing extreme or unexplainable about her. She was just a normal young person whose hands did the work of her eyes and ears, with skills built of necessity and practice.[10]

In May, Helen and Annie were still finalizing their plans for the summer, Helen wrote to John Hitz with an update on May 17:

Do not imagine that I am overworking. Teacher has arranged for me to take a ride twice on my tandem every week. I enjoy my "spins" in the parks immensely, and I find my work easier after a ride on my wheel. We also go to Wrentham almost every Sunday. Last Sunday the country was beautiful beyond description. Bettie and I took a long tromp through the woods and came home with our arms full of wildflowers, dogwood, lady-slippers, Rhodos, violets, and other woodland beauties. It seemed as if the world had never been as beautiful before! But of course you know all about it; you have seen the fruit trees covered with a mass of soft pink blossoms; you have heard the birds singing, and listened to the life-music which Nature's orchestra pours forth in the spring-time.

We went to see the little cottage, which mother is to occupy this summer. I call it the Nest of Delight, in anticipation of the good times we shall have there. It has six tiny rooms, and a nice, wide porch, and is surrounded by trees. Also, it is only a few feet from the lake, and I intend to take a swim every morning before breakfast! Oh, won't that be fun?

We were very sorry indeed not to see Dr. Bell, when he stopped over in Boston the other day. He sent a telegram, inviting us to lunch with him at the Parker House, but we could not possibly go, so we sent him word, begging him to come to us; but bless me, we didn't hear any more from him. . . .

By the way, Teacher wishes me to ask you if you have said anything to Dr. Bell about our summer plan, and if he is going to help us carry it out. She would like to know, as she is going to cut her cloth according to the material she has.

She sends her dear love. We are looking forward most eagerly to seeing you this summer.[11]

On June 29 and 30, 1899 Helen took her final examinations for Radcliffe College and passed all of them. Helen's accomplishment was extraordinary in itself but even more so considering that the examination process was fraught with additional challenges for her, especially in algebra and geometry, as she later described in her book *The Story of My Life:* "The college authorities did not allow Miss Sullivan to read the examination papers to me; so Mr. Eugene C. Vining, one of the instructors at the Perkins Institution for the Blind, was employed to copy the papers for me in American braille. Mr. Vining was a stranger to me, and could not communicate with me, except by writing braille. The proctor was also a stranger, and did not attempt to communicate with me in any way."

Helen reported that "the braille worked well enough in the languages, but when it came to geometry and algebra, difficulties arose." Her previous math studies had used the English (British) braille system, and its symbols were different from the American system of braille, which the exam now used. She wrote that

two days before the examinations, Mr. Vining sent me a braille copy of one of the old Harvard papers in algebra. To my dismay I found that it was in the American notation. I sat down immediately and wrote to Mr. Vining, asking him to explain the signs. I received another paper and a table of signs by return mail, and I set to work to learn the notation. But on the night before the algebra examination, while I was struggling over some very complicated examples, I could not tell the combination of bracket, brace and radical. Both Mr. Keith and I were distressed and full of forebodings for the morrow.

One can imagine the panic and frustration Helen must have felt the night before the examination, as the symbols and signs that she had learned were suddenly presented in a foreign notation. As she wrote, "Consequently, my work was painfully slow, and I had to read examples over and over before I could form any idea of what I was required to do. Indeed, I am not sure now that I read all the signs correctly. I found it very hard to keep my wits about me." Charitably, she added, "But I do not blame anyone. The administrative board of Radcliffe did not realize how difficult they were making my examinations, nor did they understand the peculiar difficulties I had to surmount. But if they intentionally placed obstacles in my way, I have the consolation of knowing that I overcame them all."[12]

Helen's experience with the Radcliffe examination process would receive much attention—and very public discussion—in the future.

With the examinations behind her, summer at the rented cottage in Wrentham lay ahead.

On July 4, 1899, Helen received her Certificate of Admission to Radcliffe. But suddenly the college authorities balked; they objected to the requirement that Annie would need to be present to read examination papers to Helen, and her admission was delayed indefinitely. To her extreme disappointment, Helen would not be allowed to enter college with the freshman class that fall.

Despite the delay, Helen tried to enjoy her summer. Relaxing with her family and Annie in the Wrentham area, she wrote to Annie Pratt in late July:

I know you think me a very very naughty girl for allowing all these weeks to pass without sending [?] . . . so I am going to "screw up" courage and write to you, and take your well-deserved scolding with a humble, contrite spirit, and try not to let the country make me forget my manners again. . . .

Thus far my vacation has been sweeter than anything I can remember. My mother and sister and little brother have been here five weeks and we are as happy as happy can be. Not only have we the joy of being together, but we have also a most delightful little house right in the woods, a few steps from Lake Wollomanapoag [sic], *which you may remember. I wish you could see the view of the beautiful lake from our piazza, the islands looking like little emerald peaks in the golden sunlight, and the canoes flitting here and there like autumn leaves in the gentle breeze.*

We go bathing every day and I swim longer and longer each time. . . . We also row a good deal in my little boat especially in the evening when the sun is sinking down low behind the hills and the stars come out one by one, like the forget-me-nots of the angels, "and night, gliding embraces the earth with her dusky rings." I wander a good deal in the woods with Mildred and we sometimes come home with our arms full of golden-rod, ferns, bright red berries and other woodland beauties. So you can easily imagine how my cup overflows with happiness.[13]

During his visit that summer, John Hitz had asked Helen to write a "souvenir" of her life—a longer, more elaborative piece than her autobiography that had appeared so many years ago in *Youth's Companion* when she was only twelve years old. She wrote to update him on the progress on September 4: "I thought I'd send you a blithe greeting this glorious morning, and tell you that I am working on the 'souvenir,' but I am afraid it will take me some time to finish it. In fact, I have feared at times that I should have to give it up altogether. You see I have never written a paper such as you want, and I am only nineteen years old, so I find it hard to write anything interesting about my simple, girlish self for so many distinguished people to read."

Even late in the season, Helen noted, "we still go in swimming, though the water is somewhat cold. The lake is so shallow, that we can swim almost clear to the big island and touch the bottom." While Helen enjoyed the waning days of summer in her cottage, life at Red Farm was not going well. In her letter to Hitz, Helen reported that "poor Aunt Ida has been very poorly indeed. Last Tuesday she sent away all her family, and had an operation and since then she has been having a hard time; but now she is more comfortable."[14]

This was the first in a series of mentions of Ida's ill health by Helen. Subsequently, over the next few years, Helen often noted that Ida required frequent periods of bedrest due to serious illness of an unspecified nature.

Later in September, Annie and Helen returned to Cambridge to await the next phase of their lives. Meanwhile, two other young women, both American Indian, were folded into the Red Farm community. In early September, Ida reported to Fred Holland Day, the publisher and photographer, that the Sioux violinist Zitkala-Ša (also known by the Anglicized version of her birth name, Red Bird, or her mission school name of Gertrude Bonnin) and the Winnebago artist Angel De Cora were living with them.[15] But soon after their arrival, the two women were "sent off grounds" due to Ida's operation.[16]

They returned a few weeks later, once Ida had recuperated sufficiently. These new friends of the Chamberlins may have been introduced to them by Reverend Edward Hale, who was active in the Indian Rights Movement, but they could also have been introduced by Day or the painter F. Luis Mora, with whom they had artistic connections in common.

As it had been for Helen and Annie, Red Farm became a sort of second home for De Cora and Zitkala-Ša, and they added a potent new element to life there. Ida and Ed promoted Zitkala-Ša's writing efforts and expressed pride when an article she wrote based on "memories of her Indian childhood" was accepted for publication in *Atlantic Monthly*. Ed wrote to Day in September 1899 that "Zitkala-Sa has been with us all summer and has developed intellectually, I think, a great deal. Her written impressions of her childhood are natural, clear, and significant."[17] Many years later, Helen praised the stories of Zitkala-Ša's childhood, writing to her that her children's book "should be in every home," as "they are so young, so fresh, so full of the odors of the virgin forest."[18]

De Cora and Zitkala-Ša were frequent subjects of celebrated photographers, including Day. After a mission school education, Zitkala-Ša had moved to Boston to study violin at the Conservatory of Music, where she and Day struck up a friendship. Historian Linda M. Waggoner describes her as "artistic, attractive, assertive, passionate, and outspoken."[19] She also quickly became a close friend of Ida. Later, Zitkala-Ša became controversial when she encouraged young American Indians to embrace their traditions rather than adopt or conform to the ways of the White culture. Some White men would call her "ungrateful," since she had received a mission school education, but she remained a vocal advocate for a return to tradition and cultural pride for American Indians.[20]

A much quieter personality than Zitkala-Ša, Angel De Cora had been taken from her family as a child through trickery and brought east to be educated at the Hampton Institute, a mission school in Hampton, Virginia. After graduation at twenty-two, she traveled north in 1891 to attend art school in Boston, eventually enrolling at Smith College and graduating in 1896 as their first American Indian graduate.[21] An artist who worked in several media, she also studied in Boston with the American Impressionists Edmund Tarbell and Frank Benson. She was considered the most prominent American Indian artist of her generation and, like Zitkala-Ša, became a vocal supporter of Indian rights.[22]

De Cora was also influenced by Ed and Ida Chamberlin. Historian Elizabeth Hutchinson describes their relationship and its impact, saying, "De Cora's familiarity with [the] ideas [of art as moral force] came not only from her teachers, but also from her patron and landlord, Joseph Edgar Chamberlin. De Cora's relationship with Chamberlin and his wife, Ida, became deep and long-lasting."[23]

As Ed nurtured the careers of his two newest protégées, his writing also flourished. He continued his "Listener" columns and work for *Youth's Companion* but also wrote independently for other publishers, magazines, and newspapers—work that included a new biography of the abolitionist John Brown, published as one of the Beacon Biographies of Eminent Americans series published by Small, Maynard & Company. Edward Everett Hale Jr. (Reverend Hale's son) and the Chamberlins' friend Charles Waddell Chesnutt were among other authors who contributed to the series, which included biographies of Reverend Phillips Brooks, Aaron Burr, Frederick Douglass, Nathaniel Hawthorne, Robert E. Lee, Daniel Webster, and Thomas Paine.

Ed was well suited to write a biography of John Brown as he was deeply familiar with Brown through his family's abolitionist history. In addition, Boston society of the 1860s figured prominently in Brown's story. Dr. Samuel Gridley Howe, founder of Perkins, had been one of the "Secret Six" conspirators who supported Brown in his revolutionary antislavery agitations. Howe was able to emerge unscathed from Brown's eventual conviction and hanging—but the trial and revelation of his role in supporting Brown necessitated that he flee to Canada for a time.[24] With his wife, Julia Ward Howe, composer of the Battle Hymn of the Republic, he played a definitive role in the nation's march toward war. Another member of the "Secret Six" who supported Brown had been Ed's friend and Annie's rescuer from Tewksbury, the Honorable Frank Sanborn. He and Howe were fearless, visionary, bold men.

Ed revered John Brown, as illustrated in the preface to the book:

To present a picture of the man, separating him as much as possible from the controversies and hatreds which commonly rise up at the mention of his name, and to tell the story of his life plainly, without inquiry into the effect of his work, or any further estimate and comparison, would be quite enough to attempt in a biography of John Brown of Osawatomie as brief as this one must be. . . . Yet the story of Brown is so strongly simple, so utterly governed by an ideal, so glowing and tragical, that any one who follows it closely is likely to find himself kindling before he is aware of it.[25]

At the end of the book, Ed described the final hours of Brown's life before his death by hanging, quoting one of those who had imprisoned him: "'They are mistaken,' Governor Wise of Virginia said . . . in a public speech at Richmond, 'who take Brown to be a madman. He is a bundle of the best nerves I ever saw,—cut and thrust and bleeding and in bonds. He is a man of clear head, of courage, fortitude, and simple ingenuousness. He is cool, collected and indomitable . . . and he inspired me with great trust in his integrity as a man of truth.'"[26]

Meanwhile, Helen waited for further word from Radcliffe. Even though she had passed the entrance examinations, the college continued to stall on admitting her. The decision hinged on the approval of Dean Agnes Irwin, the same woman who had assisted with the search for an appropriate tutor after Helen and Annie's Cambridge School experience. The expressed concern now was over how Helen would manage the rigors of college coursework and examinations.

In late July, an article appeared in the *Boston Transcript* that discussed Helen's examinations for Radcliffe. Lucy Derby Fuller wrote to Helen on August 6 about the account. She was overwhelmed with the article, saying, "Whoever wrote that article (and of course we suspect it was Mr. Chamberlin) wrote it with his heart for a pen, and it has gone straight into the hearts and eyes of those who read it." She encouraged Helen to "please thank Mr. Chamberlin for his beautiful account of it all." Further, she noted, "Teacher has the hearts of people from all over this country for what she has done and ever is doing for you."[27]

Helen wrote a reply to Fuller in October. Her disappointment in the Radcliffe "hedging" was obvious. She had talked to Irwin recently and reported on the conversation:

You know it has long been my ambition to go to Radcliffe, and receive a degree, as many other girls have done; but Dean Irwin of Radcliffe, has persuaded me to take a special course for the present. She said I had already shown the world that I could do the college work, by passing all my examinations successfully, in spite of many obstacles. She showed me how very foolish it would be for me to pursue a four years' course of study at Radcliffe, simply to be like other girls, when I might be better cultivating whatever ability I had for writing. She said she did not consider a degree of any real value, but thought it was much more desirable to do something original than to waste one's energies only for a degree. Her arguments seemed so wise and practical, that I could not but yield. I found it hard, very hard, to give up the idea of going to college; it had been in my mind ever since I was a little girl; but there is no use in doing a foolish thing, because one has wanted to do it for a long time, is there?[28]

It must have been heartbreaking for Helen to be put off again since she had passed all of her examinations and had previously been so encouraged by the college.

Wrentham once more served as a welcome distraction. Helen was in their rented cottage on October 20 as fall descended on the region. She wrote to Pratt:

You may be surprised to hear that my teacher and I are still in the Nest of Delight. Our summer has passed away like a lovely dream. My mother and the children have already been at home in Tuscumbia three weeks, and we have been keeping house all by ourselves. Nearly all the people who came out here for the summer are gone, and we rarely see anyone, except the men who bring our provisions; but we are not lonely, for there is a peace and sweetness and quiet tenderness about these October days, which satisfies the spirit, and fills the heart with contentment.

The wind has just stripped the trees of nearly all their leaves, and the birds have flown to warmer climes, but we have had some beautiful days which we shall never forget! One afternoon about two weeks ago, we stepped into my little boat, and rowed slowly around the lake, our minds and hearts full with the beauty of the landscape.[29]

Helen tried her best to stay optimistic.

Meanwhile, Ida was ill and bedridden, and it does not seem that she was able to offer much help to Helen and Annie.[30] The pair faced an uncertain future, and the anxiety took its toll. Lingering clouds of the Frost King and Gilman episodes continued to haunt Annie. She wrote an angry and frustrated letter to John Hitz from Wrentham at the end of October—hinting that Gilman still sought to cultivate sympathy for his cause in Cambridge and Radcliffe circles. She declared,

I find people hateful and I hate them. Mr. Gilman seems to me a fair specimen of our noble race, while such men as yourself and Mr. Chamberlin are exceptions so rarely met with as to be almost incomprehensible to the average man or woman. . . .

No word yet from Dean Irwin with regard to Helen's work!! Helen is restless and disappointed and I am utterly discouraged. How absurd the idea of a souvenir such as you are getting out seems at this time. Here is the subject of it clamoring at the door of a nineteenth century university for instruction and getting splendidly snubbed for her audacity. . . . The mention of the Frost King story shows he [Gilman] has been consulting Mr. Anagnos, who

I understand is shortly to publish another statement in regard to that episode.[31]

Helen was working on the "souvenir" for Hitz, though Annie clearly did not relish its publication, and Annie frankly shared her thoughts with him:

You know, I told you last summer that I did not believe in enlightening the public further as to what we had done, were doing and intended to do. . . . Helen and I have suffered more than you or any one else in the world can ever understand, through the publicity that had been given to her education. I am not saying this because I blame you in any way, far from it, but simply to explain my lack of enthusiasm in something which has been in Helen's and my best interest. I cannot think the new Souvenir will unravel the tangled web of truth and falsehood that over-zealous friends and enemies have drawn about us. Time will only do that, and, as far as I am concerned, I am more than willing to work and wait, knowing that right and justice must triump [sic] *in the end.*[32]

Despite Annie's objection to further public comment, Merton Keith was also composing material to contribute to the souvenir. He submitted an exhaustive article in 1899 about his instruction of Helen from early February 1898 until June 1899. From his summary, it is clear he was both scholarly and a sensitive teacher. Like Ed, Keith had seen deeper qualities in Helen, writing, "But with all her innate and acquired powers of mind she could not have attained her present eminence, had it not been for the moral, or quasi-moral qualities of her soul. Ambition, undaunted courage, defiance of or glorying over obstacles, obstinate refusal to admit defeat, hope rising from incipient despair, self-respect and self-trust, patience and faith in planning or working or waiting for the consummation of effort—these constitute her armor of victory."

In summary, he continued, "Great as have been her accomplishments, equal results are, I believe, within the reach of many others. The merely intellectual qualities needed are not rare; it is their combination with moral powers that produces the seemingly magic results. Ambition stimulated by obstacles, persistent will and patience explain many of the wonders of Helen's achievements."[33]

The public still craved news of Helen and Annie, and the Chamberlins and other friends were sought-after sources of information for journalists. On occasion, Ed reported selected news of the pair to the *Transcript* and other outlets. The releases were most likely discussed with Annie beforehand, as they never compromised their friendship. Often these reports were reprinted in other newspapers across the country.

In October, William Wade, the Pittsburgh industrialist in whose home Helen and Annie had once spent time as guests—and who harbored unconcealed disdain for Ed and for newsmen in general—wrote a belligerent letter to Bell. Wade had sided with Gilman against Annie during the Cambridge School debacle, so it was not surprising that he would have a response to a glowing article about her teaching methods. He was raising a brouhaha about Helen's confusion regarding the algebraic symbols used for the Radcliffe examinations, and he told Bell that "I really fear that Mr. Hitz does not at all comprehend the surroundings Helen now has, and the flood of falsehood let loose over her examinations. . . . That wretched mass of rot that appeared in the *Transcript* has started the nonsense about Helen, and how any intelligent man could write of Helen passing examinations when the questions were written in a print unknown to her, passes my understanding: How could she answer questions without knowing what the questions were? How could she know what they were if she was unacquainted with the print they were written in?"[34]

Wade's letter was apparently forwarded by Bell to an acquaintance who worked in the U.S. Census Office and provoked a response on November 21, 1899. The unnamed writer had received several letters from Wade who said "the nonsensical stuff about Helen Keller provokes him all the more because it was published in the *Boston Transcript,* and was apparently written by Mr. Chamberlin, one of the editors, in whose house Helen had been a guest for nearly a year."[35] Wade also wrote disparaging letters to the editors of several newspapers regarding Helen's examinations, as well as national publications for the deaf.

Helen, meanwhile, was happily oblivious to this exchange over her examinations, reporting to Hitz on December 1 from their apartment in Cambridge:

We are now settled for the winter, and our work is going smoothly.... There is only one check to my pleasure in my work, and that is the pain in poor Teacher's eyes. She has been suffering greatly the last few days, and it becomes more and more plain, that she must have some one to help her or we must give up our work. The trouble is she can not easily find any one who can use the manual alphabet with sufficient facility for reading purposes; but we hope we shall succeed before the New Year.

We like our new home very much. I do not think that we have ever had a prettier room than the one we study in. From the windows we have a pleasant view of lawns and trees and pretty houses. Inside, there is our little world of pictures, and bric-a-brac and books; so we do not miss the country quite so much as we at first feared we should, though I do long for the fields and meadows, and the freedom of Wrentham.

Although Ida had been ill since at least September, Helen and Annie went to Red Farm for Thanksgiving. Helen continued,

We spent Thanksgiving with the Chamberlins, as usual. We had a very pleasant time, but poor Aunt Ida was not well at all, and it made us very sad to see how slowly and painfully she was recovering, if it can be called recovery, but we hope and pray most earnestly that she may be well when spring comes round again.

Yesterday morning half a dozen of us took a long walk in the woods, and I was much impressed by their beauty at this late time. Of course all the leaves had fallen; but in many places the ground looked like a picture, all covered with moss, pine-needles and oak leaves, which though withered, still kept their bright colors. There was no sun, but the air was sweet and fresh, and the soft gray sky felt to me like the embrace of a beloved friend. You may be sure that such a delightful walk as this gave us a very keen appetite for our dinner![36]

Helen continued to enjoy the fall weather but finally she heard from her tutor of the disparaging comments that had appeared in the press regarding her and the *Transcript* article. William Wade apparently wrote letters to the editor of the *Transcript* in response to Chamberlin's piece, and while no copies of those survive, in his correspondence to Gilman, he called Chamberlin "a cur" and "a dupe." Wade said he had "been aching for a chance to get at that fellow and if I don't make his hair fly now, call me a Dutchman." He also wished his comments could have gone "into *The Globe*, for that would probably provoke a fight, when I could fight with a free hand." He called Chamberlin's writing "bombastic exaggeration" and had contemptuous and scornful names for those whom Helen was close to: "Hon John" (John Hitz), "The Whisperer" (Ed), "Bellites" (Bell and his assistants), and "feminine jackass" (Eleanor Hutton). Wade clearly despised Ed, probably jealous that the Chamberlins were such trusted friends of Helen, a role that Wade had sought for himself. Local readers even accused Wade of "abusing" Chamberlin.[37]

In a letter to "My dear Mr. Wade" in early December, Helen reacted with tears, anger, and hurt:

How can I beat out on these keys what I have to say to you when my heart is so heavy with grief, and disappointment and rebellion at the cruel indignities, which you have showered upon me and those who are dear to me! My fingers will scarcely obey my will! I have loved you so truly and trustingly all these years, and looked up to you as a father. My heart has been too full of love and gratitude to hold even the suspicion of a doubt of your sincerity and affection for me. I knew two years ago that you took nearly, if not quite the same views as Mr. Gilman did, before and after I left his school; but I felt sure that you had been persuaded by him, and that in time you would see the mistake you were making, and be sorry for it. I thought your heart was true and generous, and I waited for the dear Heavenly Father to let the light of His beautiful truth shine upon the darkness that was in your mind; but, dear friend—I must still call you by the dear old name, though now it brings the bitter tears to my eyes, it is evident that you have now taken up your position among my enemies. How little did I dream, when I first knew you, that I should have an enemy, and least of all an enemy in you! And yet, as I sit here alone with my typewriter and my thoughts, I must acknowledge that I have three enemies, two of whom I loved as a little child, and shall always love, no matter what they do—I mean you and Mr. Anagnos. I have resolved to try to forget the wrongs you have both done me and my teacher, who is dearer to me than my life, and remember only the love and kindness you have shown us in the past. My third enemy is Mr. Gilman, and for him I feel only contempt and indignation. . . .

I am writing to you in this way, because Mr. Keith has just read to me your letter in the "Mentor." It is really outrageous, and I would not believe at first that you wrote it.

Helen further explained that in addition to the *Transcript* article, another reporter's account of an interview with her and statements from Ida Chamberlin, Kate Keller, and Annie had been printed in the *New York World* in the form of a conversation, a style Annie had strenuously objected to before publication, to no avail. That article was also being discussed in Wade's correspondences. Helen ended her letter to Wade: "I implore you with my tears, not to attack my friends any more. I cannot bear it any longer, and I know it will recoil upon you some day, if you do not check yourself now. My heart aches so I can write no more." She signed off with a "sad farewell."[38]

Wade's opinions could be dismissed—though with a heavy heart—but the reality was that Helen, Annie, and many of their friends and supporters were all experiencing great frustration. The uncertainty of Helen's future—and differing opinions as to what that future should look like—would test many friendships in the coming months.

PART III

CHAPTER ELEVEN

Dreams and Challenges

Beginning in December 1899 and continuing over the next year, the advocacy that emanated from Red Farm took a different turn. While well intended, it would challenge the relationship between the Chamberlins and Helen and Annie in a nearly catastrophic way.

Ida had been ill for months when she wrote to John Hitz from her sickbed on December 15. In her letter, she proposed an idea: Helen and Annie should become the heads of a residential school for deafblind children to be named "The Helen Keller Home." Days and months of bed rest had given Ida a great deal of time to think about Helen and Annie's future.

She was still ill and in pain when she wrote that she had "waited from day to day hoping to have some good news to write, but it does not come. I am waiting now with what patience I can command, to gain strength to go through another operation. This time there will be no great danger but it will be extremely painful in the healing. I have had a nurse all but two weeks of the time since Sept. 26. Just think of it."

In writing to Hitz, Ida pledged him "to the utmost secrecy." She had an idea that had been inspired months before, when Annie told her of a plan suggested by a Boston friend named Goodhue for a school in Cuba for the deafblind to be named the Helen Keller School for the Blind. Ida told Hitz that Goodhue's suggestion had "started her thinking," as "Helen has talked with me a good deal about what is to be her life-work." She said that Helen "wants to *do* something that will make her feel her active usefulness to her fellow-creatures. She told me one time that she would like to give her life to College Settlement work. I don't quite see how she could do much, except by the use of her name, and that would mean little to her as she does not value the use of a name. It is something greater that she is groping for."

Ida further wrote, "Now, for *my secret*. I want to see Helen and Annie at the head of an institution or home, for the deaf dumb and blind children, the triply afflicted only, to be known as the *Helen Keller Home.*" Ida had ruminated on her plan; in her words, she had "thought over this until I am so familiar with it that it seems as though everyone must have thought of it too." Armed with intimate familiarity with the pair from their many years in her household, she continued,

You know Annie Sullivan has a wonderful amount of power for this work, which should not be lost to the world. Her active work for Helen is nearly over. She can no longer teach Helen, and ought not to do the reading even which she is doing now. Her eyes are very bad again. It is hard to say it, but few of the people interested in Helen, have a second thought for Annie other than as Helen's teacher. You and I love her, know her true worth, and know her tremendous force. She has told me, and I fully believe her, that if blindness comes to her again, she will kill herself. The directing and training of another teacher or teachers, she would be able to do if she were blind, as well almost as with her sight. At any rate if she were doing something of this kind she would be more likely to keep the sight she now has. You can see as well as I her peculiar ability for this kind of work. She has said a good many times, that lack of force in his teachers was a potent factor working against Tommy Stringer's development [the young boy in whom Helen had taken an interest and for whom she had helped raise funds to send to Perkins in 1891]. It seems to me the PROPER *thing for Helen too. She would then feel that she had a part in the world instead of just existing, which I know to be her great hope. She is very beautiful with children, and could have certain duties later on in direct connection with them. Until that time should come her study could continue. Of course I know that all this takes time, but until a definite object is found, nothing is ever done in forming a life work. The lawyer and doctor are many years reaching their usefulness after they have decided what they are to do. I know both girls so well that I feel sure they would be happy. I don't think I need to put out any more reasons, for I feel that you will understand and appreciate this proposition.*

Ida confessed, "I feel 'a call' to go into this." She had "a great desire to see these girls strong and useful in the world, not living on the caprice of a few wealthy ones, who, even now are showing less interest. Mrs. Hutton cannot raise that fund, and I do not really think she *ever* can. I think that this object is so great and good, that it must, through that very strength and goodness, live and be.... My illness is holding me back, but I have a conviction, and a very strong one too, that I shall, sometime raise enough money to make a beginning, after that it will grow of itself."

Having presented her idea for Helen and Annie's future, Ida solicited Hitz's help in making it a reality:

Now, will the Volta Bureau be willing to be a helper, or can it be. You see, in the eyes of the world, especially in the eyes of those who have befriended Helen, I am nobody. Then, too, we must admit, painful as it is, that Helen, through animosity toward Annie, has enemies. I should like to feel the courage of the support of one, be it a business concern or individual, whom these various elements could both have confidence in and FEAR *too. If I were to raise money in small amounts, could the Volta Bureau on Helen's behalf, be custodian.*

Then, Ida revealed that her vision for the pair's future was not entirely altruistic. She also wanted credit for the authorship of the idea—even perhaps a copyright: "I don't know much about the business part of such an undertaking, but is there not some way of my copyrighting, as it were, this scheme of mine, so that another person or company could not encroach on my territory, and also, to protect supposed contributors against me. But dear me, this is way in the future. Again, begging your secrecy, I am lovingly, Ida Chamberlin."[1]

Hitz's response to Ida is not preserved, but within a few days she confided her plans in a letter to Helen. With her deep and almost decade-long familiarity with Helen and Annie, Ida felt qualified to help decide their future. On December 20, 1899, she wrote to Helen, her "dear *Little Girl*." She had resisted telling

Helen of her idea for months but now wanted to share it with her, though she must "not speak of it to anyone but teacher." Ida was bold in her belief in her scheme and confident of its merits, writing,

I am sure I am not wrong when I assert that no one, not even yourself, has given more thought to what you may do in the future than I have. It is my most earnest desire, that you shall become an important WORKER *for the general good. Heretofore you have been, in the eyes of the world an interesting experiment. The world has gone out in love and sympathy to you in your great deprivations, but I do not think the world has looked upon you as anything but a loving charge, to be made as happy as could be. It has been proved that you are as capable of imbibing knowledge as the best with sight. Now I want to prove that you are capable of more than that, for I know you are. I know, too, that you will never reach your greatest happiness if you are* ALWAYS *the recipient. It is only in the giving, only in being a working part of the universe that the fullest satisfaction is to be found.* NOW FOR MY SECRET.

I want YOU *to be at the head of a school, to be the one whom others afflicted as you are, may look up to for help and love and sympathy. This school to be for deaf dumb and blind children only, and to be known as the* HELEN KELLER SCHOOL. *It seems to me to be the most fitting thing, that the future* HELPER *of such, should be the one whom the whole world has watched during her development,* AND WHO WAS AS THEY. *Then, to look ahead down the years, I can see you surrounded with such children, not many we hope, who look up to you as to a mother, because your love and care must of a necessity mean more than the love of one who* KNOWS NOT.

But I think the feature of this idea which will appeal even more, than this picture does to you, is this. It is a work where teacher's peculiar strength and ability would tell.

Ida assumed that Annie was reading the letter to Helen, as she added a note for Annie: "No (read *every bit* of this to Helen even if it is about yourself) other teacher has shown the strength and force necessary to control the little savage that she has, and no one else seems to really know how to combine love and perseverance.

No one else has had the obstinacy necessary. She has the endowed gift for this work." Ida went on:

I am as sure of it as I live. A school of this kind would be as much for the development of the person into the proper teacher for such a child, as for the teaching of the child. Looking at it as a work for teacher, and without her ability we could do nothing, it would be a good thing, for it would not be a tax on her eyes and by that means lessening the danger to her, which is always in the minds of those who love her.

Now, dear, this, of necessity, is a long way ahead.

Ida closed the letter, saying, "I hope you will have a lovely time in New York, and I am sure you will. I shall miss you very much at our tree, and all will be saying, 'if only Helen and Annie were here.' I send you a little shell pin to keep up the 'scolding locks' behind. I am assured it is the proper caper. You are such an impossible young lady to give presents to. You don't seem to need anything. I hope all good things you desire come to you." She signed off "with heartfelt wishes for a very Merry Xmas."[2]

Helen's specific response to the letter is unknown, but it would appear from subsequent actions that she did not respond in a way that stifled Ida's energy for the idea. Later, Helen would say that at first she was "enthusiastic" in her support.

Helen and Annie spent Christmas in New York, but on returning to Boston, took the train to Wrentham and spent a Sunday afternoon with the Chamberlins. Sometime before the Christmas holiday, Ida had her second operation. Helen subsequently wrote Hitz that "it was very good to have a little rest in the country, after the whirl and excitement of New York. But you will be sorry to hear that poor Aunt Ida is still anything but well. She has just had another operation, which we hope is the last; but we fear that she will not recover entirely for a long time."[3]

Several months later, on March 12, 1900, after an unusually long time away—almost three months—Helen and Annie visited Red Farm and, as Helen reported to Hitz, found Ida much improved. She wrote,

Last Saturday Teacher and I went down to Wrentham for Sunday. You will be glad to hear that Mrs. Chamberlin is improving rapidly. Not long ago she spent a week with some friends in Boston, and now she can go anywhere she wishes without too much fatigue; so we feel sure that she will be perfectly well and strong when spring comes. Indeed, we never saw her looking better than she does now.

Poor Teacher is very tired and nervous after her winter's work. Her eyes trouble her constantly, and the heat of the fire in our study room aggravated them sorely. Accordingly, we have been considering how she may get the most restful vacation this summer. We have decided to stay in our old home on Lake Wollamanopoag [sic] *and have a servant do the heavy work. A nice, bright young lady, Miss Kinney, whom you may have seen while you were at Wrentham, has promised to spend the summer with us. This will be so convenient as she can spell rapidly on her fingers and read to me. I am now thinking of going to college in the autumn, and if I am to do that, there must be a great deal of preparatory work done this summer. Miss Kinney will help us very much in study as well as in the jollities of our country life. Will it not be lovely?*[4]

Ida's health continued to improve, and Helen was jubilant and relieved when she and Annie visited in April. She reported to Hitz,

Teacher and I have just had a pleasant little vacation. We spent Easter, as usual, with the Chamberlins. They were all well. Aunt Ida has improved wonderfully this spring, and looks as well as ever. It rained a good deal while we were there, but we seized every possible opportunity to wander about in the woods. We found song, fragrance, and growth everywhere. We drank in the delicious air, as if we would drink in Wrentham, and our hearts simply ran riot with delight! Easter meant a double resurrection—the rising again of the soul from the sickness and sorrow of past years and the renewal of the world.[5]

Helen wrote a formal letter to the chairman of the Academic Board of Radcliffe College on May 5, pleading her case for taking regular courses at the college. She acknowledged that "the conditions under which I work require the presence of Miss Sullivan, who has been my teacher and companion for thirteen years as an interpreter of oral speech and as a reader of examination papers. In college, she, or possibly in some subjects some one else, would of necessity be with me in the lecture-room and at recitations," but Helen would do all her own "written work on a typewriter, and if a Professor could not understand [her] speech," Helen could "write out answers to his questions and hand them to him after the recitation." She asked if it was possible for the college to "accommodate itself to these unprecedented conditions?" She realized that the obstacles in the way were great but closed the letter with the comment that "a true soldier does not acknowledge defeat before the battle."[6]

Helen was thinking ahead to the summer. She wrote to Alexander Graham Bell on June 2 and, after wishing him well on an upcoming trip, which she presumed to be to the Paris Exposition of 1900, solicited funds to help finance their summer plans:

My teacher and I have also been planning how to spend our summer. We have decided to take the little cottage we had last summer, when my mother was with us. A very nice young lady is going with us, to be a sort of companion to me, and help me do some studying for next year. You see, I am still thinking of going to Radcliffe, and I must do a good deal of preparatory reading before I can take the regular college course. If we can do all that we intend to, we shall have a most delightful summer. But this plan will be somewhat more expensive than boarding, and we are obliged to ask our friends to help us out. Perhaps you will help make it possible for us to carry out our plan successfully, as you were so kind as to do last summer. If so, you will make very happy indeed one who loves you; but if you think I am asking too much, please do not pay the slightest attention to this. I only want my dear teacher to have a perfectly restful vacation, and nothing can be better for that purpose than a little cottage, where we can "camp out" and be as free as the breezes which play on the lake only a few feet away.[7]

As requested, Helen and Annie's plan for the summer was generously funded and they spent it in the rented cottage in Wrentham.

Frustration mounted into the summer, with still no word regarding the hoped-for fall 1900 admission to Radcliffe. Helen wrote to Eleanor Hutton in New York on June 9 that she had

not yet heard from the Academic Board in reply to my letter; but I sincerely hope they will answer favorably. My friends think it very strange that they should hesitate so long, especially when I have not asked them to simplify my work in the least, but only to modify it so as to meet the existing circumstances. Cornell has offered to make arrangements suited to the conditions under which I work, if I should decide to go to that college, and the University of Chicago has made a similar offer; but I am afraid if I went to any other college, it would be thought that I did not pass my examinations for Radcliffe satisfactorily.[8]

Finally, after almost three more months with no response from Radcliffe, enough was enough. Ed Chamberlin was compelled once again to step in on Helen's behalf. With characteristic humility, he called upon what influence he had and wrote to Dean Agnes Irwin on August 31:

I am in a kind of despair about Miss Sullivan and Helen Keller. Are you willing to help me out of it? Helen wishes very much to go to Radcliffe, and Miss Sullivan wishes to have her go. But can Miss Sullivan go with Helen there (as surely she must if Helen goes) if she is completely shut out from the chance of giving examinations, even in an emergency, to Helen? Do you not think it would be an unbearably hard position for Miss Sullivan to be in, and a poor acknowledgement and crown of her remarkable work? Is it really true that such a condition is imposed?

This decision must be made at once. Meantime Helen is asked for at Chicago and Cornell, and there no such condition is imposed. Cannot we keep them here?

I am encouraged to appeal to you in this way because you were good enough to accept me, when you were out here last summer, as a sort of friend and counselor in the business. I have been and am most grateful to you for showing me that confidence.

Faithfully yours, J.E. Chamberlin[9]

In a postscript, Ed noted that he was going on a short vacation and that his address for the next seven days would be East Corinth, Vermont, where the Chamberlin family frequently spent their vacations. The request to Irwin would incubate in his absence.

CHAPTER TWELVE

Battle Lines

A month after Ed's letter to Agnes Irwin, Radcliffe relented and offered admission to Helen. She would be permitted to attend the regular first-year courses with other students and Annie could interpret for her. Chamberlin family lore tells that when Helen left for college—perhaps from vacationing in the rental cottage in Wrentham—Ed rode the train with her and Annie to Cambridge. Once there, he may have visited the dean and thanked her for her favorable decision.

Per usual, Helen made the news. On October 8, 1900, the *New York Times* reported in a headline: "Helen Keller at Radcliffe—The Blind Deaf-Mute Passes the Examination and Is Admitted." The article stated that she had chosen "French, English, and German courses, and in addition a course in history. At the lectures Helen is invariably accompanied by Miss Sullivan, who sits close beside her and gives her in the manual language whatever the instructor may be saying."[1]

But Radcliffe was not necessarily all she had hoped for. Helen wrote in her later autobiography:

I remember my first day at Radcliffe. It was a day full of interest for me. I had looked forward to it for years. . . . I began my studies with eagerness. . . . But I soon discovered that college was not quite the romantic lyceum I had imagined. Many of the dreams that had delighted my young inexperience became beautifully less and "faded into the light of common day." Gradually I began to find that there were disadvantages in going to college.

The one I felt and still feel most is lack of time. I used to have time to think, to reflect, my mind and I. We would sit together of an evening and listen to the inner melodies of the spirit, which one hears only in leisure moments when the words of some loved poet touch a deep, sweet chord in the soul that until then had been silent. But in college there is no time to commune with one's thoughts. One goes to college to learn, it seems, not to think. When one enters the portals of learning, one leaves the dearest pleasures—solitude, books and imagination—outside with the whispering pines, I suppose I ought to find some comfort in the thought that I am laying up treasures for future enjoyment, but I am improvident enough to prefer present joy to hoarding riches against a rainy day.[2]

She added, "I am frequently asked how I overcome the peculiar conditions under which I work in college. In the classroom I am of course practically alone. The professor is as remote as if he were speaking through a telephone. The lectures are spelled into my hand as rapidly as possible, and much of the individuality of the lecturer is lost to me in the effort to keep in the race. The words rush through my hand like hounds in pursuit of a hare which they often miss."[3]

Annie's ever-worsening eyesight created a serious problem, and Helen was acutely aware of the burden on Annie. The reading required to assist Helen in her studies taxed Annie's eyes to the extreme.

While they studied at Radcliffe, Ida remained concerned for their futures and continued to work to realize the Helen Keller School for the Deaf and Blind that she envisioned, apparently now to be established on the Red Farm property. She began actively raising funds and garnering support throughout October, November, and December 1900. The experience of the *Transcript* in raising funds for the Kindergarten for the Blind over the years certainly must have attuned her to the process, politics, and nuances of philanthropy in the Boston area, but she also traveled to other large cities, including Chicago, Washington, and New York, seeking support. By October, Annie Pratt reported to Alexander Bell that Ida had raised dollars and pledges totaling $30,000.[4] Several prominent Bostonians had agreed to serve as trustees, Edward Hale had promised money for housekeeping, and others had donated furniture. It is possible that Ida's aunt Nancy Atwood Sprague in Chicago helped in the effort, as she could have handsomely contributed and would have had many wealthy connections.

Helen may have had some interest in the scheme but not Annie. It was clear that the pair had much to lose if they offended Aunt

Ida, so Annie did not specifically tell Ida that she did not support the effort. Instead, Annie seems to have adopted an "ignore it and perhaps it will go away" approach to the problem, at least in the early months of discussion.[5]

Ida's efforts soon created a distraction for Helen—one that was not appreciated by Annie, who wanted Helen not only to succeed at Radcliffe but to achieve highest honors. As Helen had said, college was not the "romantic lyceum" she had imagined, and when the coursework became difficult, she became frustrated and daydreamed of other places and pursuits. For Annie, who was investing so much of herself in Helen's education, at great cost to her own eyesight, it was frustrating to have to continually refocus Helen on her studies.

Ed's position on the matter at this juncture is unclear. Only later correspondences revealed his view of Ida's efforts toward the school.

But there was one person who had no fears about insulting Ida, and that was Annie Pratt, the employee of Bell in Boston and a close friend to Annie Sullivan. Pratt wrote an urgent letter to Bell on October 5, 1900, including, among other topics discussed, a long explanation of Ida's scheme. Her description of the school was scornful, describing "little cosy wooden cottages" with loving "mother-teachers" as key features. She went on: "Further details it is hardly worth while to endeavor to describe, suffice it, they are all in line, in Mrs. Chamberlin's fertile brain, and her ready tongue can give the reply to any inquiries." The letter continued in a similarly derogatory vein: "Funds for this—Yes, Dr. Bell,—this to me is the grandest of all—the funds to be raised, and annually contributed, by the hearing school children of the world, in sums not to exceed five cents each or less than one cent—always voluntary contributions, to be, (in the United States), arranged for, by the State Superintendent of Schools or by the Governor in each state and territory. An appeal, announcement, prospectus, or whatever it may be termed, is to appear 'right away' in all the newspapers on this subject." She closed the letter, "I must stop writing and start my rather long letter on its way to New York, or it will not come to your notice on the Steamer, as I intend."[6]

Pratt's description of Ida's plans for the school brought an immediate and authoritative response from the great inventor, who was on board a transatlantic steamer:

October 13, 1900

ON THE IRISH SEA

. . . The last part of your letter relating to Mrs. Chamberlain's [sic] *plan for Helen Keller and Miss Sullivan came to me as a sort of shock and I hardly know what to say about it.*

I like to think of Helen fighting her way through Radcliffe College in competition with hearing and seeing young ladies, and then startling the world as a great authoress or even poetess. With her gifts of mind and imagination there should be a great future open to her in literature, and I believe that as an authoress, she would not only move the world, but make for herself all the money that might be necessary to keep her in comfort all her life and give her the means to do any good she chose. But for Helen to become joint superintendent of a special school for Deaf and Blind children would be a "come-down" indeed.

So far as Helen is concerned, I should like to see her take her proper place among hearing and seeing people. She can, if she chooses, associate with the best minds of the world upon equal terms. I have no hesitation in saying that the proposed joint superintendency would NOT be the best thing for Helen herself. Whatever should be her sphere of usefulness, she should always be interested in the deaf and blind—her sympathies would naturally go out to those who have been afflicted like herself, and I am sure she could do a great deal more to aid them indirectly than directly.

With Miss Sullivan, of course, it is different. It would be a great thing if she could be placed in a position to impress her ideas upon other teachers,—not simply teachers of the deaf-blind, but teachers of the deaf generally, and I would be glad to see some scheme elaborated that would lead to this result.

I have spoken above from the point of view of Helen Keller herself and Miss Sullivan. But I must say that from the point of view of the deaf-blind themselves, I do not think that a special school for their benefit would be the best thing. From my point of view, the larger and more comprehensive the school, the worse it would be, and the proposal to admit pupils from foreign countries, worst of all.

In Bell's opinion, deafblind children should, as much as possible, be educated among sighted and hearing children. He believed "the blind become blinder by exclusive association with one another, and the deaf and dumb are made into a class apart by themselves. Now, the creation of a special school for those who are both blind and deaf is, in my opinion, to be avoided, if possible. I could write a great deal upon this subject, but this is neither the time nor the place."

He continued, "My heart is deeply moved in the matter because I feel that a gigantic blunder is about to be made and I am away and cannot prevent it." He proposed a constructive rechanneling of Ida's energies toward the establishment of an association to promote the education of deafblind children. Like Ida, he too was interested in helping Annie Sullivan develop the ability to support herself and to contribute to the education of larger numbers of children:

Let me, however, say a few words as to what I think should be done, rather than what should not be done. . . . I would say that it would be better to send the teachers to these children, rather than send the children to the teachers. It would be better to associate together THE PEOPLE WHO WISH TO BENEFIT THESE CHILDREN, *than to bring the children themselves together.*

I would have this association provide funds that would enable Miss Sullivan to qualify others to become teachers of the deaf-blind and then send these teachers to the deaf-blind children in their own homes and among their own people, as Miss Sullivan herself was sent to Helen. It should only be the duty of these teachers to instruct—not simply the deaf-blind children themselves—but their parents and relatives and friends. They should teach the people at home, so that through their agency, the children would have in effect many teachers in their own homes.

I can't go on elaborating thus in the dining room of a transatlantic steamer, but I cannot allow your letter to pass unanswered, lest you should think that I approve of a plan that seems to me to be a great mistake.

Just one point in conclusion. So much individual instruction and care is required that the instruction of a deaf-blind child will necessarily be expensive. Each child will necessarily require a teacher to himself. Now, looked at simply from the point of view of expense. Suppose we have a special school. We must provide the buildings and grounds; we must board the pupils and teachers. The money necessary for these things is over and above what is necessary for the education of the children. If we send the teachers to the children, we have only to provide the teacher, salaries of the instructors, for the parents would provide board and lodging for the teacher and pupil, and the expense of the school buildings would be saved.

From the point of economy, as well as efficiency, I would say that the money provided should be expended, as much as possible, in the salaries of teachers, (exclusive of board) and as little as possible upon board and lodging and buildings.

Bell closed the letter to Pratt with his final word on the matter: "Send the teachers to the children, not the children to the teachers."[7]

Apparently Ida was not informed of Bell's objections to the plan for the school, for on October 17 she sent him a copy of an appeal she planned to use to solicit funds from the schoolchildren of America. The appeal read,

Sisters, little children, you who can hear and see all the wonderful, beautiful things in this great, bright world; listen, and you shall hear how you may share your blessings with many little children, who lack everything that makes your lives sweet and happy.

These children are deaf, and dumb and blind. They are little prisoners, while you are free. The outside world is a blank to them, there is nothing for them to do all day long but fret, and cry and feel things they do not understand. It is the one great desire of my heart to ransom these little captive souls. I want to give them a home and educate them.

Will you help me? I am sure you will; your loving hearts cannot fail to respond to the cry that goes up from their darkened lives for

sympathy and help. It is your privilege, little children, to make it possible for them to receive their rightful inheritance of thought, knowledge and joy.[8]

Drawing on their close relationship, Ida also enlisted the help of Reverend Edward Everett Hale. She enclosed "a copy of E. E. Hale's certificate, vouching for the school." It was to be "a home in Massachusetts to be started for the care and education of the Blind & Deaf and to be known as the Helen Keller Home. Miss Sullivan to have the supervision of teachers of such children, Helen Keller to love and care for them." Hale added to his certificate the statement: "This home approves itself to me in all its details."[9]

Shortly after her letter to Bell, Ida wrote to Pratt. By now, she had heard of Bell's objections, most likely from Pratt herself but also from John Hitz, because Ida referenced a letter from him as well. Ida boasted of her "triumphal march" to gain support for the school. Ida had told "W. D. Howells, Dr. Greer, Henry M. Alden, editor of Harpers, and many others" of Helen's supporters that Bell had said he thought a position in a school for the deaf and blind would be beneath Helen. According to Ida, they were "amazed that Dr. Bell *could* think such a great work a 'come-down' for Helen." She was very direct, even audacious, with Pratt, writing,

John Hitz thinks that if I can once have a long talk with Dr. Bell he will change some of his opinions. I don't much care. But—there is one thing I will say, that I have not done all this work, and I have worked terribly hard, to raise what promises to be a large sum, to exploit Graham Bell's theories. I am audacious enough to THINK *I am nearer right about these little children, not grown-ups, than he is. As for Helen, I* KNOW *I am. I am more interested in her literary abilities and am hopeful for her, but I work from an earnest spiritual standpoint. . . . I have been meeting great men every day now for two weeks, men who do as valued thinking on mental development, broad men not specialists, and, with the exception of Dr. Greer, they think a mistake is being made in sending Helen to College. They all feel that a higher & broader development lies in this course. Dr. Greer said, "what Helen wishes to do is the thing, and I will help all in my power, as I have done, to accomplish her desires." He thought my idea a beautiful one.*[10]

The two women began exchanging angry letters. Pratt was furious that Ida had quoted Bell's "come-down" statement to others. A subsequent letter from her chastised Ida for having taken advantage of a letter to Ed that contained a copy of a letter from Bell. It is noteworthy that Pratt had sent a letter regarding Ida's school plan to her husband. Perhaps she hoped that Ed would talk some sense into Ida.

Pratt scolded Ida: "I am surprised and disappointed that you did not more carefully read my letter to Mr. Chamberlin, enclosing copy of Dr. Bell's personal letter to myself. I do not think that you had any authority to quote any expressions Dr. Bell may have used in his personal letter to me. I am sorry now that I sent you a copy of his letter; my object was to aid you, and I have only succeeded in creating an unwise and erroneous prejudice."[11]

In turn, Ida wrote a November 15 letter to "My dear Mrs. Pratt." She discussed an upcoming conversation that was scheduled between herself and Bell. She did not intend to offend him and "wagered that he would agree with her when they had their talk." In addition, a pupil had already been identified for the school.[12]

Ida had spread far-reaching word of the plan and in late November received communication from an education superintendent in Texas regarding the potential student, a young deafblind girl named Ruby Rice. The situation had escalated to the point that Helen and Annie could no longer ignore it. They discussed the plan with friends during a visit to New York—where much of the funding for Helen's education was being raised. The New York response was immediate and negative.

On November 26, Helen wrote to John Hitz:

[Not] until I went to New York Wednesday night did I begin to realize that a school for deaf and blind children maintained by money obtained from the public and perhaps managed more or less by committees might involve dangerous complications and unforeseen difficulties which I have not the experience or ability to deal with.

Still I hoped that my friends in New York might be able to make suggestions as to how these perplexities might be averted.

On our arrival in New York we went straight to Mr. Rhoades' [a longtime friend, banker, and benefactor who had a daughter who was blind] house and took breakfast with him. To my surprise and disappointment he emphatically disapproved of the scheme from the first and declared that it must be stopped at once. He said that it really meant that my name was to be used as a means of raising money for the erection of school buildings and for the education of children. Of course I knew that was not the real object. Neither Aunt Ida nor I were considering the advantage to me only, and I told him so; but he went on to say that if my name was used in that way, I should lose the sympathy of my friends—lose their support and find myself without the means of accomplishing anything. He pointed out the financial problems and other questions which Teacher, as the head of such an institution, would be called upon to solve, to say nothing of the tremendous expense we should incur each year.[13]

Helen included the remainder of her letter to Hitz in her later book *The Story of My Life.* She redacted Ida's name, indicative of her respect for Ida and her desire not to embarrass her dear friend publicly. In the letter, she admitted that she had originally been very supportive of Ida's scheme. She even referred to it as "her and my plan," saying,

At first I was most enthusiastic in its support, and I never dreamed that any grave objections could be raised except indeed by those who were hostile to Teacher; but now, after thinking most SERIOUSLY *and consulting my friends, I have decided that ___'s plan is by no means feasible. In my eagerness to make it possible for deaf and blind children to have the same advantages that I have had, I quite forgot that there might be many obstacles in the way of my accomplishing anything like what ___ proposed.*

Helen felt a deep need to help other deafblind children, desiring "passionately" that all who are "afflicted like myself shall receive their rightful inheritance of thought, knowledge, and love." But finally, Helen wrote, "I could not shut my eyes to the force and weight of their arguments, and I saw plainly that I must abandon ___'s scheme as impracticable."[14]

Meanwhile, Helen's New York friends were developing a plan to better control her future. An "advisory committee" to whom "she should always turn for advice" was created, consisting of six trusted family members and friends: Kate Keller, Annie, Eleanor Hutton, John Harsen Rhoades, Dr. David H. Greer, and Henry H. Rogers.[15] The committee did not include Ed Chamberlin or Ida, nor Dr. Bell and his associates for that matter. The members were all—aside from Teacher and her mother—Helen's financial supporters from New York and would help manage the pair's financial affairs and the money contributed for her support. As for the Chamberlins, Bell, and Hitz, Helen and Annie had direct lines of communication to them, so their advice was always accessible.

Once back in Boston, Helen and Annie met with Ida and Bell. As he had previously suggested in his letter to Ida, he proposed that "energy" be put into development of an association to aid deaf and blind children rather than the creation of a school. Helen summarized the conversation in her letter to Hitz:

We had a long talk with Dr. Bell. Finally he proposed a plan which delighted us all beyond words. He said that it was a gigantic blunder to attempt to found a school for deaf and blind children, because then they would lose the most precious opportunities of entering into the fuller, richer, freer life of seeing and hearing children. I had had misgivings on this point; but I could not see how we were to help it.

However Mr. Bell suggested that [Ida] and all her friends who are interested in her scheme should organize an association for the promotion of the education of the deaf and blind, Teacher and myself being included of course. Under his plan they were to appoint Teacher to train others to instruct deaf and blind children in their own homes, just as she had taught me. Funds were to be raised for the teachers' lodgings and also for their salaries. At the same time Dr. Bell added that I could rest content and fight my way through Radcliffe in competition with seeing and hearing girls, while the great desire of my heart was being fulfilled.[16]

Bell had proposed a plan that all parties involved appeared to be able to live with. Helen exulted, "We clapped our hands and shouted; [Mrs. C] went away beaming with pleasure, and Teacher and I felt more light of heart than we had for sometime." She finished her letter with a final request to Hitz: "Do tell me what you think about Dr. Bell's suggestion. It seems most practical and wise to me; but I must know all that there is to be known about it before I speak or act in the matter."[17]

CHAPTER THIRTEEN

Crisis

On November 26, 1900, the same day that Helen wrote to John Hitz regarding the outcome of Helen and Annie's recent meetings in New York, and the subsequent meeting with Dr. Bell and Ida, Ed was experiencing a crisis at home. He sent an urgent note to Annie Pratt that morning. He was terrified for his wife's health:

On the train, Monday morning.

Dear Mrs. Pratt:

Mrs. Chamberlin came home Saturday night very ill, and though she is now in less pain, she is completely prostrated, and nervously in a bad condition.

She longs to see you, and though I know how busy you are, I am going to beg of you to come out to see her if you can. She is racked and torn with the thought that Annie and Helen have turned their backs on her, and I am sure you are the only one who can help her to look at all sides of this matter. You may not be aware [two lines deleted] and I have many fears.

Ed included a ticket and the local train schedule and suggested on the note that Pratt come and be prepared to stay overnight if needed, adding, "I would not urge you so, if I did not feel that some one who knows about this and has sympathy with Ida, must come!"

Two lines were deleted in the letter—perhaps by Annie Pratt before sharing with Bell archivists—and must have included the information that Ida was pregnant and in precarious health. A mention of pregnancy was considered personal information at the time and was likely obscured to protect the Chamberlins' privacy. The letter, archived among the Alexander Graham Bell Family Papers at the Library of Congress, also contains the notation: "Copy of letter from Mr. J.E. Chamberlin to Mrs. A.C. Pratt, written November 26, 1900, and received the same day, at noon."

Further, the notation reads, "Mrs. Pratt went to Wrentham from Boston on the 3:27 p.m. train. She found Mrs. Chamberlin in bed and quite ill, she was exceedingly nervous, very much disturbed and excited. When Mr. C returned at evening from Boston, he found his wife's condition much improved."[1]

Despite Ed's concerns, Ida's pregnancy, and the meeting with Bell, Ida continued with her campaign. Her contacts had been far ranging over the previous few months.

She wrote a rambling letter to Bell on December 2, referencing their recent meeting. Despite Helen's earlier, joyful summary of the meeting, Ida seems to have misunderstood him. She had found the campaign for the deafblind school to be a heady experience and hard to let go, and was encouraged by the possibility of bringing in students from elsewhere in the country. But there had also been a heated exchange between Ida and Annie, and Ida was growing weary of the crusade in some ways. She "felt she should set the whole thing aside." According to her, Annie had told her that she had not understood Bell, that he was "strongly opposed to a school of any kind," that Ida could not "do anything these New York men oppose," and that she would never have Bell's support.

Ida's letter went on. It is hard to tell if she was drawn to the fame she might receive through creating such a school or relieved at the possibility of not having to experience it. She told Bell that if he opposed the school, her "last reason for continuing it would be taken" from her. Still, though she seemed to acquiesce and stated that she had given up the idea of the school, she continued to argue for it, at length.

She reported that Annie "told Mr. Chamberlin that she had a hard time 'prodding' Helen, that it seemed to her as though Helen was losing her interest in her college work, that for the first time since she came to Boston Helen was crying to go to her mother." Comments such as that surely tugged at Ida's heartstrings and fortified her in her desire to build the school and provide Helen with what she thought would be a more fulfilling life. Ida closed the many-paged letter by saying, "Won't you please answer this letter as soon as you can" and "I wish I might have a talk with you."[2]

This letter was clearly shared with Pratt, for on December 6 Pratt wrote a nine-page, authoritative letter to Bell, coaching him in detail on how to put an end to Ida's campaign. She wrote that

any letter [from him] should be very carefully and guardedly written—to heal wounded pride is no easy task—to arrange the poor woman's affairs in such a manner as to preserve to her all the glory she felt was to be hers in the carrying out of her original scheme and at the same time do no injury to any is yours to accomplish—You are the only one person who can bring order and harmony out of what is now chaos . . . through the exercise of your wonderful ability to solve all perplexing problems and your great-heartedness which always aids you to suggest plans based on the fundamental principle of the greatest good to the greatest number.

Pratt offered patronizing verbiage for Bell to use, proposing that he could say that "Mrs. Chamberlin with her excellent motherly instincts and experience surely does not require any advice on this subject."

Pratt closed the letter by writing, "If, after Mrs. C____ had studied your letter carefully, she still thinks she will go on with her school, and proceeds to do so—I am sure it will not be anything harmful, because her ideas are already so modified and dwarfed from their original design, as to render the effort she will make of little value. If she adopts the association plan—the forming of the organization will probably close the record for the present—I enclose Mrs. C____'s last letter to me."[3]

Meanwhile, Reverend Edward Everett Hale had come to Ida's aid in the conversation with Bell. In view of the revised plan to establish an association instead of a school, she had asked Hale to serve as its president. He declined. At the same time, word had spread of "alarming statistics regarding the number of deaf-blind children in the United States." Hale addressed both issues in a letter to Bell on December 14. Dr. Hale did not want to serve as president of an association; he urged Bell to take on that role. Ida had clearly garnered his sympathy but not his commitment of time.[4]

Dr. Bell must have written the letter to Ida as urged by Annie Pratt. On December 18, Ida responded to him regarding Helen's "overwork" at Radcliffe and the matter of the "scheme" for Helen and Annie's future work. Her letter was long, argumentative, and difficult to follow. Often she contradicted herself.

After thanking Bell for his kind words regarding her own abilities, Ida expressed concern for Helen. She was privy to information about Helen's workload and corresponding fatigue at Radcliffe and shared that with him. Friends were confiding in her regarding Helen's coursework. She wrote, "There are several things which should be explained to you. In the first place I wish to put myself right about my position with regard to the college course. First—with the exception of the Fullers here in Boston, the New York people and yourself, not one of Helen's friends nor her mother, nor Dean Irwin of Radcliffe approves of the full college course, which calls for *four* studies a year."

Ida noted that "Dean Irwin, with whom I had a long talk, said that the work as done now, was very unwise, and that before long some change would *have* to be made." Ida went on:

> *I should not have presumed to dictate to Miss Sullivan. She told Mr. Chamberlin that she had to prod Helen continually to get her to do the required work. Helen works all day on studies, the evening being reserved for writing her daily theme. Of course she is very tired and it takes her so long to write, she often works till 10.30 or 11.00 o'clock. I do not think you have ever known how much harder just in point of time this work is for her.*
>
> *She is not succeeding in the literary part except when she writes about herself.*

By speaking with Helen's instructors and Dean Irwin, Ida was now actively involving herself in Helen's education. She told Bell, "When I told Miss Sullivan what these educators had said, she answered: 'I snap my fingers at all of them. I have done as *I* pleased with Helen and shall continue to do so, Dean Irwin included.'"

Ida expressed concern again about Annie's problematic eyes, the issue that had perhaps motivated her most to develop a plan for the pair's future:

Miss Sullivan's eyes are in a very precarious condition. I honestly thought and still think if she were at work in the proposed school, she would have work to do which would not injure her eyes, and would make it possible for a reader to be employed who could do the mechanical work. All of this idea SHE KNEW *but did not tell these New York people, for she is absolutely determined to prove that Helen can do the work of the seeing girls, and also, she is not capable of perceiving the harm to Helen. . . . I am sure if I had not been ill when you were here you would have seen the wisdom of this after hearing in detail these ideas.*

Ida claimed that she had "never for one instant thought of Helen giving up College, nor would there have been any need of it [though she had said in her letter to Annie Pratt of October 26, 1900, that she and others believed a mistake had been made in sending Helen to college]. I never supposed that Helen would be 'brought actively into the enterprise.' It seemed so clear . . . that she would not, that I am afraid I did not make myself quite clear to you. I most certainly must have done so to Dean Irwin to have her endorse the idea."

She now even considered a specific individual as director of the proposed school, writing that "a woman incomparably stronger than Miss Sullivan, in some respects, is ready to take charge of it. Miss Greeley for 13 years Superintendent of the Kinder-Garten for the Blind at Jamaica Plain. . . . Could a better one be found?"

She continued emphatically, "I wish I could make myself understood with regard to the Association." It is hard to know whether Ida was being purposely ignored by those to whom she wrote or was actually misunderstood. She may also have changed her mind to suit objections as they were raised in order to placate people, and in so doing was unclear and confusing, even while convincing herself that she was not being inconsistent. It seems likely that Annie had campaigned among her own friends and supporters against Ida's plan and that they were "under orders" to ignore Ida's letters. Ida was alone and swimming against a tide of opposition from Bell and Annie.

Ida was flattered that anyone should think her capable of being president of an association for the deaf and blind—since others had refused and suggested instead that she do it herself—and also asserted, "I do know my limitations in spite of appearances. I feel that I have exhausted my possibilities, and to do with my eyes open something of which I know absolutely nothing, in this frame of mind, would be disastrous in the extreme. Apparently this same frame of mind makes me appear willful and headstrong. Please do not think so."

She implored Bell to serve as president of the association for which he had advocated, since Dr. Hale had refused "on account of increasing years." Hale had told her, "Dr. Bell of all the world is the one to be president of such an association." Ida agreed and told Bell, "It seems truly so to me. No one has so complete a knowledge of everything connected with the deaf-blind. Why *will you* not do this thing, which you think is easy for Dr. Hale?" After all that Bell had said on the topic, Ida was still deluded in believing he would even entertain the idea of serving as the association's president.

Finally, Ida gave a hint of Ed's feelings regarding her scheme. In an earlier letter to Bell, Ida had mentioned the possibility that the Chamberlins would take the first student into their own home, which she said "was all a feeling of my own which I expressed to you, before I had even consulted Mr. Chamberlin who naturally thinks I have done enough already." In closing, she ostensibly deferred to Bell's authority, saying, "Now—I await your advice as to the first work for me to do. Please be very explicit to the details, and allow yourself to be president."[5]

Throughout November and December, Ida wrote and even campaigned with the knowledge that she was pregnant—and that heading a school or an association for the deaf and blind was likely out of the realm of what she herself could do with her own children and a newborn to care for. Clearly Ida believed in the school, and that it was right for Helen and Annie. The support for it seemed wedded more to her enthusiasm and persistence than to the actual prospects for success. Her wavering over the form it would take and false denials of personal interest must have been exhausting to those around her and those with whom she communicated by letter.

Through it all, Ed appears to have said little, though conversations were swirling around him and letters on the subject were directed to him. Perhaps Ida's passion for the school was beyond his capability to defuse—his gracious manner may have prevented him from dictating to his wife, especially when she seemed so set on the idea.

Helen wrote to John Hitz on December 23, and it is clear she was worried that the events of the previous few months had harmed her relationship with the Chamberlins. However, she now reported that she was pleased Beth Chamberlin had sent her "a little Japanese tree for Christmas" and also that "a few days ago Aunt Ida wrote to us asking us to come out to Wrentham for Christmas. Another lovely surprise. We should certainly have gone, only we had already invited some friends to spend the day with us. Nevertheless, it is a joy to know that Aunt Ida still loves us, and we feel sure that it is all well between us there."[6]

She wrote another friend the next day: "Now we are feeling happier than we have been for some time. There is not a cloud in our sky, only hope and gladness; so we are anticipating a delightful Christmas."[7]

While Helen was relieved about the state of the friendship, there was extreme tension between Annie and Ida. Annie had been in close communication with Pratt, and they were in agreement regarding Ida's scheme. Letters collected by Pratt record bits of conversations among Annie, Helen, and Ida—and reveal anger and frayed nerves.

One letter from Ida described Annie as having "given the hardest blow yet. She told Mr. Chamberlin last night, that as a friend she could get along with me, but in a school it would be utterly impossible. She also said that I would find Dr. Bell entirely with the Hutton crowd, and further, that I had entirely misunderstood Dr. Bell, that he was strongly opposed to the school, and I would find him so."

Ida added that Annie had "impressed upon Helen so completely [the foolishness of the school] that when I had a few words with her she was very nearly impertinent and did tell me that I would have no help from Dr. Bell *she* knew." Further, Ida related that she had responded to Helen, "Young lady, you have shut the door on yourself, and if the school is started your withdrawal will be the only change."

Ida went on:

I feel today, as if no power on earth could make me continue in this work. My condemnation of Annie is so great I cannot feel or do for her ever again. Her conversation with me, entirely free from excitement of any kind, was absolutely more than I could allow myself to bear again. The result of this is that it has completely unnerved me again. I must end this once and for all, or it will end me. I then think of the little children. I could not make or coax Helen to say she desired to help them. . . . The work of the Hutton men has been well supplemented by Annie. I think it is the most painful revelation of all.

Wearily, she closed the letter, "*How* is it going to end[?]"[8]

A very dark cloud hung over the friendship. But it was Christmas, and Annie made an overture toward reconciliation. She wrote to Pratt on December 26: "We went down to Wrentham on the 12:30 train, as we thought we should, and had a very pleasant time. Mrs. Chamberlin received us affectionately, gave us a nice luncheon, and talked about everything except the *School.*" The letter continued,

She was evidently surprised and glad to see us. I was very careful indeed not to refer to anything that might lead to discussion of any sort. I did not even say the conciliatory things I had planned to say. She looks dreadfully, and I felt very sorry for her. She asked me if you had returned and I said, I suppose so, not wishing to tell her I had seen you, for I was sure that would lead to discussion of Dr. Bell's suggestions, and I did not want to excite her or myself either. I told her that we were going to spend Sunday with you, so please do not refer to our Sunday evening call. You can't imagine how happy we feel tonight. . . . A great load is lifted from my heart, for whatever Mrs. C. may feel inside, it is evident she is not going to banish us out of her life, which I think would have been the saddest thing that could happen for all concerned.[9]

Although frustrated with the situation, Annie did not want to lose the Chamberlins as friends. Her statement that being banished from the Chamberlin household would be "the saddest thing that could happen for all concerned" is telling and reinforces the importance of the Chamberlins and Red Farm in her and Helen's lives. So many of their fondest memories and pleasures of the past decade had taken place within the embrace of that family and that home. Banishment would have been very distressing.

Relieved, Annie closed the letter: "Well dear little Aunt Polly I guess the worst of the tempest is passed and we shall get to shore safely. What say you?"[10]

Still, even while Helen showed Annie a compliant front in opposition to Ida's scheme in Wrentham, she was expressing support for helping deafblind children in some fashion to others outside of Boston. She wrote to Eleanor Hutton on December 27 that a gentleman in Philadelphia had written to Annie about a young deaf and blind child in Paris. Helen told Hutton that she wished she could "do something for him."[11]

On December 28, two days after Helen and Annie's visit to Wrentham, Ida was in a desperate condition at home. Her health was declining rapidly. In addition, she was worried about her relationship with Annie and confided in Pratt by letter:

I am so nearly blind at present that I do not read, write or sew. What do you think of that for me? Miss Sullivan and Helen are to be with you over Sunday they told me. Will you please not tell them of anything concerning Dr. Bell and me? I will explain when I see you. I particularly desire that she, Miss S., should not know that Dr. Bell and Dr. Hale ever desired that I should be the president of a proposed organization. Miss S. has said such contemptible things that I wish nothing further said about the deaf-blind from my point of view.

Meekly, Ida closed the letter, "Can't you come to see me soon? I have so much to talk over with you and I shall probably be confined to bed by next week." She signed the letter, "With fond love, Ida C., Friday A.M."[12]

Ida's letter contradicted Annie's feelings that the icy relations between them were thawing. The two women were avoiding all discussion of the school and keeping a wary distance from one another. And Annie Pratt was privy to the confidences of both women—though her allegiance was entirely with Annie Sullivan.

Following the posting of her letter that day, Ida nearly died of complications of Bright's Disease and eclampsia. She also lost her unborn baby.

It would be two weeks, on January 12, 1901, before she was sufficiently recovered to dictate a letter describing her situation to Pratt. Angel De Cora and Zitkala-Ša were still in residence at Red Farm and now providing assistance in caring for Ida, who wrote,

My friend Zitkalasa [sic] *is writing for me, as I am crawling slowly back from the grave. The whole of last week is a blank. Previous to that I failed very rapidly, completely losing my vision, the result of Bright's Disease, consequent upon pregnancy. Friday the fourth convulsions set in and my doctor had to force delivery to save my life.*

We had three doctors. Two nurses are still with me. I find it rather hard to gather up the lines again. And of course the Deaf & Blind business is waiting. I am anxious to talk about the matter with you. . . .

As I must take great care of my eyes, the vision coming back slowly, I fear I shall not be able to write to you for months.

I would enjoy a visit from you should you come out.[13]

Even with her grave health issues and the loss of her baby, Ida was still thinking of the school for the deaf and blind.

The trauma Ida described in her letter was extreme: blindness, convulsions, and subsequent coma, combined with forced delivery of the baby. Even in more modern times, the situation would have been grave. At the turn of the century, it was an almost hopeless scenario.

At the time, the term "Bright's Disease" was used to describe inflammation of the kidneys, a condition that would now be described as nephritis. Symptoms were usually severe: back pain, elevated blood pressure, vomiting, and fever commonly signaled an attack. Edema, varying in degrees from slight puffiness of the face to an accumulation of fluid sufficient to distend the whole body, and sometimes severely restricted breathing were common. Acute Bright's Disease was often treated with methods such as "depletion" or bloodletting (with leeches or cuts to the skin) to reduce blood pressure, warm baths, diuretics, and laxatives. Other "treatments" involved methods that created steam and sweating, followed by the application of cold and rubbing alcohol.[14] Most of these methods probably did more harm than good.

Kidney disease could possibly explain Ida's confinements and illnesses of the previous few years, as well as the almost manic energy apparent in her long letters to Bell and Pratt. The medical profession at the time advised that women with kidney disease never marry, in order to avoid pregnancy, which was considered very dangerous. The effects of nephritis on the mind were described as mood changes or "hyper-excitation of the nervous system almost maniacal in character."[15]

In addition, Ida was fortunate to have survived the condition known as eclampsia or toxemia—a life-threatening condition caused by high blood pressure during the later months of pregnancy. Although details of Ida's pregnancy are scant, she must have been in her last trimester, with the baby probably deceased when the delivery was forced. Even if the baby had survived the delivery, as a premature infant in those times, its chances of survival were severely limited.

The pall cast over the household by Ida's health emergency and the death of the baby, coupled with the fears over so many days that Ida would also surely die, must have been dark and heavy. Perhaps the Chamberlin children were sent away during those frantic days, as Ida clung to life at Red Farm, surrounded by doctors and nurses and close friends.

Ida was forty-five years old. Over twenty-seven years of marriage she had had at least eight pregnancies, lost three children at ages varying from stillborn to adolescence, and suffered through long and painful illnesses possibly related to hypertension. She had four surviving children: Helen, now twenty-seven and married with a baby of her own; Beth, fifteen; Raymond, eight; and Dolly, aged five. The Chamberlins' adopted son, Phil, was twenty-two.

The death of the Chamberlin baby—a boy—was recorded at the Wrentham town office. The office was a short walk from Red Farm but would have seemed a long one for the sad bearer of the information—most likely Ed himself. Returning home, he must have felt the dark mantle of depression descend on him as it had at times of loss before. Surely he mourned deeply. He was fifty years old. He had just lost a child—again—and this time he knew there could be no more children, as Ida could not risk another pregnancy.

Even as she recovered from her near-death, worries for Ida's health continued. On February 8, Helen wrote to John Hitz from Cambridge: "The few weeks past we have been much worried about poor Aunt Ida. Since we saw her she has been extremely ill. She was beginning to recover when she had an attack of pneumonia. However, when we saw Uncle Ed last Wednesday she was on the mend and now we hope there will be no more relapses."[16]

But still more change was in store for the Chamberlin family.

CHAPTER FOURTEEN

Upheaval and Recovery

On March 11, 1901, Helen wrote shocking news about the Chamberlins to John Hitz: "You will be surprised to hear that Beth Chamberlin has come to live with us. It all happened within a few days. A great sorrow has come to Aunt Ida, and she has been obliged to break up her home and send the little ones away."

Helen reported,

Several weeks ago Uncle Ed went to New York, on business for the "Transcript" as we supposed, but now it appears that he did not intend to return. Several days later certain letters were received by his friends from St. Paul [probably Minnesota, as he had family members there] where it seems he had previously sent them to be re-mailed to persons addressed. In them he said he had to go away or to kill himself. Aunt Ida thinks he has committed suicide, but no one can solve the sad mystery. Poor, dear Uncle Ed! This strange disappearance has grieved many friends deeply.

Aunt Ida is quite ill at Wrentham, where she is staying with some friends. Dolly and Raymond have gone to Vermont. Both Teacher and I are so glad we can offer Beth a home, and thus return the generous kindness Aunt Ida showed us three years ago when she opened her home to us after the Gilman affair. Beth is a dear, sweet little girl, very brave and full of hope. I think she believes that her father will return soon.

She helps us quite as much as a grown-up person, both in the reading and about the home. Besides, as you know, she is full of fun and frolic, and we always have beautiful times together. . . .

With dear love from Teacher and Beth (I know she would send her love if she knew I was writing to you).[1]

The news of Ed's disappearance must have startled Hitz—and many others. It was true that Ed had withdrawn abruptly from his work and domestic life before; he had left the *Chicago Times* in

1880 for reasons of "breakdown," and he had made frequent and even lengthy escapes to Vermont and New Hampshire from the pressures of work and grief and for "nervous exhaustion" or other health reasons during his Boston years. This time, though, his leave-taking was different—and far more concerning and disruptive. As Helen noted, Ida believed Ed had actually committed suicide—so tumultuous were the circumstances, so odd his behavior.

Another friend, Alexander Graham Bell, learned the Chamberlin news in a different way and wrote of it to his wife, Mabel, on March 15, just a few days after Helen's letter to Hitz. Bell had been in Northampton, Massachusetts, for a meeting at the Clarke School for the Deaf and then come to Boston, planning to see Ed. He wrote,

In Boston I went down to the Transcript Office to call upon Mr. Chamberlin, the husband of the lady who is so much interested in forming a school for Blind-Deaf children. The clerk in the Transcript Office looked at me in a very peculiar manner, and said Mr. Chamberlin had not been there for some days, and he did not know when he would return, so I left my card and went out to 3 Chelsea to see Mrs. Pratt. . . .

From her I learned of the tragedy in the Chamberlin household. I think you saw my letters to Mrs. Chamberlin concerning her plans for the education of blind-deaf children, and know how I tried to dissuade her from making a school of her home on the ground that her husband and children were her first consideration. Mrs. Chamberlin for many months has been almost fanatical upon the question of blind-deaf children, and very much against the wishes of her husband she has been traveling about the country to Chicago, Washington, New York, &c, when she was in no condition for traveling. I think I told you of the strange letter I received from Mrs. Pratt upon the subject with a request to burn it as soon as read, and I think I told you its contents, showing that Mr. Chamberlin was fearful of a disaster in his family and wanted Mrs. Pratt to go and see his wife.

Well, the natural results followed, and the disaster has happened, and they have lost their little boy born in January. Mr. Chamberlin has been heart broken over the matter. He has waited to see his wife out of danger, and has now DISAPPEARED. He settled up his

affairs before going and wrote several letters which he forwarded to his brother in St. Paul to be mailed from there.[2] *He threw up his position with the Transcript and proposes never to return again.*

Mrs. Chamberlin is evidently determined to go on with her plans as I have a letter from her reopening correspondence . . . upon the subject. Her daughter, fifteen years old, has been employed by Miss Sullivan as an interpreter for Helen at five dollars a week, and the two younger children, seven and five years old are to be sent to live with a married daughter in Vermont, leaving Mrs. Chamberlin all to herself in Wrentham, Mass. She is still unable to leave her room, but I understand as soon as she recovers she proposes to open a school for blind and deaf children and to earn her living in that way. Altogether a most extraordinary condition of affairs.

Bell told his wife that he had subsequently had a long talk with Michael Anagnos at Perkins. Bell continued, "I am worked up about Mr. and Mrs. Chamberlin. I am afraid she cannot be all right mentally. She has certainly acted in a very eccentric fashion, and perhaps this may be the true explanation of the whole matter, at least it is a charitable way of looking at it; but if that is so, surely Mr. Chamberlin would not have left her. He is one of the kindest hearted, most sympathetic men I have ever met, and was sincerely devoted, I am sure to his wife and children."[3] Bell was shocked and concerned.

Somehow, in spite of the situation, Ida managed to find a temporary balance. While waiting for news of Ed, she tried to regain her own physical health and kept up a brave face in public and with her children in their respective locations. Contrary to Bell's statement that she planned to support herself with the school on the Red Farm property, Ida had given up that idea. Since the Chamberlins had only rented the property at Red Farm, she abandoned the lease, put her household possessions in storage, and went to live temporarily with friends in the area.

How hard it must have been to leave so abruptly, and especially for the Chamberlin children. The family had lived at Red Farm for years, and it had been their home and where the children had grown up. Their long-term guests, Angel De Cora and Zitkala-Ša, were uprooted as well. Life for the Chamberlins—and their many friends for whom Red Farm had been a social hub for over a decade—was shattered. The days at Red Farm were over.

Helen wrote to Hitz again on March 24 and included an update on Beth Chamberlin's presence in their household. She was being paid five dollars a week for reading assistance—help that was desperately needed, as Annie's eyesight was ever more strained by the demands of Helen's Radcliffe coursework.[4]

Beth was fifteen, six years younger than Helen, and was now being called by the more grown-up name "Betty." Helen delighted in her companionship, writing, "Betty and I are working away merrily as two bobolinks. As fast as we can finish a play in French or German, another is required, and we have to read French novels by the best authors, which means the most difficult French composition. . . . Betty would send her love if she were here. She was delighted to get your letter."[5]

The Chamberlin family events created distraction and worry for both Helen and Annie while they pursued Helen's studies. Finally, in April, after weeks of waiting and concern, Ed resurfaced. Helen told Hitz of new developments in a letter on April 16: "Dear Uncle Ed has just been heard from. He is in New York, and I see no reason why he should not return to his family before long. As yet I know nothing definite about him, but I hear that he is going to work for the 'Transcript' as before."

She and Annie had also seen Ida recently, and Helen shared details of the visit: "We had a very pleasant Easter in spite of the frowning sky and chill rain which ushered in the day and led her out leaving the world in starless night. Aunt Ida, who is much better, spent Easter with us, and all day our little home was full of friends and of music."

Ida appears to have continued to discuss plans for the school for the deaf and blind. By now, it must have been a serious social embarrassment. Helen went on, "Poor Aunt Ida, we feel very sorry for her and for her children. Her mind still seems to be affected on the subject of the school scheme, and we despair of being able to make her see the impossibility of carrying it through."[6]

Despite Helen's belief that Ed would be back with his family soon, he was still absent in late May. In a revealing letter written on May 23 to her friend Fred Day, Ida confided her own account of recent events: "Your letter of April twentieth reached me on my arrival from Bermuda, where I spent three weeks. Your dear words of comfort did me good, as much as words can. Everything, even now, seems so dark and unpromising that my heart is weary. It is so hard to just live and wait. It is all so very strange, and I know no more than you what it all means. I only know, 'we is one,' that I am the object of his aversion."

Ed had left, at least in part, because he could no longer live with Ida. In her letter, she further related that "on business points, that is newspaper business, Mr. Chamberlin seems to be all right." She shared that "he told me that he could no longer endure being with the trees, that they looked to him like an idiot does, no soul, no life. To me this shows how 'out' his mind is."

She continued,

I am up on the farm [in Vermont] with Helen [Dodd]. . . . Raymond and Dolly are very happy here on the farm. They think it all play. I wish you could see them, they are so rosy and strong. My sight is coming back very slowly, but the doctors think I will see as well as ever some day. My general condition is not very good. Three doctors say that it is largely a mental result, that I cannot hope for much till my mental state improves—and there you are. I am very grateful for your offer of help. There is nothing now that any one can do, but if at any time I need help, I shall be only too glad to call on you. Please believe me gratefully yours,

Ida Chamberlin[7]

The Chamberlin marriage had crumbled. Ed had spared Ida what embarrassment he could by saying publicly only that "he had to go away or to kill himself." The outward reason for his leaving would be his own delicate nature and limitations, not Ida nor the breakdown of their marriage.

But beyond leaving his family—as scandalous as it was for the time—Ed left the larger Boston literary world and a trusted role in that arena.[8] There would be talk—in front of and within the edifices of the Washington Street broadsheets where he had worked for almost two decades, in literary circles, in clubs, at the universities, in shops, and in genteel, lace-curtained parlors. Suddenly, Mr. J. E. Chamberlin, the "Listener" columnist, was no longer with the *Transcript.*

Not far from the *Transcript*'s Newspaper Row office, behind the Romanesque facade of the *Youth's Companion* offices on Columbus Avenue, a less public ripple would be felt. But the void left there by Ed Chamberlin's departure was quickly filled by a younger rising star from among the large editorial staff.

And certain men found the Chamberlin separation of particular interest: Arthur Gilman still communicated regularly with the belligerent William Wade. On April 5, Wade wrote to Gilman that he "had not heard of Mr. Chamberlain *[sic]* scooting."[9] Days later, on April 18, he wrote, "I am glad that Mr. Chamberlin has turned up, for Helen's sake, as Mr. and Mrs. C were among her 'dears'; Of course she must come to learn that lots of her idols are of clay, and the tumbles they get off the high shelf she has perched them on, will smash lots of crockery, but I don't want to see that knowledge come to her any sooner than maybe."[10]

Gilman and Wade took perverse pleasure in the situation. On May 25, Wade responded to a letter from Gilman, writing,

The story about Mr. Chamberlin was most thrilling. I never met him, but I did meet his wife once, and—well, I really do think the poor man had more excuse than some people who run off and leave their families. Poor Helen wrote me that a very sad thing has happened to "dear Mr. Chamberlin." He has mysteriously disappeared, and although she did not know the circumstances in the case, she could not help hoping he would soon return to "his dear ones." I couldn't help wondering what his "dear ones" would do if he did return. I am afraid my inclination would be to "fire something at his head."

Five subsequent lines of text are blacked out. A postscript discusses "The Listener" further and ends with Wade's comment: "I thought he was the injured angel, hen-pecked, in fact."[11]

Ed's generous friendship with Helen and Annie had embroiled him in a world of jealous and vicious men.

About the same time Ida was writing to Day, Helen and Annie were making alternate arrangements for their summer since they could no longer stay at Red Farm nor benefit from its proximity and circle. Helen wrote to Hitz on May 26 that they had decided to stay in Cambridge and noted, "Of course we shall miss beautiful Wrentham sadly, but it is really quite like being in the country here, and when we feel like it we can take little trips to the suburbs of Boston. Among the pleasures of the summer we [missed] your visit, and we beg you from our hearts not to disappoint us this time. We are ready for you now, or any time you choose to come."

She provided an update on Ed:

I must tell you that Uncle Ed is not working for the "Transcript," but for the "Mail and Express" in New York. It is no pleasure to read the "Listener" now, for it is in the hands of an uninteresting writer. Aunt Ida has just been to Bermuda, and returned full of enthusiastic accounts of its varied beauties and mild climate. She was with us the other day and said in reply to my "How are you?" "I am well." She is in Vermont at present, and Beth will go up there after the Examinations. Oh, how I shall miss her! I cannot tell you how much sunshine she has brought into our little home, or what a help she has been to us both! No one can fill my little sister's place as she does.[12]

Another month went by and on June 21, Helen again updated Hitz about the Chamberlin family. It had been five months since Ed had disappeared. Helen wrote, "We have seen Uncle Ed lately. He spent last Sunday with us, and we were all very happy. Just think, none of us had seen him since the early part of January. Another bit of good news, Aunt Ida has found a delightful home in Newbury, Vermont, right near the Connecticut River, and after she is settled she and the children will be very comfortable. Bettie *[sic]* left us Wednesday, and I miss her terribly; but I know how glad she is to get back to her loved ones, and I am happy in her happiness."[13]

Ida had finally abandoned her plan for the school; certainly, it was even less practical than ever due to her own severely changed circumstances. Soon after Helen's June letter, Annie wrote to Hitz in a temperate mood, saying, "I feel sorry for Mrs. C. She has worked hard to carry out her plan. . . . Her whole heart was in it, and naturally she could not give it up without a struggle." She speculated "that [Ida] should be disappointed and hurt, is not strange; for Helen gave her enthusiastic support to the plan from the beginning and withdrew only at the eleventh hour."[14]

Although Helen had hinted at early support for Ida's plan, many years later she shared in an account of her Radcliffe years the story behind her own and Annie's reaction to the idea of establishment of a school for the deaf and blind, describing it ultimately as "another attempt to divert me from my education." She wrote,

> *I was assailed on the affectional side of my nature, and I wished that I might be free to help liberate them [deaf and blind children] from the double dungeon of soul and body I had once dwelt in, but it was my right as well as my duty to complete my college course so as to demonstrate how doubly handicapped children could be developed.*
>
> *Teacher was determined that I should not be deflected from my schoolwork. I mention this merely because it was among the many upsets which we encountered, and which caused Teacher such disappointment over my failure to attain highest honors in every subject I studied. She was rent with emotion and overwrought by my apparent lack of zeal in obtaining the* SUMMA.
>
> *It is thanks to our strenuous apprenticeship under Teacher that . . . I have been able to clear away the plans of those who would dominate us and keep our position as free, self-reliant women.*[15]

Annie Sullivan's vision for Helen's education and future was pioneering and intractable. The orphaned girl who had carved a future for herself out of the wreckage of life in the Tewksbury Almshouse would never be deterred from reaching her goals for herself and her charge.

As Helen reported in her last letters of 1901, the uprooted Ida found a house in the picturesque town of Newbury, Vermont. Newbury was the ancestral home of Ed's family, but nonetheless Ida chose to move there with her children, probably because her daughter Helen and Helen's husband, Walter Dodd, were busy establishing a Vermont-based cottage industry in a house they were restoring there called Twinflower. They were both talented designers and artisans, she with an MIT architecture degree and Walter with his passion for woodworking, furniture making, and crafts.[16]

In Newbury, Ida received a warm welcome. She was related through marriage to one of the founding families, her own family had originated in the nearby town of Barnard, she had an aura of fame about her, and she had engaging and lively children. The town had a social scene that was surprisingly cosmopolitan. It was home to several elegant hotels that were popular summer destinations for Bostonians and others seeking mountain views and fresh air.

As chance would have it, the move brought the separated Ida and her children into the orbit of a future writer who would record the Chamberlins' arrival: the young Frances Wheeler, who was fifteen years old at the time. Wheeler soon married a much older man named Henry Keyes, who was then a state senator and would later become governor of New Hampshire. Eventually, she would become a novelist writing under the name Frances Parkinson Keyes. Later works set in New Orleans, such as *Dinner at Antoine's* and *Steamboat Gothic,* made her world-famous.

In her memoir, *Roses in December,* published in 1960, Keyes picked up the Chamberlin story post-Wrentham. She and her widowed mother had moved to Newbury from Boston just prior to Ida's relocation. Keyes wrote that the Chamberlins' arrival "roused actual excitement" in "that village where nearly all the families had lived for several generations." Betty Chamberlin was close in age to Keyes and fascinated her, as "she was as pleasant as she was pretty . . . and she was pretty as a picture."

According to Keyes, almost everyone in Newbury knew that Betty's "father was the celebrated journalist who wrote the feature called 'The Listener' in the Boston Transcript. Now he and her mother had separated, though there was no divorce nor any talk of one." Betty's "elder sister, Helen and her husband, Walter, had moved to an abandoned farm near West Newbury, which they were bent on reclaiming."

Frances continued, "We all knew about 'The Listener' and the Dodds and were greatly impressed with their achievements" but "were all the more impressed by what we soon learned of Betty: young as she was, she had mastered deaf-and-dumb language and had been the great Helen Keller's interpreter and companion. But this connection, though an honor, had also been a strain and it had been decided that Betty must have a rest from it."[17]

Presumably the demands of living in the small apartment with Annie and Helen and having to assist with Helen's college reading and studies on a constant basis were stressful for fifteen-year-old Betty. A return to life with her mother and siblings was perhaps a welcome relief.

Frances Keyes also gave two other bits of crucial information: first, "a family by the name of Sanderson, which Ida had known in Boston and who had spent many 'sojourns' in Newbury, upon hearing of Ida's separation had written 'numerous letters bespeaking a welcome.'" Second, Frances had become good friends with a girl named Jeannie Darling, who visited her grandmother in Newbury and had a brother named Richard. According to Frances, "the first time Richard Darling laid eyes on [Betty], he asked her if he might see her home from church. He was not quite eighteen then, and . . . as far as I know, he never looked at another girl with any real interest from the time of that first walk." So not only was Betty the lovely and interesting newcomer in town but she "also had the aura of romance around her" and quickly became a "favorite member" of Frances's group of friends.[18]

Ida and her children would make the best of their new life in Vermont.

Far removed from his former life, at his desk at the *Mail and Express* offices on Broadway in New York, Ed must have contemplated the path that had brought him there. Perhaps he felt deep shame at abandoning his wife—especially as she struggled to recover her health and grieved the loss of their baby. That, and leaving his children, whom he adored, must have tortured him.

Where he had once sought escape from his work, it now became his salvation. Ed remained in New York City over the next fourteen years, working at the *Mail and Express* as literary editor and art critic. When he joined the paper in 1901, it was an established daily that covered international and national news while also focusing on

New York City and its boroughs. With its gentle tone and features, daily literary reviews, a poetry section, and even a "Young Readers' Page," the paper was perhaps comfortingly similar to his past work at the *Transcript* and *Youth's Companion.*[19] Throughout his time in New York, Ed would do his best to maintain close ties with his children through letters and visits.

CHAPTER FIFTEEN

The Intervening Years, 1901–1915

Although distance separated them between 1901 and 1915, Helen, Annie, and Ed were often in one another's thoughts.

Ed's vacated editorial position at the *Youth's Companion* was soon filled by a young Harvard-educated writer named John Macy. He was a socialist and, like Ed, would have a major influence on Helen's political leanings. He developed a close friendship with Helen and Annie while they were still at Radcliffe and subsequently asked Helen to write an expanded "story of her life" for publication, which she agreed to do. Early chapters were featured in a series of articles in 1902 for the *Ladies' Home Journal.*

Following the publication of the articles, Helen felt a familiar worry that perhaps what she wrote might not be original. She wrote to Ed and expressed her hope that it was all her own work and not derived from something he had written. In particular, she was concerned that her image of a "City Child" might have been lifted from one of Ed's columns.

Ed read Helen's series with interest and then wrote a response on September 1, 1902, on *Mail and Express* letterhead. As in the early years of their friendship, Ed could not resist the opportunity to begin with a recent personal story. He was camping in the rugged Ramapo Mountains near Mahwah, New Jersey, forty miles from Manhattan, when he wrote, "Your most interesting and delightful letter was forwarded to me in the camp in the Ramapo mountains where I have been spending one of the loveliest vacations, in every outward respect, that I have ever known—a vacation free from all thought of the working world—from all thought even of thinking—and surrounded by every agreeable ordinary circumstance. I slept in a tent sixteen successive nights, and in all that time was not inside of any house, except a country store for a few minutes at a time."

"The only fly in the ointment," he continued, "was the presence of a large number of rattlesnakes and copperhead snakes up in the mountain above." An encounter between a small dog in their company and a large rattlesnake on their walking trail was described in colorful detail for Helen.

Then Ed turned to Helen's story, the primary reason for his correspondence: "It was while I was at this camp that I got hold of a copy of the *Ladies' Home Journal* and read the last in your series of articles. I was very much interested indeed in it, and regard the article as the most important of the series. I can never judge *critically* where my affection is concerned, but it seems to me that you have done a very good thing in this series of articles. I like them very much." Knowing firsthand how Helen was haunted by the plagiarism accusations of so many years before, Ed reassured her with his characteristic generosity of spirit:

You certainly need not have supposed that I could consider your reference to the city children as coming at all too close to my chapter on the city children in the Listener in the Town. I am touched that my picture of the little boy who seemed to be shrinking from a blow remained in your mind—but the thought was just as much yours as mine. Who knows, but I may have derived the idea from you in the first place? I don't remember that I did, but perhaps I did. You have been a great inspiration to me, and it would be an immense pleasure to me to feel that sometimes I have been an inspiration to you. I thank you with all my heart, dear Helen, for the kind things you say about me in this article. I am proud and happy that I have been of some help to you, especially of the sort you note.

Ed was wistful about being far away from Helen and Annie, but even more so about the separation from his own children. He alluded to the terrible price he had paid for his separation from Ida:

It is a great sorrow not to see you—as it is a still greater and ever-present sorrow to me not to have my children near me, whom I love, I am sure, more passionately than ever. I earnestly hope it may not be long before I see you and your dear Teacher. Give her my love. I am grieved by what you say of her eyes. Take care of her, Helen. With love always, Uncle Ed[1]

In addition to the companions he described to Helen, another familiar woman camped with Ed in the Ramapo Mountains throughout the month of September 1902: Angel De Cora, the quiet Winnebago artist who had been living at Red Farm with her friend Zitkala-Ša at the time of Ed's personal crisis and separation from Ida. Just as Ed did not mention her in his letter to Helen, neither did De Cora mention Ed in letters to her friends, though both described the same incident with the rattlesnake on the trail, and it was De Cora who had brought the little dog on the trip.[2]

Angel had come to New York in the spring of 1902, one year after Ed's move to the city, and at the time of the camping trip she was living in Harlem in the apartment of friends who were also on the camping trip.[3] Both Ed and Angel were suspiciously discrete about their friendship in their correspondences. Perhaps it was merely a convenient continuation of a mentor-mentee relationship. Ed could provide De Cora, almost twenty years younger, entrée to art patrons and galleries because of his role as art critic for the *Mail and Express* and could connect her with literary people who might hire her for illustration or publishing projects. Perhaps they were careful because people might otherwise "talk" if the estranged Ed and the unmarried De Cora were known to be in close companionship. For a young Indian woman artist trying to "carve out her livelihood" in a White man's world and to build a positive and professional image for herself and other Native Americans, whispers of an affair with a prominent literary figure could have been damaging.[4] And for Ed, a relationship with a considerably younger, Indian woman while he was still legally married to Ida might have been delicious gossip for those in the newspaper world and beyond and could have hurt his own reputation.

Still, in June 1905, the U.S. Census documented them living in the same apartment at 27 West 98th Street, with the census listing De Cora as an "artist" and "head of household" and Ed as a "boarder" and "editor." Ed was fifty-three and Angel was thirty-six or thirty-seven (her birthyear is uncertain). Also living in the household was De Cora's ten-year-old niece Madelyn.[5] At the time, De Cora was creating designs for a book project titled *The Indians' Book,* with Natalie Curtis, a writer whose uncle was editor of *Harper's Weekly*.[6]

But early the following spring of 1906, De Cora left New York to become an art teacher at the Carlisle Indian School in Carlisle, Pennsylvania. She returned to New York that summer, packed up her apartment, and enrolled Madelyn at Carlisle.[7] Except for a quiet pastel landscape of birch trees in a marsh, signed "A de C" and dated 1900, no lingering evidence of her friendship with Ed remains, nor is it certain if it was anything but platonic.

The Story of My Life, Helen's first published book, came out in 1902 and included the articles that had appeared in *Ladies' Home Journal.* It was a literary success that would provide Annie and Helen with financial independence for the immediate future. The book contained Helen's accounting of the Frost King affair and the Cambridge School events, as well as excerpts from Annie's and Ida's letters regarding the latter's plan for the school for the deaf and blind. It was impossible for Helen to tell her story without those chapters; Ed and Ida Chamberlin were inextricably bound up in Helen and Annie's lives.

Helen dedicated the book to Alexander Graham Bell, the man who had set her on a path of liberation from the darkness that enveloped her as a child by introducing her to Michael Anagnos and Perkins, and, as she wrote in her dedication of the book, "who had taught the deaf to speak and enabled the listening ear to hear speech from the Atlantic to the Rockies."[8] *The Story of My Life* was met with great acclaim, and countless positive reviews followed. The *Boston Herald* reported on March 15, 1903, that "exquisite, loving sympathy for every living thing is the characteristic of Helen Keller that makes the deepest impression upon one who reads her new book."[9]

Bell read the complete version and wrote to John Macy on April 2. Ever fascinated by Annie's teaching, he expressed his disappointment that she had not previously revealed her methods in teaching Helen:

[Annie's letters, featured in the book] . . . reveal the fact that had long been suspected, that Helen's remarkable achievements are as much due to the genius of her teacher, as to her own brilliant mind . . . and they also prove that Miss Sullivan was wrong when she gave us the impression that she acted without method in the instruction of Helen—groping her way along and acting on the spur of the moment. They show that she was guided all along by the principles of the greatest importance in the education of the deaf—that she did have a method and the results have shown that her method was a true one. These principles properly compiled can be carried out by any intelligent person in the education of other children.

In issuing a second edition of the work, I think it would be a good plan to bring together in an appendix, the passages you italicized, with a few others, so as to present in concise form, the principles that underlay her instructions.[10]

Especially after the publication of *The Story of My Life*, Bell tried to convince Annie that she should dedicate her life to teaching deaf children. It was her "duty," he pleaded, to use her "brilliant abilities as a teacher FOR THE BENEFIT OF OTHER TEACHERS." He further urged, "You must be placed in a position to impress your ideas upon other teachers. YOU MUST TRAIN TEACHERS so that the deaf as a whole may get the benefit of your instruction."[11]

The similarity of Bell's efforts to mold Annie's future to those of Ida is ironic. Ida had wanted a school exclusively for the deaf and blind; in contrast, Bell believed in "sending the teachers to the children, not the children to the teachers." However, both acknowledged the importance of training teachers to work with children with disabilities—and saw a future role for Annie in development of that training. But, as she had with Ida, Annie seems to have ignored Bell's pleas. Annie Sullivan would make her own decisions regarding her future.

Helen and Annie spent Easter 1903 in Wrentham with friends, despite the fact the Chamberlins no longer resided there. Not long after, they used money from the sale of shares of stock they had been given years earlier to purchase their own home in the village for $2,700—a pretty house that "Uncle Ed had spoken of."[12] It was a natural choice for them, and a direct consequence of their longtime friendship with Ed and Ida.

Helen graduated cum laude—though not summa cum laude as Annie had wanted for her—from Radcliffe on June 28, 1904, a day after her twenty-fourth birthday. The accomplishment was monumental. Against so many odds and struggles, a deafblind woman was graduating from an Ivy League women's college. John Hitz was among the dignitaries in the audience as Helen, "tall, erect, grave-looking, rose and moved to the platform" to receive her degree. "She mounted the steps gracefully, Annie's guiding hand on her arm, bowed to the college secretary, approached the president, bowed again and stretched forward her hand and with firm fingers grasped the coveted diploma."[13]

But Helen and Annie avoided commencement festivities other than the ceremony itself, sensitive to the possibility that Helen's accomplishment would be diminished by the presence of Annie at her side and that the media focus on Helen would detract from the accomplishments of other graduates.

Per usual, the press misinterpreted their absence. On June 24, 1904, the *New York Times* reported the headline, "Helen Keller Breaks Down." According to the article, Helen was "broken down" and "on the verge of prostration" in her dormitory room, "while her sisters in Radcliffe's class of 1904 are in the midst of their graduation festivities." Further, the paper reported, "She began to fail two months ago and was ordered by her physician to abstain from college work. It is believed she will get a degree in spite of her inability to fill all the requirements."[14]

Just as the press had lapped up and exaggerated any suggestion of overwork and exhaustion when she was a child at Perkins, they now sensationalized any hint of the same in the adult Helen. How Annie—who had worked so hard to prove Helen was capable of academic success on par with seeing and hearing young women students, and who invested so much of herself toward that goal—must have chafed at the suggestion that Helen would be "given" a Radcliffe diploma.

A reporter at the *Transcript* noted more kindly: "It is greatly to the credit of both Miss Keller and her instructors that while she has studied, so to speak, in competition with other girls, there has not been the slightest difference of treatment in her favor. She was awarded her degree with high standing because she had accomplished what anyone else must do to receive such an honor."[15]

Immediately following the commencement, the pair took the train to their new home on East Street in Wrentham.[16] Helen reported to a friend that "our chief happiness is that we have a real home of our own. It is old-fashioned, roomy and cheerful." She was especially attracted to a stone wall on the property, "overgrown with fruit trees, pines, and spruces." She "could walk there alone" and felt "rich in having all this space to myself."[17]

Other widely read publications, such as *Ladies' Home Journal,* also remarked on Helen's graduation, while noting that what she intended to take up as her life's work was the only point she had not covered in the story of her life. As historians have observed, Helen clearly could write, and the role of social activist and critic increasingly appealed to her, but the path forward remained uncertain.[18]

Later, in October of that year, the *New York Times* reported huge crowds greeting Helen during a speaking engagement at the St. Louis World's Fair: "The crowd was so dense that every aisle, window, and doorway was filled."[19]

Meanwhile, a romantic relationship had developed between Annie and John Macy, Ed's replacement at *Youth's Companion.* Eleven years his senior, Annie was reluctant to accept his offer of marriage and repeatedly refused him. In May 1905, after frequent reconsiderations, thirty-nine-year-old Annie married twenty-eight-year-old Macy at her home in Wrentham. Helen was thrilled. The octogenarian Reverend Edward Hale officiated at the ceremony. Helen described his presence and the event to Ed much later: "One of my happiest memories of Dr. Hale is the day he came out to Wrentham and married my teacher and John Macy. I stood beside him during the ceremony . . . with my hand on his arm, while he pronounced the words that united my dearest friends. I felt the strong current of life in his lion-like frame—that incalculable abundance of life, of faith, of adventure and passion which vitalized and inspired millions of his fellowmen."[20]

Despite Helen's happiness on the occasion, the marriage would be an unhappy one.

Life went on for the Chamberlins in their respective locations. The years in New York were professionally productive for Ed. Among other activities, he continued as editorial writer and art critic for the *New York Evening Mail* (the paper had changed its name from the *New York Mail and Express* back to the *New York Evening Mail* in 1904).[21] The offices of the paper were located on busy Broadway and occupied what was then considered a "skyscraper" and described as "an extraordinarily ornate and narrow 14-story slab embedded in a mid-block site, with [the] main façade on Broadway a mere 21 feet wide." One newspaper described the structure as looking "for all the world like an upright lead pencil." The building would survive until 1920, when it was torn down to make way for the AT&T Building.[22]

New York City had by this time surpassed Boston as the center of the American literary world, as "home to the nation's biggest newspapers, and also to its leading magazines and its major telegraph and telephone companies."[23] It was a distinctly urban work world for the refuge-seeking Listener, but the tone and voice required did not differ much from that employed during his *Youth's Companion* and *Transcript* years. The *Mail* was unusual among newspapers with its "refined" and even "religious" approach to news. Editorials had to be "free from wickedness," and articles included "nothing you wouldn't want to talk about around the dinner table, at least one where grace was said." The paper focused on "uplifting news of the city's charitable, religious, and educational institutions."[24] Readers perused twenty or more pages in each edition that included a weekly writing prize contest and coverage of local trials, sports events, stock market activity, recipes, society news, real estate, and copious advertisements.[25]

Ed worked from the editorial offices on the tenth and eleventh floors, and as he did in his cub reporter days in Chicago, probably still thrilled to the "din of the behemoth presses that occupied the basement and turned out 98,000 papers per hour."[26] By this time in his career, with steady employment as an editor and critic for an established big city newspaper and freelance writer for major periodicals, he was making an income that could best be described as upper middle class. He also contributed articles to large and small newspapers and nationally read periodicals.

Although Ed's letters to friends seem to indicate he and Ida were living apart, and that most of the time Ida lived in Vermont with her children, the 1910 census reported that Ed resided in Rutherford, New Jersey, with Ida, Raymond, and Dolly. Ed's occupation was listed as editor of a newspaper, and Ida's as "editress of a newspaper."[27] By this time, she was writing professionally, contributing articles on childhood, motherhood, and domestic topics to the *Evening Mail* Sunday magazine under the penname Elizabeth Atwood. She also reviewed articles and resources on those topics for the magazine.

Ed was close to Raymond and Dolly. Ed and Raymond were especially sympathetic souls in their love of the outdoors. While "a bright boy," Raymond struggled in school and his parents enrolled him in various private and public school settings in Vermont, Boston, New York, and New Jersey while trying to find one in which he could be successful. He eventually graduated from high school in Rutherford, New Jersey.[28]

During his years with the *Mail,* Ed also served as a contributing writer at *Harper's Weekly,* alongside his friend, William Dean Howells.[29]

In 1906, he wrote a lengthy article on Helen Keller for the nationally syndicated *Sunday Magazine.* Ed wrote lovingly of his dear friend whom he had now known for almost two decades. The man who worked "in the service of words" described Helen as "an embodiment of the word."

The article was titled "A Day with Helen Keller" and began with an engaging request for the reader to imagine what it would be like to be profoundly different in some way. He acknowledged, "Sometimes we dream, or like to imagine, that we are something different from what we are. . . . But no one of us can imagine what he would do, or think, or even feel, if he was a being without sight, or hearing, or speech."

Ed asked the reader to "conceive yourself, if you can, getting up some morning in a world which is totally dark, totally silent. You sit on the edge of a bed. You feel it. Something is under your feet that is hard. But what is beyond, what is above, what is about you? You cannot say which way you will go—there is no way." Indeed, this vagary and uncertainty was "the situation of one of the most habitually cheerful, and one of the cleverest and brightest of human beings: Helen Keller."

Ed wrote that day after day

I have seen this girl start out on her daily life, and have tried to put myself in her place as she stood before me with her habitual sweet smile on her face—and never been able to do so. I only know that she images such a world as I image; but she does it through others' eyes, through others' ears, and just how she does it no one can tell. Helen's inward mental world is one in which others' eyes and ears have served her, but when she confronts the physical outside world only her feet and fingers can be of use to her. So she begins with the spot where she is, and feels her way to the place she wants to go. This involves, as a general thing, following around the outside of the room.

He observed that "Helen seems to arrive at a sense of direction only by reasoning out the relation in space of one known object to another. She follows around the side of the room she knows best of all, locating herself by well-remembered objects on the walls and shelves."

After years of sharing meals with Helen and Annie, Ed described what it was like to dine with her:

No one comes in [a] blither mood to the table than Helen Keller. Her little helplessnesses there may trouble her inwardly; but she good-naturedly puts them aside as things not worthy of any show of attention from herself or others, thereby unconsciously rebuking the form of egotism by which we consistently ask the pardon of others for our little awkwardness and blunders.

She thinks of the table as a place where everybody is having a good time, and seeks to join in this good time at once. Of course the person next to her, who is presumably her teacher, or some other friend who communicates with her in the sign language for the deaf made upon her hand, must act as her ears for what is said; and her own words are in her half-chanted, peculiarly uttered speech. Of course, she does not know when others are speaking, and depends on the fact being signified to her by her neighbor. She waits with a smile of sweet patience until others are silent.

Sometimes, in merry companies, it is a long time before Helen gets the right of way; and when she speaks, what she says is generally well worth listening to, and generally starts the table off on another tack with its suggestion.

Yet it is an odd thing that no one's talk is less introspective, less egotistic, less of the talker, than Helen Keller's. She is plainly thinking herself into the people around her. What they have been saying and doing, what they are going to do, what their ideas are about this, that or the other thing—this is her ordinary theme. She is fond of relating a story, or repeating a witticism or clever thought that she has read. I have never heard a person who is as invariably pleased by other people's jokes as Helen Keller.

According to Ed, Helen's cheerfulness and energy were prodigious: "She is no sooner up in the morning than her fingers, her nostrils, and her perception of vibrations begin to open to the world of sense. She seeks the veranda, her every day place of promenade, or if some one will conduct her (she never ventures off the veranda alone), the lawn or the field. She touches things, inhales, tosses her head to feel the wind the better in her hair or upon her face, all with as keen a sense of enjoyment as that of any seeing person who revels in a beloved landscape."

Without the sense of hearing, Helen had developed "a way of feeling for sounds." She spoke to Ed of "feeling the faint noise of a fly's wings." On the porch one morning—the house was a mile from the railroad, a lake lying between—she said, "The 8 o'clock train is going through." How do you know? "I smell the smoke." Ed smelled it then himself but had not noticed it before. He believed "it is not that the senses which Helen possesses are keener than ours—it is simply that having no others, she gives these closer heed."

Ed believed that Helen's happiest moments each day were spent speaking with others. As sentences "shape themselves" for her, he wrote that "she has a little trick of making quick starts of pleased surprise." But her "greatest, wildest pleasure" was swimming.

Finally, Ed described Helen's "most beautiful moments" each day, both in terms of how they seemed to affect her own state and as they impressed her friends, as "the half-hours—hours sometimes—at the end of the day, that she passes reading her books, not for the purposes of study, but of inward delight." Reading for Helen required books written in braille, and many had been translated especially for her. They were a "particular pleasure."

Helen was "especially and unwearingly fond" of Oliver Wendell Holmes's *The Autocrat of the Breakfast Table.* Ed related that "when she reads it her face wears an expression that it never wears at any other time. She is always expecting something funny, and when the funny thing comes her half-suppressed laugh always comes too. She has read the book so many times that she knows it almost by heart."

In summer, Helen often sat on the Red Farm veranda with one of her big braille books in her lap,

> *reading as the shadows gather, reading on after darkness has fallen—it is all one to her—and smiling, or knitting her brows, or gravely shaking her head, as the images that enter her mind through the tips of her fingers succeed one another, grave, and gay, tender, poignant, or absurd. . . . Sometimes she laughs aloud in her singular, individual way. Around her, people sit or pass, intent upon their own affairs. Sometimes they jostle her in their play, and Helen, smiling, extends an inquiring hand to "see" who it is. Children bury their heads in her lap, or come to her and ask for a story, for she is a capital story-teller, repeating for instance, most of Kingsley's "Greek Hero Tales" almost word for word as they stand in the book.*

All children quickly learn to understand her somewhat indistinct spoken words with readiness. Her good-night, as she rises at last to go away to bed, is softly spoken, but it is answered with caresses.

Ed closed the article with a gentle summation: "Helen's life has its vexations, its griefs, and its hard passages, but these leave no residuum of bitterness or ill-nature, for some reason that is hard to fathom."[30]

In early May, Annie had shared one of Ed's articles about Helen with her in Wrentham. Helen had then written to Ed in New York, telling him that she appreciated that he had spoken in the article of the "delightful walks we used to take together in the woods" and noted that "somehow, everything that brings you to my thoughts brings also the beauty and fragrance of growing things and the cherishing warmth of the sun." She lamented that Ed had "to work so hard and constantly" but wrote that he was always near to her heart.[31]

In other letters around this same time period, Helen wrote to Ed describing her advocacy work and the improvements they were making to their home and property. She begged him to come visit, saying, "can you not overcome your shrinking from dear old Wrentham" and make a visit? She believed that despite his expressed worries, "Wrentham people feel nothing but kindness towards you," and she wanted him to "remember how happy we have all been here together in the past." She and Annie longed to have Ed with them in their own home.[32]

In 1907, Ed published one of his most enduring books, *The Ifs of History*. Considered a "classic text" today, with chapters such as "If Queen Elizabeth Had Left a Son or Daughter," "If George Washington Had Become a British Midshipman," and "If Abraham Lincoln's Father Had Moved Southward, Not Northward," it remains a thought-provoking look at the role chance has played in history across the ages. The book was widely distributed and reviewed positively across the country.[33]

Fluent on a broad range of subjects, in 1909 Ed contributed to an *Evening Mail* homage to his personal hero, Abraham Lincoln, on the forty-fifth anniversary of Lincoln's death. Ed's pieces in the thirty-page pamphlet were sympathetic themes for him: "Lincoln and the Black Soldiers: Story of Robert Gould Shaw, the Heroic Leader of the First Colored Regiment from the North" and "Lincoln's Use of Scripture." In a subtitle, the latter article elaborated, "He employed Bible phrases as the backbone of his eloquence, and made use of them in demolishing the structure of treason." Ed observed,

It is well known, of course, that Lincoln did not belong to any church. He did not even claim the name of Christian. But he was as deeply religious in feeling as any man could be. He was a Bible man—not in the sense that he arranged his views according to any particular interpretation of the Bible, but in the larger sense that he read the Bible as he read no other book, knew it almost from cover to cover, and spoke and acted on its inspiration. The spirit of the book had flowed into his very soul, and its words came out on his lips whenever he spoke seriously.[34]

Ed was well suited to write the essay, as he emulated Lincoln's spiritual example in his own life. He had studied the Bible intently as a boy and used it to guide much of his literary style and thought, but he did not personally belong to any organized religion or church.

In the spring of 1913, women's suffrage and Mexican political upheaval were among the front-page headlines at the *Mail.* Ads for rust-proof corsets, Wrigley's spearmint gum—"slip a stick in your mouth before a goodnight kiss for minty freshness"—and "Wanamaker's News Page of New Things" competed for space in the densely typed pages. A young cartoonist named Rube Goldberg's work was featured prominently.[35]

The now-legendary New York Armory Art Show of 1913 merited Ed's critical review. The show brought groundbreaking contemporary art by artists such as Pablo Picasso and Marcel Duchamp to American shores and "marked "a reordering of the rules of art-making."[36]

Ed was contemporary in his views on how photography was changing art, writing in the *Evening Mail* that the camera was now the tool for recording nature and that it freed the artist to "paint only abstractions, gigantic symbols, ideas in broad lines, splotches of color that suggest the thoughts that broke through language and escaped."[37]

Probably in May 1913, Ed wrote to Fred Day at his home in Massachusetts, updating Day on his life in the city and the activities of the family. Day had invited Ed to visit him in Maine, and Ed was having difficulty arranging his schedule to do so. He told Day,

I have thought of you often through these years in New York. For four or five years I have been doing the art criticism—oh Lord, I don't call it criticism; just art writing for the paper, and the work has brought me in connection with the artists in photography, like Coburn and White and Steichen and Stieglitz, and all of them call you Master, with a huge M, and in reverent utterance. You are inextricably woven with the whole subject—there is no thinking of photographic art without thinking of you. And quite aside from that, innumerable recollections of our old pleasant association are continually arising.[38]

Vanity Fair benefited from Ed's viewpoint in a December 1914 article about the now famous Rube Goldberg, titled "Foolish Question: Who Is Goldberg?" From personal knowledge of his colleague, Ed brought readers into the newsroom and told the story of the discovery of the iconic cartoonist and writer. Although hired by a skeptical editor, "the public found the pictures immensely funny; and the highbrows, who liked them just as well, accounted for their liking by saying—which is true—that Goldberg is not like the other funny artists—that his things have a significance—as art and literature."[39] Goldberg's cartoons sold papers, and he was paid handsomely: in 1915, he earned an astonishing $450 per week, equivalent to over a million dollars a year today. And he later brought the same genius to the invention of overly complicated machines and devices that performed simple tasks.[40]

Helen Keller continued to try to establish herself as a serious writer. Perhaps purposely, Ed's nationally syndicated 1906 article "A Day with Helen Keller" presaged Helen's second book, *The*

World I Live In, which was published in 1908. The new book complemented the autobiographical *The Story of My Life* but was a collection of more introspective essays about Helen's life and her innermost thoughts.

The book was met with genuine respect by critics. Now in his mid-seventies, Mark Twain responded personally with admiration and invited Helen and Annie to visit his Connecticut mansion for a conversation and tour. Helen wrote of their friendship, "He never made me feel that my opinions were worthless, as so many people do. He knew that we do not think with eyes and ears, and that our capacity for thought is not measured by five senses. He kept me always in his mind while he talked, and he treated me like a competent human being. That is why I loved him."[41]

That same year, Helen and Annie's dear friend and confidant John Hitz died at the age of eighty. Helen wrote a memorial tribute to him in *Outlook for the Blind* in which she spoke of his "constant message . . . that I should 'contribute a share to the inalienable treasures of enlightenment, the betterment of man, and the praise of God.'" Further, Hitz "believed in the advancement of women" and expended "unceasing effort to foster in us a larger activity. He exhorted us to think, that we might develop a greater capacity for usefulness. He disapproved our shrinking from independent, fearless thought and reflection."

In a reference to Ida's scheme, which had distracted Helen during her Radcliffe years, she told of Hitz's view of the situation: "When I abandoned a certain scheme for work which appealed to the affectional side of my nature, but which would have interfered with my college studies, he expressed his strong approval."[42] He had been a grandfatherly figure for Helen and Annie since his investigation into the Frost King affair in 1892, and his death was a severe loss for both.

Less than a year later, in 1909, their longtime friend Edward Everett Hale also passed away at the age of eighty-seven. Ida and Ed too would have mourned this loss, as Hale had been such a central figure in the Red Farm circle. Active and involved until his death with many religious and social causes, he was memorialized in May 1913 with the placement of a bronze statue inside the Boston

Public Garden. Former President William H. Taft spoke at the installation service.

Helen reconciled with William Wade several years after her angry letter to him in 1899. A memorial tribute written by her in *Outlook for the Blind* in 1913, upon his death at the age of seventy-five, noted that "he often got into controversies with the people who essayed to speak and write with authority about matters of which they were obviously ignorant. He loved a fight when it was a just one." In regard to their reconciliation, Helen wrote, "At last he understood what had happened and came back to me, and that was a happy day for us both."[43]

The mentors and benefactors, the men of genius, were aging and passing away.

Helen followed *The World I Live In* with publication of the poem "The Song of the Stone Wall" and the book *Out of the Dark* in 1913. The latter was a collection of Helen's essays and magazine articles, many of them focused on the issues of the blind and deaf in society. Readers were shocked by other writings about why she had become a socialist, her alliance with the women's suffrage movement, and her belief in the importance of the use of nitrate of silver in the eyes of newborns to prevent blindness caused by venereal infection. Reviewers often discounted her writings on economic, social, and political subjects. As her friend and Annie's biographer Nella Braddy Henney noted in a later book, the "image of Helen Keller as a perfectly radiant creature happily rolling along in the best of all possible worlds seemed to be firmly established." Further, "people had trusted Helen to be sweet and resigned when she spoke of affliction."[44]

Ed must have observed Helen's literary efforts from afar and applauded her social and political writings. After all, he had instilled in her much of her understanding of those subjects. His influence was widely known. A colleague of Ed's at the *Evening Mail,* Charley Edson, informed his sister Rita that he shared an office with Mr. J. E. Chamberlin, "the man who put the hell in Helen Keller."[45]

Ed and Helen shared a bond of mutual admiration that was strong. In February 1912, she wrote a tribute to Ed in *American*

Magazine. In the article, titled "Joseph Edgar Chamberlin," she told of how he influenced her:

Thirteen years ago, when I was preparing for college, my teacher and I were guests at Red Farm, which overlooks a beautiful lake in Wrentham, Massachusetts. What a solace it was to turn from the harassments of learning to the frolicsome company of that household! What a joy it was to desert the wanderings of the "Anabasis," and go with three lovely children on real excursions by the shore of the lake and into the dusky woods!

But that summer we were all lonely; for the master of the house was far away in Cuba. Mr. Chamberlin was war correspondent of the New York EVENING POST. *He was following the fortunes of an army less celebrated than the army of the Ten Thousand. My teacher used to read me what he wrote for newspapers and in his letters about our inglorious war with Spain. . . . I must say that Uncle Ed's accounts of battles and sieges were very disappointing. The letters of some of the other correspondents abounded in thrilling adventures and picturesque situations.*

Mr. Chamberlin told us of men underfed and dying of fever, of polluted streams and wells, of mismanaged commissariats. When we asked him to make his reports more heroic and patriotic, he replied that he could not describe what he did not see, or narrate what did not happen. When word came by telegraph that our men had driven the Spaniards from their strongest positions, we imagined a fierce army of Weylers, black-bearded desperadoes overcome by the superior valor of American soldiers. A few days later Mr. Chamberlin's letter described a handful of Spanish boys, mild-mannered, soft-voiced, willing to shoot and be shot but with no very clear idea of what the war was about.

"The Listener in the Town" and "The Listener in the Country" brought to a battlefield an intellectual honesty, a sense of justice, a tender humanity which were wasted upon readers who preferred exciting fiction to disillusion and truthfulness. That Mr. Chamberlin knows what true heroism is, his excellent life of John Brown bears eloquent witness. Yet I think he is a better biographer of bird, tree and flower.

How glad we were to get him back from Cuba, and to walk with him again in the fields and woods, whose inhabitants were his life-long friends. For forty years he has been a busy journalist, working in Chicago, Newport, Boston and in New York, where he is now editorial writer and critic for the EVENING MAIL. *His vacation hours he has spent in the heart of nature, and he has told me more than any other of my friends about shy creatures that love shady places and hide in the hollow of tree and wall. He knows all the plants that grow, and all the birds that fly between Newbury, Vermont and Wrentham, Massachusetts. The collection of his sketches from the well-known column of the Boston* TRANSCRIPT, *called "The Listener," contains as fine flashes of descriptive writing as any I have read. "The Whippoorwill," for instance is the expression of a man with rare gifts of style and still rarer gifts of perception. His portraits of dogs have the quality so remarkable in Maeterlinck's essay and in "Rab and His Friends"—truth to the personality of the dog without false imputation of human characteristics to our four-footed comrades.*

Mr. Chamberlin's newspaper work has made it necessary for him to live in many parts of the country. Wherever he has set up his household gods, he has surrounded them with a little garden, and although his tenancy was to be brief, he always planted trees for later comers to enjoy. At Wrentham he gathered about him a host of friends—men and women already distinguished in their profession, as well as young men and women hoping to become famous and much in need of his unfailing help. Many young writers owe their start to Mr. Chamberlin. But of course I have no right to express their gratitude. All I can say is that I am still learning from that book of nature, that special page in it which he first interpreted for me. He is so inseparably associated with this corner of Massachusetts that I regard him as a habitant here and only a visitor in New York.

I understand that newspapers are not hospitable to radical and progressive ideas. Mr. Chamberlin's thought, as he expresses it to his friends, is far in advance of his written work. His conscience is alive to the wrongs and perils of our social institutions. Long before I knew what it all meant, he talked with us about Socialism and William Morris's "News from Nowhere." The work of a journalist is for the greater part anonymous, so that Mr. Chamberlin's name may be unknown to many readers of these words. The affections and services of friends are also anonymous. The influences which most enable and sweeten my life may be hidden from fame; but they live immortal in other lives.

A photograph accompanying the article shows Ed in casual hiking clothes seated on the grass, his back leaning against a tree, with legs stretched out before him and a slouchy, felt hat on his lap. The photo caption reads, "Joseph Edgar Chamberlin: A daily newspaper journalist of high ideals whom Helen Keller writes about in these pages. As representative of the New York *Evening Post* in Cuba, Mr. Chamberlin, alone among war correspondents, showed up the pettiness and uselessness of the war."[46] In his characteristic, humble way, Ed most likely felt such a tribute unwarranted.[47]

Despite the publication of her books, the lack of public interest in Helen's more serious work led to the eventual realization that she could not support herself on the basis of her writing. In 1913, Helen and Annie began a lecture tour on the vaudeville circuit, something they had long resisted due to its "freak show" nature and reputation but which now became a necessity if they were to survive financially.[48]

By this time, Annie and John Macy's marriage had unraveled and they were spending increasing amounts of time apart. It was a marriage complicated by the strong personalities of both Annie and John, and by Helen's constant presence and complete dependence on them. The couple would eventually separate but never officially divorce.

In early 1914, thirteen years after the Chamberlin family's abrupt exodus from Red Farm, Ida fell ill in Chino, California, and died on February 1 at the age of fifty-seven. Obituaries did not reveal the cause of death but stated that she had been visiting her stepmother Sophia at the time of her death. Ida had made numerous trips to and from California in recent years to visit Sophia.[49]

Ida had faced myriad challenges during her lifetime: losing her mother when she was a young child, her father when he was forty-seven, her teenage son Charley, and her four-year-old daughter

Corda. She had suffered several miscarriages or stillbirths and the loss of another baby and her own near-death during her last pregnancy.[50] She was afflicted with severe and chronic health issues throughout midlife, if not earlier. Those losses and hardships were overlaid by her husband's own personal crises over many years and his frequent need for escape from stress. Still, she brought optimism, energy, and generosity to her world, raising five children to adulthood and creating, along with Ed, a household renowned for its hospitality and the brilliance of its guests.

An obituary appeared in the *Pawtucket [RI] Times* that praised Ida as "a woman who for many years was a prominent figure in the life of Wrentham, and whose home was always open with royal hospitality to all classes and conditions of people." She had gathered "a brilliant coterie of literary people, who were figures of national importance." Helen Keller and Annie Sullivan were listed with others who had been part of the Red Farm circle. Also noted were Ida's contributions to magazines and newspapers. Her "work on the magazine page of the Evening Mail was a feature of unusual interest to women and many of her stories of child life were masterpieces of force and brilliant English."[51]

Helen had appreciated Ida's "loving, motherly ways."[52] Historians almost exclusively cast Ida as "meddling," a pejorative that sadly discounts the welcoming and embracing role she played in the lives of Helen and Annie, for whom she provided a second home at Red Farm for over a decade.

As time wore on, Annie became increasingly visually impaired. She and Helen now needed additional assistance with daily life. In 1915, they hired a young Scottish woman named Polly Thomson to live with them in Wrentham. She became a devoted and indispensable companion. Helen would grow to love the "true-in-all-weathers Scotch Lassie" whom she described as "hardly out of her arms' reach" for the remainder of her life."[53] The pair was now a trio.

In June 1915, a year and a half after Ida's death, Ed married Leonilda (Nilda) Farness Lowry in Lyme, Connecticut. The wedding was reported in several newspapers and in *American Art News*.[54]

In late July, however, Ed resigned from the *Evening Mail.* The paper was now a harder-edged publication with dark and blaring headlines, ever-denser type, and a decreased literary emphasis. War in Europe dominated much of the front page, though it would be two more years before the United States entered, and articles on women's suffrage and "automobiling" captured readers' attention. Hundreds of employees were on the payroll, from editors down to newsboys. Ed was making $70 per week as editor, and with freelance work on the side, he was making equivalent to between $150,000 to $200,000 per year in today's dollars.[55] Twenty-two-year-old Raymond Chamberlin had recently joined the staff as a reporter and was making $12 a week.[56] When the paper sold on June 1 to Edward Rumely, widely suspected of "German interests," Ed stayed only a few more weeks. According to his daughter Dolly, he came home one day and announced, "I quit! The paper stinks of Germans."[57]

The announcement of his departure was widely reported in newspapers across the country. His New York associates held a "big" farewell banquet in his honor at Little Hungary restaurant on East Houston Street.[58] The writer of a nationally syndicated column, O. O. McIntyre, wrote, "Joseph Edgar Chamberlin long an editorial writer on the Evening Mail has gone back to Boston—his first love. He will edit the editorial page of the Boston Transcript. Chamberlin takes with him his celebrated hat." Ed had become known in news circles in New York for his distinctive, slouchy, outdoorsman's hat, which he wore tilted back on his head with the front brim tipped up. Apparently, he always wore it when he wrote, and "it was just as necessary as his pencil."[59]

Once again, a confluence of circumstances had forced a major life change: the sixty-three-year-old Ed was perhaps exhausted by a decade and a half of churning out a major daily newspaper in one of the largest cities in the world. But he was also his own man and would not write for an entity whose ideals did not match his own, just as he would not yield to pressure to write what he was not personally inclined to write. On an earlier occasion in his life, one of his stories had been under consideration by *Century* magazine, recognized as the best general periodical of its time, when editor

R. W. Gilder suggested major changes to the story. In response, Ed thanked Gilder for the recommendations but said he was "going to keep it as it is rather than force it into any other shape."[60] On another occasion, in 1899, Ed wrote a letter to the editor of the *Boston Transcript* (for whom he worked at the time) disputing reports of "orders being given that no prisoners should be taken—that is, that they should be shot," during the Spanish American conflict. He called the "prominent publication and repetition of such statements of barbarity and unsupported by identification or evidence . . . in my mind exactly on a plane with the worst feats of yellow journalism."[61] That letter was also reprinted widely in large and small newspapers across the country.

And so Ed moved back to Boston, though not to Wrentham, and resumed work for the *Transcript,* the venerable paper "considered the very essence of traditional Boston."[62] Ed now added a new column called "The Nomad," which allowed for a broader scope of subject matter including travel and interviews with prominent people. When he had left in 1901, his "Listener" column had been taken over by the *Transcript*'s editor, E. H. Clement, who continued to write it even after Ed's return until 1920, whereupon Ed resumed its authorship.

Helen, Annie, and Polly Thomson were still living in the house on East Street in Wrentham.

In January 1916, Raymond Chamberlin followed Ed to Boston and began working as a reporter for the *Transcript.* Even more so than when Ed had entered the field almost fifty years before in Chicago, journalism promised an exciting future as newspapers continued to grow in size and influence.[63] Ed was proud of Raymond's character and his blossoming career, and both men savored the opportunity to live and work near one another.

PART IV

CHAPTER SIXTEEN

Souls Tried and Greatened

In April 1917, the United States entered World War I. Helen's voice would be heard as an outspoken critic, while Ed's would be that of the father of a soldier and a chronicler of the war for the *Transcript.*

In May, Raymond Chamberlin enlisted with a fellow reporter in the Boston Company of the National Guard. "It is the only thing for a man to do," he told his father when the summons went forth for America's participation.[1]

Ed must have been heartbroken at his son's enlistment. He had seen firsthand how the Civil War had affected his older brothers and had witnessed the realities of war in Cuba. He was realistic about the horrors awaiting Raymond and his comrades and could not have been eager for Raymond to serve. But his son was a grown man, patriotic and determined, and he had no choice but to support him. Raymond would not leave a timid and wavering father behind.

Ed wrote that "unquestionably, all Raymond's instincts were patriotic." He related in a later history that "Raymond had long admired his Uncle Preston who had fought in the Civil War. With all the rest of us, his wrath rose at the outrages of Germany upon the world, upon our country, upon our people. The flame began to burn brightly in his heart. His thought was just to go. He said nothing of glory, not a word of expectation of advancement. Never for a moment did he contemplate any other course."[2]

During the years of America's involvement in the war, Helen Keller tried to remain neutral, stating that she "loved the Germany of thought and culture." She was a well-known socialist, and to many she appeared pro-German when she refused to condemn Germany and the war. Her views alienated many Americans. Neutrality—especially in an avowed socialist—was an unpopular stance. Hecklers awaited her at her lectures. "I am neutral, yes," she replied to critics, "but I consider my second country the land of Beethoven, Goethe, Kant, and Karl Marx." She claimed "to like the people of all nations, but not their armies and navies."[3] It was a difficult position to maintain for a woman dependent on book sales and lectures for her livelihood.

Raymond's battalion drilled at the Commonwealth Armory in Boston until September 21, 1917, when it departed by train for Hoboken, New Jersey, and then to sail for France. Writing for the *Transcript,* Ed described his son's leave-taking on the train from the Framingham Station—verbalizing the pain of departure experienced by thousands and thousands of American parents:

At last one day—the 21st of September—the call came to me by telephone from Raymond, "We're going! Come out!" By mid-afternoon we were all there at the camp. Officers bustled about. Up and down strayed the tearful fathers, mothers, brothers, sisters, sweethearts, pausing, wringing hands.

The bugle sounds, the men fall in. The tramp of feet is a kind of deep measured music. Voices are hushed and tears are pouring. The emotion of that bugle call to the march to the far-away death can hardly be borne. We are all on the way now; by the side of the boys in the company, at the end of the files, march the parents, the brothers, the sisters, the sweethearts. Every one knows well what it means.

A steady, palpitating march to the railway station, and then a tedious and heartbreaking wait. . . . We are there, near him, as he stands at rest with the others, a long time. Slowly they move up to the train. It is an hour, perhaps two hours. The boys sing and whistle—bluff, heroic bluff!

At last an empty car comes alongside. It is his. In the boys go, waving a hand at the car door. There is to be but a brief pause before the train is off. . . .

There he goes to a seat. He is at the window, smiles, waves his hand—his head drops out of sight, we know it is bowed with emotion. It is the last look on earth, and though, with our illusion of a sure and special return, we put the intimation aside, and say, "Come back all right, boy!" Our sinking hearts somehow seem to prophesy. . . .

We had a fleeting, almost unreal glimpse of him as the train moved along across the main Framingham street a little later, but it was but little more than a flickering wave of a handkerchief; the train rolled away through the night, and the battalion was gone . . . the boy was gone.[4]

Just as Ed had waited with his parents for letters from his brothers, now he waited for those from his son. Raymond's letters home were detailed, and he tried valiantly to communicate, sending messages that the family would understand but which would not merit censorship. With Raymond everything was "all right," no matter what discomforts or privation there might be.[5]

For Ed and those at home in Boston, "letters from the men in the battalion were read aloud at the eager weekly meetings of the Company A Welfare Association—a body composed of the parents and other relatives and close friends of the soldiers. These meetings were very pleasant—until the casualty list began to come in, and this and that family, bowed with grief, began to drop out, or attended in mourning and tears, still in quest of the meager information that the official records denied. At those mutual readings of soldiers' letters, one boy's letter often supplied the details that another had omitted."[6]

During this time, Ed wrote a column for the editorial page of the *Transcript* entitled "Over There," which consisted largely of letters from soldiers in the field and incidents gathered from other sources connected with their service in France. Due to the column, as well as its broader coverage of the war, the *Transcript* was considered the "war paper of the time in Boston."[7]

Before long, Raymond's battalion received its "baptism of fire" as they moved into a "sector of plateau, rough, steep carps, and ragged forest land that formed a bastion of the German defensive line." The battalion had begun to see signs of German demolition in villages, shell holes, old trenches, and graveyards. The countryside was "all shot to hell."[8]

In early July 1918, the battalion was summoned to the point of greatest strategic importance, north of the Marne River. Artillery fire was heavy, and the troops on the outpost line were raked by machine-gun fire. Many casualties resulted from gas, but Raymond came through.[9]

On July 5, Ed printed a "Nomad" column for the *Transcript,* "a sort of representative letter from a war father to his son" called "Your Souls Will Be Tried and Greatened." Ed had a vision of Raymond's triumphant return from war: "I saw you of larger intellectual stature and broadened understanding and sympathies. I saw you graver than before, but not sad. . . . I saw you coming nearer to me than you had ever been—as if this that has made both of us bigger and stronger had carried each one of us closer to the other's life and soul. I believe that the vision was true, and that our relation in that great day when you come back will be much more than one of fatherly or filial affection."[10] The letter was lengthy and full of Ed's thoughts on God and nations—a deep conversation with a son away at war.

Raymond replied to the letter on August 6, writing to Ed,

I wish I had time to discuss in detail all the subjects that you have raised. . . . First, is the new attachment that you believe will be formed. Somehow, it is hard for me to conceive of a closer attachment than that which we have already between us. I have always felt about as close to you as it is possible to feel. Still, there has undoubtedly been added something more by this experience. It IS *as though we were one, for I constantly feel that I am representing you here as well as myself. You need never feel as though you were "not doing your bit," for you are here with me. That is the way I feel.*[11]

There was one more letter—dated September 25, the day before the battalion went into battle at Marcheville. The letter was long and full and spoke of several private matters. Raymond asked Ed for his current sentiments about the war and wrote of his expected return to the *Transcript* after the war was over, speculating as to whether it would be necessary to seek some other employment.[12] That was the last letter.

A dark period followed during which the family had no letters and no resolution regarding Raymond's whereabouts. The Spanish Flu pandemic raged in Boston and around the world, but the

Chamberlin family was consumed with greater worry for Raymond. Then, on November 1 came the telegram from Washington: "Deeply regret to inform you that Private Raymond Chamberlin, Machine Gun Battalion, is officially reported as missing in action since September twenty six. Will report first information received."[13]

The news, with Raymond's picture, was published in the *Transcript* that same day. It fell to Ed to deliver the sad news to family and loved ones. They could not believe Raymond was dead. He must be a prisoner! Kind letters from dear friends sustained them during the dreadful time of waiting. The family continued to write letters to Raymond, imagining he was alive and in a German prison camp. But as some of the wounded soldiers from his company began to return home, one of them told Ed the truth "squarely": "Blown to pieces by a shell!"[14]

Raymond's diary was brought back to Ed by a private into whose hands he had placed it and other articles before the fateful day. Later known as the Battle of the Argonne Forest, the fierce fighting between September and November would culminate in the German surrender on Armistice Day, November 11, 1918.

Official confirmation of Raymond's death finally arrived by telegram on March 22, 1919, five months and seventeen days after he went missing.[15]

Raymond's death left Ed bereft. Every day of the following winter, he clung to his youngest daughter Dolly's arm as they walked slow and sorrowful miles around the Chestnut Hill Reservoir near her home outside of Boston.[16]

Finally, Ed turned to writing to assuage his grief. In 1921, he published a small book tribute to Raymond entitled *The Only Thing for a Man to Do*. It was a father's ode to a precious son. He shared Raymond's life story and letters from the front and told of Raymond's eternal optimism, humor in times of stress, and love for his fellow soldiers. Raymond's life was personified by a special gift for love: "Love—that was his genius, love of his country, love of family and kindred, love of the man's duty, and the tenderer love whose brooding presence left him neither night nor day." Ed closed the book with the confident assertion that if Raymond "had known just what was coming, there would not have been one smile less, nor one shrinking step."[17]

Even as American casualties mounted, Helen Keller maintained her neutral stance on the war. After it was over, as a further demonstration of her expressed impartiality and feeling toward the people of Germany, Helen requested that the publisher of the German translation of her book *The Story of My Life* turn the proceeds over to charities serving blinded German soldiers.[18]

CHAPTER SEVENTEEN

Reconnection

Ed must have had a sense of déjà-vu as he wrote to Helen on *Transcript* letterhead on May 9, 1930, and asked if she would be willing to write a piece for an upcoming celebration of the three hundredth anniversary of the founding of the city of Boston. Nearly forty years had passed since Ed had written his request for Helen's "little story" for *Youth's Companion* in 1892.

Now, Ed was in his late seventies, still mentally alert and professionally productive. He was now writing both the "Listener" and "Nomad" columns for the *Transcript,* regarded as affectionately as ever by his readers.

Helen was a spry almost fifty-year-old whose story was known throughout the world. She was active in multiple causes, tirelessly advocating for people with vision loss and others who were overlooked in society. Annie was sixty-four and in poor health. They had sold their house in Wrentham in 1917, about the same time as Raymond went off to war, and were residing in Forest Hills, New York, closer to Helen's work with the American Foundation for the Blind, which had been founded in 1921 by M. C. Migel, a philanthropist who wanted to help the large number of veterans blinded in World War I. Helen began working with the organization in 1924.[1]

Helen and Annie's dear friend and advocate Alexander Graham Bell had passed away in August 1922 at the age of seventy-five, from complications of diabetes and anemia. At the news of his death, every AT&T telephone in America fell silent for one minute in tribute to the great inventor.[2]

Sometime after 1924, Ed's second wife, Nilda, passed away. But he did not remain alone for long. On October 30, 1926, at age seventy-five, Ed married Jenny LeRoyer. She was sixty-three, of French origin, and taught her native language at a private school in Boston. The couple purchased a home in the Boston suburb of South Hanson but maintained two residences—moving into town during the school year for her work. In Jenny, Ed found himself "highly blessed with a most kind, devoted, attentive, companionable, cheering wife, with a mind as well as a heart, who fills his days with interest as well as cares for all his wants."[3]

As he began his letter to Helen on that May day in 1930, Ed picked up the threads of friendship with facility:

Dear Helen:

We do not hear much from each other in these latter days of the world, but I am sure we often think of each other; and Uncle Ed is still at the accustomed desk where—or very near where—you and Teacher sometimes used to visit him. But no Wrentham nowadays; I have transferred my country allegiance to a little place with a garden and orchard down in the general direction of Wrentham, but over in Plymouth County near a little village called South Hanson, where I cultivate more roses than memories. It is very nice. And I am well, and as "happy as the law allows." . . . While I have joy in saluting you and Teacher, I have to confess that this letter is not primarily ascribable to that purpose.

He described the book that the Tercentenary Committee was putting together and hoped that Helen might contribute to it, as "we want to put some life and sentiment into this supplemental volume, which is expected to hit the high spots of Boston's life in the times since you were born." Before closing the request, he assured her, "You will be in good company in its pages, for some distinguished people are going to contribute chapters."[4]

Ed's letter reached Helen in Cornwall, England, where she was touring Great Britain with Annie and Polly—a visit made even richer by Polly's return to her native Scotland. Helen responded several months later with the requested article and a lengthy letter to her longtime friend:

Dear Uncle Ed,

I am sending you something for the Boston Tercentenary Book, as you requested. Neither Teacher nor I feel satisfied with it. I find it impossible to put new life into these old memories. I have already written about Boston in "The Story of My Life" and "Midstream," and you know how hackneyed a subject becomes when it is gone over and over. Even the loveliest experiences become tedious by too much retelling. Repetition makes one self-conscious and over-critical. One is afraid of emphasizing what is unimportant and making little of an important matter. Besides, the people one admires seem quite different from one mood to another according to the moment of recording, which is another way of saying that whatever one writes is all about oneself.

I want you to feel free to make any changes you may think advisable—if indeed these recollections seem worth bothering about at all. It will not hurt my feelings if you consign them to the wastebasket.

You will see that I have confined myself to the Boston of my childhood and youth. I have tried very hard to keep the rosy glow of first love. The years have rudely brushed away some of the bright illusions of the young girl, and tarnished the golden dream of a city of friends and lovers of liberty.

In later years I have had little patience with the intolerant, self-complacent attitude of Boston towards liberal ideas. Every atom of me protested against the execution of Sacco and Vanzetti, and I still feel that some terrible retribution will overtake Boston for that monstrous deed. The harshness of Boston's censorship of literature is another black mark against the city. But those sins are of a later day, and I felt that they had no place in my recollections. The Boston of my dreams—the City of Kind Hearts—is real to me, and will, I believe, outlast the reactionary and spiritually blind city of the present day.

Helen then turned to the subject of her renewed acquaintance with Ed: "Yes, dear friend, Teacher and I often speak of you, and we were glad to get your letter and to hear such pleasant news—that you are well and reasonably happy. I have a dear picture of you in your garden and orchard, just as I used to know you. I never think of you as part of the crowded life of cities, I see you always in a quiet village where nature talks to you in the language of sunbeam and falling dew, bird and blossom."

Helen, Annie, and Polly had spent ten weeks in Cornwall before going to Ireland and then Essex. Helen gave glowing descriptions of the villages and cities they visited and lamented that they "must soon return to New York, and I must break myself in to the desk again. . . . It will cost us a wrench of the heart to leave this isle so rich in peace and rustic charm. As soon as we get back, my work for the blind will take me far a-field, first to Detroit, where I am to speak at the opening of a training cottage for sightless children."

Before signing off, she detailed a recent trip to Edinburgh and then finished, "The trio sends you affectionate greetings. To me you remain the friend whose universal sympathy woke an echo in my heart that has never been silent since the lovely days I spent at Red Farm."[5]

Helen's piece for the tercentenary was thirteen typewritten pages and included fond recollections of times at Red Farm. There, she had been "initiated into the mysteries of trees and wild flowers, the stone walls and green pastures of New England." She reflected on the personalities of the Chamberlins' circle of friends and their contributions toward her lifelong love of nature and the out of doors. She was grateful for Ed's belief in her ambition to attend Radcliffe and support of her "in the face of strong opposition."[6]

Ed was traveling abroad—also in Europe—when Helen's letter arrived in the editorial rooms at the *Transcript*, but he responded when he was able on November 29, thanking her for the Boston piece, which he said "really was a beautiful thing."

Ed was overwhelmed with joy at renewing the friendship with Helen. The difference in age between them, and the years in which they had not seen each other, all fell away. These were two sympathetic souls in deep and intimate communication with one another in a friendship ripened by time and experience. They reveled in it. He wrote,

Your letter to me . . . has gladdened my heart for all the rest of my life. The dear old days when you were with us all are brought back by it, and old delights live again. I thank you, dear Helen, for the words, the thoughts, the sentiments, which you have here committed to paper, and I shall value your letter among my most prized possessions. Some few good friends here read the letter and they cannot say enough in praise of it. I want to say that I am absolutely in sympathy with what you say about the Sacco and Vanzetti case and about Boston's other moral derelictions, and I am not sorry that I allowed the powers that be at City Hall to read the words. Perhaps your kindly but indignant message will do them good.

As in the "old days" of their friendship, Ed went to lengths to make his description of his own recent European travels illuminating for Helen. He had been to France and Spain and described his new appreciation for El Greco, who "paints the depths of the soul." He wished he could help her to see them.

Finally, he closed the letter: "I have lost track now of your programme after your return, but I know that you have been busy and have been shedding light on the paths of your countrymen and countrywomen. Bless you for thinking of me in the midst of your activities! . . . My best love to Teacher, and greetings to all who are with you and are good to you. I simply cannot thank you enough for complying so kindly with my request about the article and for your splendid letter."[7]

Work always beckoned. Among other projects, the year 1930 saw Ed preparing a history of the *Transcript*, eventually titled *A History of the Boston Transcript: Its First Hundred Years.* Some believed that selecting Ed, the paper's "grand old man," to write the history was "an unfortunate choice because his own part in the making of the newspaper was modestly kept in the background."[8] By 1930, the *Transcript* was known as the Brahmins' favorite newspaper, but Ed noted in his book that "the ear the *Transcript* sought from its first day was 'Genteel Boston,' meaning not just its old stock Brahmins, but the entrepreneurial middle and upper middle classes aspiring to live more like them."[9]

The paper was traditional, cherished, and venerable. And T. S. Eliot added additional cachet with the publication of his poem, "The Readers of the *Boston Evening Transcript,*" in *Prufrock and Other Observations.*[10]

As Ed was composing his *Transcript* history, an editor named Nella Braddy Henney was writing a comprehensive biography of Annie Sullivan. She had contacted Ed in 1927, asking if he could provide any insights or material for the book, which he did.[11]

Following publication of *Anne Sullivan Macy: The Story behind Helen Keller* in 1933, Ed wrote to Henney, praising the work and asking her if "at your first opportunity, will you give my deepest love to Annie and Helen? They are often, very often, in my thoughts. You have written a great book in this story of Annie, and I thank you for making mention of me in it."[12]

It was only just prior to the publication of the biography that Annie shared with Helen for the first time the details of the poverty and horror of her own childhood. Since the book would bring out that history, she knew she must tell Helen herself before it went to print.

The story of Annie's rescue from Tewksbury and subsequent education at Perkins before going to Tuscumbia to work with Helen was now known the world over. Annie was often called a miracle worker for her teaching and instruction, but Helen had an understanding of the altogether different miracle wrought from Annie's pitiful beginnings and the devotion of her life to Helen.[13]

In his "Listener" column for January 5, 1934, Ed reviewed Henney's book. He knew Annie as few others did, having met her as a young woman in her early twenties and having lived with her intermittently over many years as she matured in her own right. Ed's public and private praise for the book would affect both Helen and Annie deeply. He wrote,

A book of very considerable local interest is Miss Nella Braddy's [sic] *"Anne Sullivan Macy, the Story Behind Helen Keller." It portrays the rise of a poor girl born in western Massachusetts of a pair of destitute refugees from the Irish famine and brought up chiefly in the Tewksbury Almshouse to a unique position of credit and honor as the teacher of Helen Keller. Boston figures of great interest march through the pages of this book, but its principal feature of interest is the picture of the overcoming by an honorable career of a handicap of humble and institutional life portrayed in the life and education of Anne Sullivan. . . .*

In Miss Braddy's hands, Annie Sullivan is at once the most individual and the most positive observer, and the most modest. She has sunk her personality in that of Helen Keller all her life, but her highly positive and even dogmatic character and opinions have never been lost. . . . There is no question that the genius that is attributed to Helen is in great part the product of Annie Sullivan's phenomenal power of concentration and her iron determination. It is true, as Miss Braddy in one place intimates, that Annie Sullivan and Helen Keller really constitute a single personality and are to be thought of as one person.

When Annie Sullivan endowed Helen Keller with language she really endowed her with life.

As he had years before in various articles, Ed once again expressed his belief that Helen was not intellectually exceptional but instead possessed a different sort of genius, writing that

Helen Keller's natural gifts were very good but in no way exceptional. Perhaps her only "natural gift" was her deprivation of sight and hearing, for this deprivation relieved her of the endless observation of and subservience to details which scatter and dissipate the average human intelligence. The absence of these faculties concentrated at one fell swoop the mind of Helen Keller on her use of the language of the finger. . . . All the world passed through the tips of the fingers, and the power of getting it in that way became with its development a new power of rationalization which revealed a new form of genius.

Ed addressed the much-discussed "moment at the water-pump" when Helen discovered language: "It was a tremendous experience. Religions have been founded on less. But if April 5, 1887, was a momentous day for Helen, it was no less so for her teacher, not because Helen had at last got a firm grip on the key to language, but because that night Helen, for the first time of her own accord, snuggled into bed with her and kissed her." Ed knew that "up to this time all had been mere mummery in Helen's instruction. Her soul was still alone, still cold toward the author of this jugglery. Now an idea had passed to her from another, and she realized what her teacher was doing for her. Her gratitude and love were aroused." Ed added, "Annie Sullivan records it: 'I thought my heart would burst, it was so full of joy.' The loneliness that had tracked her since her little brother Jimmie's death was gone now. Struggle and sorrow and disappointment lay ahead, but there was someone to share it. Nothing could be as dreadful as it had been."

Ed Chamberlin understood Annie Sullivan as few others did. And he believed that the biography by Henney captured her singular brilliance.[14]

A year after Henney's book came out and a month after Ed's "Listener" column on the subject, on February 2, 1934, Helen wrote to Ed from South Arcan, Scotland, where the trio was staying with Polly's brother and his family:

Dear Uncle Ed,

Mr. Allen [retired director of the Perkins School] has sent me "The Listener" containing your comments on Nella Braddy's "Anne Sullivan Macy." It is splendid! I have not seen Teacher so moved since the book came out. She exclaimed "O Helen, is it not wonderful that Uncle Ed should write so appreciatively of me after all these years!"

As for myself, I feel it is just like your dear self who looks so tenderly into human hearts and records so sincerely what you see in them. I am gratefully happy that such a discerning friend has set the seal of highest approbation upon Teacher.

Helen praised the freshness of Ed's writing: "What I marvel at is the vigor and resiliency of your style. It is now more than thirty years since Teacher and I began reading 'The Listener' with delight. Since then how many of our friends, bipeds, and quadrupeds, have lived again in that column. How often your wise interpretation and gentle humor have explained to me strange happenings and perplexing traits of character! . . . Mr. Allen tells me you are looking well, and he thinks you are writing better than ever. You are simply wonderful, Uncle Ed!"

She continued her reflections: "The biography has been a revelation to most of our friends. No one in the world knew the whole story, and very few even a small part of it. The aridity of the first fourteen years of Annie's life has astonished everybody, even myself. . . . And despite all this penury and neglect Annie caught from somewhere a sense of beauty, the harmony of words and a desire for knowledge." Helen could not help but feel anger that Annie had languished for four years in the almshouse before finally being rescued—though philanthropists and supposed do-gooders often visited. To her it was "an atrocity."

Helen then reminisced about times at Red Farm and spoke again of how grateful she was for the experiences they had there—in "the circle of charming hospitality" where they enjoyed intellectually stimulating and satisfying conversations with "persons who had done large things." She wrote that they both looked back on those days as the "richest and brightest" experiences of their lives.

Helen was confident she and Ed would be aligned in their views on current events around the world, telling him, "Oh Uncle Ed, there is so much I should like to say, and time presses, and I want to get this letter to you while my impression of your review is still fresh. I am hungry for a good talk with you about the strange times we are living in—times that bring soul-shaking doubts and profound disillusionment. But amid the wreck selfish interests have wrought in America I think—I hope we are learning something. If we discover how our marvelous resources have been wasted and misdirected, that will be a step forward."[15]

The year 1933 had seen Helen in world news as her book *How I Became a Socialist* was banned by the Nazis and burned in a mass book burning in Berlin. Helen wrote a sharp letter of protest in the *New York Times,* boldly addressed to "the Student Body of Germany": "History has taught you nothing if you think you can kill ideas. Tyrants have tried to do that often before, and the ideas have risen up in their might and destroyed them. You can burn my books and the books of the best minds in Europe, but the ideas in them have seeped through a million channels and will continue to quicken other minds. I gave all the royalties of my books [to blinded German soldiers] with no thought in my heart but love and compassion for the German people."[16]

"Do not imagine your barbarities to the Jews are unknown here," she added. "God sleepeth not, and He will visit his Judgment upon you."[17] She rebuked both Hitler and Mussolini "for their ideologies of hate" in subsequent essays and statements, and particularly feared for individuals with disabilities.[18]

Helen shared more of her political and moral views and then closed her letter to Ed: "With affectionate greetings from our nest in the heather, and with the wish that we may sometime give you an idea of what Scotland means to us in renewed energy and happiness for the future, I am, as always, Faithfully your friend."[19]

He responded eagerly a few weeks later:

It is a great joy to get into communication with you once more—my own fault, I am sure, that we have been out of touch so long. I cannot tell you how deeply I have been delighted to receive your lovely letter from the far-away Scottish village. And your "Dear Uncle Ed" falls upon my ear as the sweetest melody of which the human voice is capable. It brings back the dear old times when we explored the stone walls and canoed the lake together. It has been a long separation, but I know there has never been a day in all that time when you and Teacher have been absent from my thoughts.

Ed continued on the subject of the Annie Sullivan biography: "I took it up really with apprehension, but was soon struck and overcome by its remarkable power. I can imagine that Teacher herself has had certain misgivings about it, but she may dismiss them—she comes out of the book greater than she could ever have appeared without it, and nearer and more deeply esteemed by all her friends."

As always, Ed's affection for Annie was obvious: "I read with delight, dear Helen, every word you wrote [in your letter] about Teacher. . . . I send my dear love to her. I sorrow for the affliction of the terrible impairment of her eyesight. I have myself nearly lost my hearing—distressing enough, but mild in comparison with her affliction. I can't hear the robin singing on the apple tree over my head, but anyhow I can see him!"

Ed could not pass up the opportunity to talk of world politics with Helen, and shared his views of recent events abroad, and was "glad to read in your letter the evidence that you retain your faith in the regenerating force of mankind."

Finally, he wrote, "I too yearn for a good talk with you and a chance to get a little of that inspiration with which you always abounded. I thank you earnestly for your letters—there is a lot of inspiration in that—it chirks me up wonderfully."[20]

A month or so later, on April 15, 1934, Helen wrote to Ed's wife Jenny from Ross-shire, Scotland, perhaps because Ed was ill. She referred to the deafness that now quieted Ed's days:

It was lovely to receive with the spring-time of birds and the first daffodils of the garden two letters from you and Uncle Ed. Teacher and I wanted to be ever there with you and tell you, as one can tell only with smiles, how sweet it is to have you both understand us so truly and give us a place in your household thoughts.

Please tell Uncle Ed, I was glad to have news of his family and his home in South Hanson where his spirit is really at liberty. I am thankful that his eyes are still quick to follow the robin flitting in and out of the apple-trees, but I cannot get used to the idea of his deafness. It is strange to find myself in thought holding out one hand to him in a world of silence and the other to Teacher in the dark! But life need not be dark or void while we see and hear with our hearts. It is a comfort to know that he keeps well, and that you are his "Listener" to the confused voices of the outer world.

Helen was concerned for Annie, who had been ill since December, writing that "despite my anxiety . . . it has been a blessed experience for me to have real leisure, read at length and shake long quiescent thoughts out of the closets of my mind. I have just finished 'Pepys's Diary,' (thirty-one volumes in Braille!) and I am hoping to read 'Boswell's Johnson.' If things are good to us three, we shall soon visit London, and under its fascination throw off our moods 'sicklied o'er' with nursing and the sense of pain."

As usual, Helen was enjoying vigorous health and thriving on hiking and fresh air, accompanied by Polly:

We are living through a Highland spring the beauty of which defies any but a Poet's description. Polly and I had a glorious two hours' "hike" over wild moor-land and through the woods looking for gulls' nests (The gulls come in by the firths and breed on the edge of ponds in deep woods.) On the way I found a lap-wing's egg in one of the furrows of a ploughed field. Do you know, those eggs are delicious? Many lap-wings flew over us. . . . When we reached the tiny loch where the gulls were, we found that their nests were in the middle of it, on little islands, and we could not manage wading to them, but it was a darling spot surrounded by pines, with exquisite reflections in the water of boughs and gull-wings. We visited another pond overshadowed by birches.

It was a physical exhilaration to clamber up the Scottish braes, to feel the heather and bracken brush against my knee and the larchee whistling in a sportive breeze. Polly kept seeing a different bird at almost every step—splendid wild geese and ducks migrating northward, wood doves, pheasants and partridges, and O the delirious joy of the larks shouting alleluias to Spring! Everywhere I caught the honey-sweet fragrance of gorse blossoms. To my great content I found the first primroses and, by keeping the soil about their roots, I carried them home fresh to Teacher. After she had seen them, they were planted under the drawing room window.

As we pushed our way over the moor and climbed over stone dykes, I kept thinking of Wrentham days when Uncle Ed's children and I used to go in search of violets and bring home great bunches that made Uncle Ed exclaim at their rich color and abundance.

I could hardly believe my fingers when reports from America were spelled to me of the bleak inaccessibility of our retreat and four feet of snow around the farm-house where hundreds of sheep had been grazing all winter! We have never had four inches of snow, and what there was of it has not been enough to cover the countryside. So we have felt that we were the ones to be envied in this mild climate while New England shivered through a bitter winter. With Teacher's and Polly's greetings to you both, and with the hope that we may all meet some wonderful day and talk as it is not possible to write, I am, Affectionately yours, Helen Keller [21]

Time and distance had only strengthened the connection between Helen and Ed.

CHAPTER EIGHTEEN

A Gentle Influence

The day that Helen had longed for, when she and Ed could be together to talk in a way that was not possible by letter, came the following winter in February 1935, when she traveled to Boston and visited the ailing Ed at his home in South Hanson. She wrote to a friend that Ed had been "very ill indeed and anxious to see me."[1] As they reminisced and talked, both must have known this would be their last conversation, and an urgency, as well as a sadness, must have hung over it. He had been so much a part of her childhood, and she had inspired him in return.

Helen wrote that she and Polly had then "motored out to Wrentham of sad and sweet memories." She found it greatly changed and observed that she doubted it was "ever a very happy experience to revisit places we have especially loved in the past."[2]

Helen was glad she had made the time to see Ed. Five months later, on July 6, he died of heart disease and pneumonia.[3]

A telegram was sent immediately to Helen and Annie on vacation in the Catskills. The next day, Helen wrote to Ed's widow, Jenny:

Dear Aunt Jenny:

I received with tender sorrow, up here in the Catskills, the telegram with the news of dear Uncle Ed's death. When I last saw him, so brave and interested in everything, I could not think that he would leave us so soon. If I could take you and the others who loved him in my arms, you would feel the sympathy no words can utter. I realize that there can be no consolation for the loss of one whose life was a part of your own, but affection will speak—the affection my teacher and I have had for Uncle Ed during many years.

We remember how he always understood and appreciated us both. The tears come as I think how bound up he is with the fateful experience of our lives, how, when an attempt was made to separate me from my teacher, he was loyal to us. I cannot express my emotion as I recall the hospitality with which he and his family took us into their home and their belief in us when we most needed faith to overcome our difficulties.

I live over and over again the merry play-time with Uncle Ed's children, the delights of woodland peace and roadside beauty we shared. What a wealth of thought he introduced me to in books and the talk of his friends who looked at things in a fresh way, so that the world grew young again with their new interpretation of it!

I loved Uncle Ed also for his intelligent grasp of my teacher's work and her problem of rendering life as normal for me as possible. One of the things that have brought me the most pleasure was his splendid review of her biography.

His attitude towards my limitations was noble. He looked beyond them to my soul dowered with imagination and the desire to know. There was nothing sense-arrogant about him, I found it easy to talk on any subject or be silent. That is a precious kind of friendship in a world where those who have the full quota of faculties too often impose their individuality upon the handicapped. Uncle Ed wished always to speak to me with his lips—that was an expression of his intense desire to see broken all barriers that stand between mankind and their heritage of freedom and joy.

We saw him seldom after he left Wrentham, but the thought of his personality shed warmth upon me, and now that he is gone, the world will not seem quite the same again.

I hope Uncle Ed did not suffer at the end. It is sweet to know he had the comfort of your ministering love. Perhaps sometime you may feel like writing me the particulars.

With my teacher's sincere sympathy, in which Polly joins, and with a touch-picture of you together that I shall ever cherish, I am,

Lovingly yours, Helen Keller.[4]

A friendship that had begun with an invitation for the young Helen and her teacher to visit his family became deep and lifelong. Ed affected Helen and Annie profoundly. In many ways, they both grew up in his care. Although later years did not allow them to be together often, they remained in one another's thoughts. He was fascinated by the bravery and optimism with which Helen faced each day. It was a friendship deeply rooted in shared sympathies, mutual respect, and love.

And now, Uncle Ed, the friend, the man who defined himself as a father, a listener, and a nomad, was at rest. He was mourned by his family, many friends, colleagues young and old, and his faithful readers. Among tributes in newspapers from coast to coast, *Editor and Publisher* magazine called him the "dean of Boston editors." A *New York Herald Tribune* editorial on July 9 commented, "He was one of the most widely recognized staff writers of his times," noting that, "he enjoyed a common touch with men of less than mighty affairs and he wrote with mellowness at no expense to his soundness and penetration." A columnist for the *Berkshire Evening Eagle* of Pittsfield, Massachusetts, also mourned his passing, saying "he was mentally gifted, well educated, blessed with an extraordinary memory, and had a fund of knowledge that was available in any newspaper office. To his associates . . . he was a joy and a comfort. Genial, friendly, sympathetic, brilliantly endowed, he made the burden easier for those who worked out with him the harsh problems of every day professional life."[5]

Among those affected most deeply by his death was Helen Keller, the woman Ed had nurtured in so many ways.

Several months later, Jenny Chamberlin responded to Helen's letter, thanking her for the beautiful tribute:

Very dear Helen,

How kind you have been to take the trouble when you were SO *busy, to write that beautiful appreciation of Uncle Ed. And how can I thank you enough! For these works of pure love which you do constantly there are no words that can express it. Any more than we can express the profound gratitude which we feel for your heroic Teacher to have given you to the world. What deep love and kind heartedness, devotion she has shown to us all.*

How many times your dearest Uncle Ed has told of your wonderful courage and the INTELLIGENT COURAGE *you have had, guided through it all with that loving heart and bright* INTELLECT OF TEACHER *. . . . When I am in tears for the absent, your names make me remember the word courage. Heroic courage. . . .*

Privy to Ed's innermost thoughts, Jenny added a provocative note, providing tantalizing insight into Ed's personal crisis at the time he separated from Ida in 1901: "Thank you dearest, kind Helen . . . to have given him such deep joy when you were a little girl, that profound peace you gave him amidst the most terrific storm of his existence."[6]

Perhaps the storm swirling around him when he left his family was Ed's "most terrific." Ida believed he had committed suicide at the time—and her fears were apparently warranted. He came breathtakingly close. Decades later, Charles J. Edson, Ed's former colleague at the New York *Evening Mail,* wrote in an unpublished manuscript: "When I was on the Evening *Mail,* Joseph Edgar Chamberlain *[sic]*, the literary editor, told me he once had reached a similar conclusion [that the only solution to his troubles was suicide]. . . . Taking his pistol, he went behind the shrubberies in Central Park. But no sooner had he put the pistol to his head than he heard the voices of his children [in his head] crying: 'Don't do it, Daddy! Don't do it for our sakes!'" Ed's disclosure of his own despondency and recovery kept Edson from taking his own life some years later.[7]

Just a year after Ed's death, in October 1936, Helen grieved the passing of her beloved teacher. Annie's health had not been good for many years, so her death at the age of seventy did not come as a surprise. They had prepared for her eventual passing by integrating Polly Thomson so deeply into their lives. Annie Sullivan was the first woman interred in the Washington National Cathedral—a pioneering teacher and world-famous figure in the field of disabilities education.

In 1937, two years after Ed's death, Jenny Chamberlin published *Nomads and Listeners,* containing selected reprints of his "Nomad" and "Listener" columns. The small volume featured a brief biography by Samuel M. Waxman.[8] He summarized a writing career that spanned nearly seven decades:

During Ed's long newspaper career, which began in 1868 . . . [his] pen was always active. In sickness and in health, in office or on vacation, he never failed to do his daily bit of writing. Although he held no executive position on the Transcript, *he was for many years its chief editorial writer as well as writer of special columns. He was in recent years its grand old man, to whom many an editor and department head turned for help and counsel. The younger members of the staff, especially, found in him a sympathetic and kindly guide. It was much easier and pleasanter to consult Chamberlin than to go to an encyclopedia. When the time came to write the history of the first hundred years of the* TRANSCRIPT, *it was Chamberlin who was assigned to do that work. "How can you write the history of the* TRANSCRIPT?*" wrote one of his friends. ["]You* ARE *the* TRANSCRIPT.*" True enough. . . . Important assignments such as presidential interviews were entrusted to him, and he once remarked that he had interviewed every president of the United States from Grant to Coolidge.*

Waxman spoke of Ed's approach to life, observing,

Chamberlin was indeed a listener as well as a nomad, listening, as he wandered through wood and meadow, to the song of a bird or to the sigh of the wind. In social groups he spoke very little, generally listening to what the man about town had to say about politics, or the arts and letters. His greatest recreation was working in his garden. I do not believe there was a species of American tree or flower, wild or cultivated, which he could not name. He tenderly loved trees and flowers and birds, and he did not discriminate against the lowliest weed in favor of the most delicate rose.

Further,

There was something tender and wistful about Chamberlin. He had more than his share of the buffetings of fate, but retained his sweetness to the very end. In spite of long periods of illness, major operations, and increasing deafness in his later years, he was never querulous. There was much that was feminine in his make-up, and because of this trait he drew to him the sympathies of many women, among them writers of note. I do not mean to infer that he was effeminate or did not enjoy the company of men. He left a trail of loyal men friends wherever he went.

Ed "regretted deeply throughout his life that he could not follow in his mother's steps as far as religion was concerned." Although he never joined a church, he was—

extremely reverent in his attitude toward the unknown and unknowable. . . . He once remarked that he was sure he had been an oak tree in a previous incarnation. Of all the religions he had studied . . . he was most strongly drawn to the religion of the North American Indian. . . . His God was closely akin to the Great Spirit of the Indians whom he knew and loved in the days when he hunted with them in Wisconsin [young Indian boys had been some of his playmates as a child]. He firmly believed that he would meet face to face in another world those whom he had loved in this world.[9]

Helen Keller lived a long and fulfilling life until she passed away in 1968 at the age of eighty-seven. After her death, she was interred in the National Cathedral beside her Teacher, and the pair's devoted friend and companion during the last years of their lives, Polly Thomson, who had passed away in 1960.

While countless people know the story of young Helen's discovery of language, many do not know of the greater accomplishments and layers of her life. She was an iconic figure and trailblazer in her time, driven throughout her life by passion such as that which caused her to lend early support to Ida's idea for a school for the deaf and blind: the hope that all who were afflicted like herself should "receive their rightful inheritance of thought, knowledge, and love." She was often controversial and confrontational in her radical politics, theology, social views, and vehement advocacy for the poor and persons with disabilities, but she was always captivating as a personality and admired for her courage and tenacity.

The house at Red Farm still stands today, though it is no longer a working farm and its many barns and outbuildings have been cleared away over time. The dirt lane in front of the house is now a busy, paved road, and Wrentham is no longer the rural, lakeside resort town it was in the late 1890s. The story of the household that Ed and Ida created there has largely been lost to history. Their circle of friends is dispersed, and their names and accomplishments mostly forgotten.

But when reading Ed's last literary contribution, *Nomads and Listeners,* one is struck by the modernity of his writing. The book remains a surprisingly contemporary soliloquy on topics ranging from war, poverty, celebrities and political figures, education, gardens, and travel to a study of the differences in personality between the family's two cats, Snowflake and Dinah. As Helen once wrote to Annie Pratt, "One cannot be with him and not feel something of his gentle influence."[10]

Kindred and fearless souls, Ed and Helen were both compelled to write the truth as they saw it in life's large and small experiences. She lost her senses of sight and hearing at a young age, but he would most generously share his own acute senses with her, giving her powerful tools of observation and thought in order to imagine and understand the world around her, and ultimately to help reveal her own strong voice.

Ed Chamberlin's pen may be silenced, but the memory of the man and his influence endures.

AFTERWORD

In a small, hidden graveyard in the town of East Corinth, Vermont, where the Chamberlins often vacationed, Ida is buried next to her children Charley and Corda. Her marker reads, "Ida Atwood Chamberlin, Wife of Joseph Edgar Chamberlin."

About ten miles away, in the Chamberlin family plot in the Oxbow Cemetery in Newbury, stands a granite monument to Raymond, the son lost to war. Next to him, Joseph Edgar Chamberlin lies quietly among the primitive, timeworn, slate markers of his ancestors.

As one of his fellow journalists wrote in a tribute to Ed's memory in July 1935, "I am fond of believing that such lives as his live on and on and on, ever regnant in their spirit, ever tireless in their interpretations of life, ever competent in their service, ever unselfish in all they do. They are a balm for hurt souls, they soothe when, on breaking hearts, the shadows fall."[1]

It would seem to be so.

ACKNOWLEDGMENTS

This book is the culmination of years of research and the helping hands of many people along the way. I have loved this project and am fortunate that so much information about Ed Chamberlin's friendship with Helen Keller was left behind for me to uncover. And so many times it felt like the story just somehow found its way to me. It was a writer's dream.

First, I owe a debt of gratitude to my longtime friend Martha Bennett Stiles, whose enthusiasm motivated me to start down this path. My son, Colin, was my first reader of the manuscript draft and has been my cheerleader every step of the way. A big debt of gratitude to my daughter, Julie, for her many talents and for never letting me give up hope. My daughter-in-law, Fon, was a buoyant spirit in late phases of writing and editing. Special thanks to my husband, Rick, for his understanding and patience.

Sincere thanks to Helen Selsdon at the American Foundation for the Blind for both her scholarship and her generous spirit. Jennifer Arnott, research librarian at the Perkins School, and her colleagues Jennifer Hale and Susanna Coit brought wonderful energy and resources to my research. Patricia Fanning was a kindred writing spirit who shared my excitement about every discovery and was so helpful in her sharing of resources. Linda Waggoner gave just the right spark when I needed it. Luz and Will Schick were fellow "information hounds" who dug up bits that I would never have found if they hadn't reached out to me. Will was also a generous technology and media assistant. Officials at the Wrentham Historical Society were most helpful and generously put me in touch with the Murray family, current owners of Red Farm. They have all been incredibly helpful.

Extra thanks and acknowledgment to my sister, Nancy Schumm, whose research into Ed's early years in Wisconsin and Chicago was so important to this story.

A big round of hugs to Carol Henderson and the women of my writers' group: Marianna Crane, Michele Murdock, Libby Puckett,

Elyse Crystal, Carol Dorsey, and the late Linda Jay. Their patience and forbearance as I read early versions aloud will not be forgotten.

Gratitude to my dear friend Tricia Willoughby. You encouraged me from the start. More thanks to Amy Spaulding, who was so supportive and connected me with Susie Wilde and a wonderful community of writers early on.

To all of my early readers, special thanks for being willing to read a long-winded version of the story: Wendy and Jim Speir, Jeanne Huntley, Amy Cunningham, Bobbi Butler, Pat Daniel, Melinda Thompson, Judy Kraska, the late Ceil Cleveland, Mary McLean, Hal Kohn, and Ken Schlect. Much gratitude to Maureen and Bob Blouin, who were eager readers and then invited me to dinner to discuss the book, thus hosting my first book discussion. I am grateful for the talent and perspective of my friend Hillary Weeks, a wonderful writer herself. Thanks also to Jane Sample and Pam Partain for friendship, enthusiasm, and literary expertise. Bob Callahan, *Boston Globe* retiree, graciously illuminated the Boston news world for me. Michelle Sherburne helped so much in understanding the Underground Railroad in New England and welcomed me to Vermont. Boston-based historian Donna Halper provided access to many archives. My cousin Michael Draelos, M.D., provided thoughtful insight into medical aspects of the story, along with unflagging enthusiasm. Peter Boshco, Dolly Chamberlin Boshco's great-grandson, graciously shared family photos and papers. Thank you.

Haben Girma, the first Deafblind graduate of Harvard Law School, was so generous to read the manuscript and offer her comments and suggestions. I owe her the biggest cinnamon roll ever made.

Many, many thanks to John Yewell and Mimi Herman, my talented Durham editors, who encouraged, cajoled, ignored my meltdowns, and labored with me over early versions of the story. The book is what it is today because of their passion for it and their belief that Ed Chamberlin deserved his rightful place in Helen's story.

Extra special thanks to my agent, Susan Schulman. From my first conversation with her, I knew I had found the perfect representation. Thank you for loving this story.

A big thank you to Brian Halley, Rachael DeShano, Margaret Hogan, and the team at University of Massachusetts Press for their commitment to the project—and especially through the challenges of a pandemic.

Finally, I thank my great-great-grandparents Ed and Ida Chamberlin for living such full and culturally and socially engaged lives, and leaving behind an incredible legacy. Because of them, and the brilliant, fascinating, and unique Helen Keller, I have this story to share. I hope I have represented Ed and Helen's friendship honestly and well.

Elizabeth Emerson
Chapel Hill, North Carolina

NOTES

NAME ABBREVIATIONS

AG	Arthur Gilman
AGB	Alexander Graham Bell
AP	Annie Pratt
AS	Anne Sullivan
EEH	Edward Everett Hale
EH	Eleanor Hutton
FHD	Fred Holland Day
HK	Helen Keller
IAC	Ida Atwood Chamberlin
JEC	Joseph Edgar Chamberlin
JH	John Hitz
JLC	Jenny LeRoyer Chamberlin
KK	Kate Keller
LDF	Lucy Derby Fuller
LIG	Louise Imogen Guiney
MA	Michael Anagnos
NBH	Nella Braddy Henney
WW	William Wade

SOURCE ABBREVIATIONS

AFB	American Foundation for the Blind, Helen Keller Archive, accessible at http://www.afb.org/HelenKellerArchive.
AGB, LOC	Alexander Graham Bell Family Papers, Library of Congress, Washington, DC (many accessible at https://www.loc.gov/collections/alexander-graham-bell-papers).
COKH article	Helen Keller, "City of Kind Hearts," draft article sent to J. E. Chamberlin and written for the Boston Tercentenary Committee, September 10, 1930, AFB Archive.
Perkins Archives	Archives, Perkins School for the Blind, Watertown, MA (many accessible at http://www.perkins.org). Collections include Anagnos-Sullivan-Keller Collection; Helen Keller and Anne Sullivan Collections; Helen Keller and Arthur Gilman Collection; Incoming and Outgoing Perkins Correspondence, 1828–1932; Kindergarten Correspondence Collection; Nella Braddy Henney Collection; Perkins Annual Reports; Scrapbooks of Clippings.

PREFACE

1. The language used to describe disabilities, and people with disabilities, has evolved and changed over time; therefore there may be inconsistencies between the language I have chosen to use and the language used by historical

figures quoted in this book. Currently, the following terms are preferred by disability activists to describe people who are both deaf and blind: deafblind, deaf-blind, DeafBlind, or Deafblind. I have chosen to use "deafblind," as it is the terminology currently being used by the Perkins School in Boston. Deafblindness is now recognized as a unique condition and a disability all on its own, as the impact of dual losses is multiplicative rather than additive. For more information, see the National Center for Deaf-Blindness, https://www.nationaldb.org.

2. Helen's early letters were written by hand in pencil, using an assistive frame, which resulted in "square-hand" lettering. After beginning her schooling at Perkins, she used a braille typewriter for much of her personal correspondence. Unless letters to Helen were written in braille, they were read to her by someone versed in the Manual Alphabet for the Blind.

INTRODUCTION

1. Samuel M. Waxman, "Joseph Edgar Chamberlin," in Joseph Edgar Chamberlin, *Nomads and Listeners of Joseph Edgar Chamberlin,* ed. Samuel M. Waxman (Cambridge, MA: Riverside Press, 1937), xvii.
2. Helen Keller, "Joseph Edgar Chamberlin," *American Magazine,* February 1912, 421–422.
3. HK to JLC, July 7, 1935, copy in author's possession.

CHAPTER ONE: THE ROAD TO BOSTON

1. Helen Keller, *Teacher: Anne Sullivan Macy* (1955; reprint Westport, CT: Greenwood Press, 1985), 69.
2. Joseph P. Lash, *Helen and Teacher: The Story of Helen Keller and Anne Sullivan Macy* (Reading, MA: Addison-Wesley, 1980), 67–69.
3. Samuel M. Waxman, "Joseph Edgar Chamberlin," in Joseph Edgar Chamberlin, *Nomads and Listeners of Joseph Edgar Chamberlin,* ed. Samuel M. Waxman (Cambridge, MA: Riverside Press, 1937), xviii.
4. Frederic P. Wells, *History of Newbury, Vermont, 1704–1902* (St. Johnsbury, VT: Caledonian, 1902), 18.
5. Eunice Miena Barber, "Richard and Abigail (Wright) Chamberlin and Their Descendants," in *Wright-Chamberlin Genealogy: From Immigrant Ancestors to Present Generations* (Binghamton, NY: Vail-Ballou, 1914), 273.
6. Wells, *History of Newbury, Vermont,* 501.
7. Chamberlin, *Nomads and Listeners,* 3.
8. Ibid.
9. Nancy L. Schumm, "Joseph Edgar Chamberlin," unpublished article, May 2015. Used with permission. Historian Nancy L. Schumm made important contributions to this chapter with her research on the Chamberlin family in Wisconsin and Chicago, and research into the Chicago journalism world of the mid- to late 1800s.
10. Chamberlin, *Nomads and Listeners,* 4.
11. Chamberlin, *Nomads and Listeners,* 12. This should be John F. Potter, representative from Wisconsin in the 35th Congress.
12. Schumm, "Joseph Edgar Chamberlin."

13. William Le Baron, *Past and Present of Lake County* (Chicago: William Le Baron, 1877), 285.
14. Michelle Arnosky Sherburne, *Abolition and the Underground Railroad in Vermont* (Charleston, SC: History Press, 2013), 10.
15. Schumm, "Joseph Edgar Chamberlin."
16. Chamberlin, *Nomads and Listeners,* 19.
17. Ibid., 20–21.
18. Peter Boshco, conversation with author, May 2018.
19. Chamberlin, *Nomads and Listeners,* 20–21.
20. Ibid., 19–24.
21. Ibid., 5.
22. Ibid., 11.
23. Ibid., 9.
24. Ibid., 13.
25. Ibid., 24.
26. Ibid., 24, 25, 2.
27. Ibid., 26.
28. Ibid.
29. "Chicago on Fire," *Chicago: City of the Century,* PBS American Experience, https://www.pbs.org.
30. Ibid.
31. Jim Murphy, *The Great Fire* (1995; reprint, New York: Scholastic, 2006), 62.
32. "Chicago on Fire."
33. "Chamberlin-Atwood Nuptials," *Chicago Sunday Times,* June 29, 1873.
34. Elisabeth Chamberlin Darling Application, Record Copy 89870, December 6, 1911, National Society of the Daughters of the American Revolution (DAR), Washington, DC; Alicia Crane Williams, "John Wood Alias Atwood of Plymouth, Massachusetts," *Mayflower Descendant* 44, no. 2 (July 1994): 137.
35. Nancy Ann Atwood, *Pleasant Memories of My Childhood* (New York: N.p., 1916), 72.
36. Everett Chamberlin, *Chicago and Its Suburbs* (Chicago: T. A. Hungerford, 1874), 273; Chamberlin, *Nomads and Listeners,* 25.
37. Franc Bangs Wilkie, *Personal Reminiscences of Thirty-Five Years of Journalism* (Chicago: F. J. Schulte, 1891), 202–205.
38. William Monroe Newton, *History of Barnard, Vermont with Family Genealogies, 1761–1927,* (Montpelier: Vermont Historical Society, 1928), 25–27; Sprague Family History, http://acfamily.org/genealogy/showmedia.php (no longer available); Sprague, Nancy Ann Atwood, 1837–1916, Papers, Schlesinger Library of the History of Women in America, Harvard University Library, Cambridge, MA, http://oasis.lib.harvard.edu; "Mrs. Nancy A. Sprague Dies," *New York Times,* March 29, 1916.
39. Gillian Anderson, "Elizabeth Sprague Coolidge," in *Notable American Women, The Modern Period: A Biographical Dictionary,* ed. B. Sicherman and C. H. Green (Cambridge, MA: Belknap Press of Harvard University Press, 1980), 160.
40. Wells, *History of Newbury, Vermont,* 504.

41. Joseph Edgar Chamberlin, *The Only Thing for a Man to Do: The Story of Raymond Chamberlin* (Boston: N.p., 1921), 2.
42. Ibid.
43. Justin E. Walsh, *To Print the News and Raise Hell—A Biography of Wilbur F. Storey* (Chapel Hill: University of North Carolina Press, 1968), 230.
44. Wilkie, *Personal Reminiscences of Thirty-Five Years of Journalism,* 202–205, 231.
45. Ibid., 239.
46. Ibid., 215, 237–242.
47. The circumstances surrounding Philip's adoption are unknown.
48. Waxman, "Joseph Edgar Chamberlin," xii–xiii.
49. Ibid., xiii.
50. J. E. Chamberlin, *A History of the Boston Transcript: Its First Hundred Years* (New York: Houghton Mifflin, 1930), 7–8. Boston was the center of American publishing and journalism in the early 1800s, though this recognition would soon shift to New York. Christopher B. Daly, *Covering America: A Narrative History of a Nation's Journalism* (Amherst: University of Massachusetts Press, 2012), 58, 106, 155.
51. Robert Callahan, *Boston Globe* retired employee, conversation with author, April 3, 2015.
52. "A History of Youth's Companion and the Pledge of Allegiance with Collectors Notes," Collecting Old Magazines.com, https://collectingoldmagazines.com.
53. Ibid.
54. Waxman, "Joseph Edgar Chamberlin," xv.
55. Patricia J. Fanning, *Artful Lives: The Francis Watts Lee Family and Their Times* (Amherst: University of Massachusetts Press, 2016), 42–44.
56. Chamberlin, *The Only Thing for a Man to Do,* 4–5.

CHAPTER TWO: HELEN AND ANNIE

1. Helen Keller, *Teacher: Anne Sullivan Macy* (1955; reprint Westport, CT: Greenwood Press, 1985), 10.
2. Helen Keller, *The Story of My Life: With Her Letters (1887–1901) and a Supplementary Account of Her Education, Including Passages from the Reports and Letters of Her Teacher, Anne Mansfield Sullivan* (New York: Doubleday, Page, 1921), 176. Note: There are multiple editions of Keller's *Story of My Life* by different publishers. In this chapter, only the Doubleday, Page version is used.
3. "Books for the Blind," Perkins School for the Blind Archives, https://www.perkins.org.
4. "Laura Bridgman," Perkins School for the Blind Archives, https://www.perkins.org.
5. HK to JEC, September 10, 1930, in COKH article.
6. Charles Dickens, *American Notes,* in *The Works of Charles Dickens* (New York: P. F. Collier, n.d.), 5:278–283. The word "dumb" is an archaic term to describe a person with a speech disorder or difficulty with speaking. Along with the word "mute," it is considered offensive.

7. Bell was the recipient of numerous honorary doctorates, beginning with an honorary Ph.D. in 1880 from Gallaudet College in Washington, DC.
8. Joseph P. Lash, *Helen and Teacher: The Story of Helen Keller and Anne Sullivan Macy* (Reading, MA: Addison-Wesley, 1980), 44, 45, 46.
9. Ibid., 48.
10. Ibid.
11. MA to AK, August 16, 1886, Sullivan-Keller-Anagnos Correspondence Collection, 1886–1895, Perkins Archives.
12. MA to AK, January 28, 1887, Sullivan-Keller-Anagnos Correspondence Collection.
13. MA to AK, January 21, 1887, Sullivan-Keller-Anagnos Correspondence Collection.
14. Kevin Hartigan, Perkins School, conversation with author and tour, July 29, 2015.
15. Keller, *The Story of My Life,* 304.
16. Ibid.
17. AS to MA, March 13, 1887, Sullivan-Keller-Anagnos Correspondence Collection.
18. Keller, *The Story of My Life,* 316.
19. AS to MA, May 23, 1887, Sullivan-Keller-Anagnos Correspondence Collection.
20. Keller, *The Story of My Life,* 325.
21. AS to MA, May 5, 1887, Sullivan-Keller-Anagnos Correspondence Collection.
22. Keller, *Teacher,* 89–90.
23. AS to MA, January 1, 1888, in Keller, *The Story of My Life,* 341.
24. Matthew Namee, "Michael Anagnos, Who Made the Sightless See," September 6, 2010, http://orthodoxhistory.org.
25. Helen Keller, "My Journey to Boston," 1888, AFB.
26. Lash, *Helen and Teacher,* 90.
27. Kim E. Nielsen, *Beyond the Miracle Worker: The Remarkable Life of Anne Sullivan Macy and Her Extraordinary Friendship with Helen Keller* (Boston: Beacon, 2009), 99.
28. Lash, *Helen and Teacher,* 90.
29. Nielsen, *Beyond the Miracle Worker,* 99.
30. *Annual Report of the Perkins Institution, 1887,* Perkins Annual Reports, 1884–1889, vols. 53–57, Perkins Archives.
31. HK to JEC, September 10, 1930, in COKH article.
32. Sara Day, *Coded Letters, Concealed Love: The Larger Lives of Harriet Freeman and Edward Everett Hale* (Washington, DC: New Academia, 2014), 109.
33. HK to JEC, September 10, 1930, in COKH article.
34. Lash, *Helen and Teacher,* 780.
35. Day, *Coded Letters, Concealed Love,* 109.
36. AS to MA, February 10, 1888, in Keller, *The Story of My Life,* 346.
37. Ibid., 135.
38. EEH to Harriet E. Freeman, May 31, 1888, quoted in Day, *Coded Letters, Concealed Love,* 136.
39. Day, *Coded Letters, Concealed Love,* 136.
40. HK to JEC, September 10, 1930, in COKH article.

41. Ibid.
42. Ibid.
43. HK to JEC, February 2, 1934, AFB.
44. Lash, *Helen and Teacher,* 91–95.
45. Mary Klages, *Woeful Afflictions: Disability and Sentimentality in Victorian America* (Philadelphia: University of Pennsylvania Press, 1999), 177.
46. Michael Anagnos, *Annual Report of the Perkins Institution, 1888,* Perkins Annual Reports.
47. "Little Helen Keller, the Blind-Deaf-Mute," *New York Times*, September 8, 1889.
48. Keller, *The Story of My Life,* 299.
49. MA to AS, March 5, 1889, Sullivan-Keller-Anagnos Correspondence Collection.

CHAPTER THREE: THE MOVE TO RED FARM

1. Lorena A. Hickok, *The Story of Helen Keller* (New York: Grosset and Dunlap, 1964), 85.
2. The Chamberlins sometimes resided at Red Farm in Wrentham and at other times in Newton Lower Falls. However, all of Helen's memories of the Chamberlins mention only Red Farm.
3. It is not clear where Helen and Annie lived during the time she was enrolled at Perkins. They were only described as "guests of the school."
4. Helen Keller, *The Story of My Life: With Her Letters (1887–1901) and a Supplementary Account of Her Education, Including Passages from the Reports and Letters of Her Teacher, Anne Mansfield Sullivan* (New York: Doubleday, Page, 1921), 55–56, 57.
5. Ibid., 57.
6. Joseph Edgar Chamberlin, *The Only Thing for a Man to Do: The Story of Raymond Chamberlin* (Boston: N.p., 1921), 5.
7. Ibid.
8. "A Brief History of Wrentham," Wrentham Historical Commission, 2019, http://www.wrentham.ma.us.
9. JEC to LIG, November 16, 1894, Louise Imogen Guiney Papers, Holy Cross Archives, Holy Cross College, Worcester, MA.
10. Sara Day, *Coded Letters, Concealed Love: The Larger Lives of Harriet Freeman and Edward Everett Hale* (Washington, DC: New Academia, 2014), 36.
11. Ibid., 2.
12. Jean Holloway, *Edward Everett Hale: A Biography* (Austin: University of Texas Press, 1956), cited in "About Edward Everett Hale," https://lend-a-hand-society.org.
13. Day, *Coded Letters, Concealed Love,* 32.
14. HK to JEC, September 10, 1930, in COKH article.
15. Bernard DeVoto, ed., *Mark Twain in Eruption: Hitherto Unpublished Pages about Men and Events* (New York: Harper and Brothers, 1940), 244. See also Paul P. Ruben, "Mary Wilkins Freeman," PAL: Perspectives in American Literature—A Research and Reference Guide, http://cstan.edu.
16. Frances Parkinson Keyes, *Roses in December* (1960; reprint New York: Third Avon Books, 1970), 332.

CHAPTER FOUR: ED CHAMBERLIN STEPS IN, 1892

1. Joseph P. Lash, *Helen and Teacher: The Story of Helen Keller and Anne Sullivan Macy* (Reading, MA: Addison-Wesley, 1980), 133.
2. Ibid., 133–134.
3. Kim E. Nielsen, *Beyond the Miracle Worker: The Remarkable Life of Anne Sullivan Macy and Her Extraordinary Friendship with Helen Keller* (Boston: Beacon, 2009), 112.
4. Helen Keller, *The Story of My Life* (New York: Airmont, 1965), 266.
5. AS to Perkins Board, June 17, 1890, Sullivan-Keller-Anagnos Correspondence Collection, Perkins Archives.
6. Matthew Namee, "Michael Anagnos, Who Made the Sightless See," September 10, 2010, https://orthodoxhistory.org.
7. Laurie Lawlor, *Helen Keller: Rebellious Spirit* (New York: Holiday House, 2001), 23.
8. Ableism is defined as "discrimination or prejudice against individuals with disabilities." Merriam-Webster Dictionary Online, https://www.merriam-webster.com.
9. Helen Keller, *The Story of My Life: With Her Letters (1887–1901) and a Supplementary Account of Her Education, Including Passages from the Reports and Letters of Her Teacher, Anne Mansfield Sullivan* (New York: Doubleday, Page, 1921), 66.
10. Lash, *Helen and Teacher,* 133.
11. Keller, *The Story of My Life* (Doubleday), 66–67.
12. Ibid., 67.
13. Lash, *Helen and Teacher,* 138, 141.
14. Keller, *The Story of My Life* (Doubleday), 71.
15. Edwin S. Grosvenor and Morgan Wesson, *Alexander Graham Bell: The Life and Times of the Man Who Invented the Telephone* (New York: Harry N. Abrams, 1997), 51–61.
16. AGB to Mabel Bell, March 10,1892, AGB, LOC.
17. Dorothy Hermann, *Helen Keller: A Life* (Chicago: University of Chicago Press, 1999), 89.
18. "The Listener," *Boston Transcript,* April 22, 1891.
19. J. E. Chamberlin, *A History of the Boston Transcript: Its First Hundred Years* (New York: Houghton Mifflin, 1930), 165–166. This emphasis mirrored the "crusading journalism" that was happening in other major cities in the United States, as described in Christopher B. Daly, *Covering America: A Narrative History of a Nation's Journalism* (Amherst: University of Massachusetts Press, 2012), 122.
20. "Seeing Helen Keller," *Boston Transcript,* December 1891.
21. The conversation is referenced in JEC to AS, March 22, 1892, AFB.
22. Ibid.
23. Lash, *Helen and Teacher,* 149.
24. John Hitz, "Helen Keller the Wonder Child," *Lend a Hand: A Record of Progress,* May 1892.
25. Adeline G. Perry, "A Visit from Helen Keller," *St. Nicholas: An Illustrated Magazine for Young Folks,* June 1892, https://www.disabilitymuseum.org.

26. As evidenced by a survey of contemporary newspaper clippings of the time; see Scrapbooks of Clippings Collection, Perkins Archives.
27. *Boston Daily Advertiser,* May 29, 1892.
28. *Boston Transcript,* May 25, 1892.
29. HK to JEC, September 10, 1930, in COKH article.
30. Equivalent dollar amount from 1892 to 2019 calculated using CPI Inflation Calculator, https://www.officialdata.org.
31. JEC to NBH, December 6, 1933, Nella Braddy Henney Collection, Perkins Archives.
32. JEC to MA, June 18, 1892, Anagnos-Sullivan-Keller Collection.
33. "Disciples of Whitman," *Boston Daily Globe,* June 1, 1892; Wenxian Zhang, "William Sloane Kennedy's Friendship with Walt Whitman and His Legacy at Rollins College," Rollins College Library Archives, November 12, 2019, https://blogs.rollins.edu.
34. JEC to Walt Whitman, March 5, 1889, "Life and Letters, Correspondence," Walt Whitman Archive, https://whitmanarchive.org. See also Joseph Edgar Chamberlin, "Walt Whitman," May 28, 1919, in Joseph Edgar Chamberlin, *Nomads and Listeners of Joseph Edgar Chamberlin,* ed. Samuel M. Waxman (Cambridge, MA: Riverside Press, 1937), 118.
35. "Disciples of Whitman," *Boston Daily Globe,* June 1, 1892.
36. J. E. Chamberlin, *John Brown: The Beacon Biographies of Eminent Americans,* ed. M. A. DeWolfe Howe (Boston: Small, Maynard, 1899).
37. Alexander Graham Bell, "The Method of Instruction Pursued with Helen Keller a Valuable Study for Teachers of the Deaf," *Silent Educator,* June 1892, 127–128, AGB, LOC.
38. ASM to JH, November 5,1892, AFB.
39. Ibid.
40. Ibid.
41. Keller, *The Story of My Life* (Doubleday), 73–74.
42. Lash, *Helen and Teacher,* 162, 164.
43. Ibid., 164.

CHAPTER FIVE: HELEN'S STORY

1. JEC to HK, December 13, 1892, AFB.
2. Joseph P. Lash, *Helen and Teacher: The Story of Helen Keller and Anne Sullivan Macy* (Reading, MA: Addison-Wesley, 1980), 164.
3. A payment of $100 in 1892 would have been equivalent to over $2,800 in 2019. CPI Inflation Calculator, https://www.officialdata.org.
4. Helen Keller, *The Story of My Life: With Her Letters (1887–1901) and a Supplementary Account of Her Education, Including Passages from the Reports and Letters of Her Teacher, Anne Mansfield Sullivan* (New York: Doubleday, Page, 1921), 212–214.
5. JEC to HK, December 21, 1892, AFB.
6. Joseph Edgar Chamberlin, *The Only Thing for a Man to Do: The Story of Raymond Chamberlin, Private* (Boston: N.p., 1921), 7.
7. In the late 1800s, nearly two out of every ten children died before the age of five. See Patricia J. Fanning, *Artful Lives: The Francis Watts Lee Family*

and Their Times (Amherst: University of Massachusetts Press, 2016), 47; David I. MacLeod, *The Age of the Child: Children in America 1890–1920* (New York: Twayne, 1998), 38; and Samuel H. Preston and Michael R. Haines, *Fatal Years: Child Mortality in Late Nineteenth Century America* (Princeton, NJ: Princeton University Press, 1991), 3.

8. JEC to AS, May 6, 1893, AFB.
9. "Volta Bureau and Laboratory," DC Historic Sites, https://historicsites.dcpreservation.org.
10. AS to JH, June 20, 1893, AFB.
11. Helen Keller, "My Story," *Youth's Companion*, January 1894, 3–4, reprinted as "Story of My Life" in Keller, *The Story of My Life* (Doubleday), 421.
12. Dorothy Herrmann, *Helen Keller: A Life* (Chicago: University of Chicago Press, 1998), 12.
13. Helen Keller, *The Story of My Life* (New York: Airmont, 1965), 18.
14. Keller, *The Story of My Life* (Doubleday), 22.
15. Keller, "My Story."
16. Ibid.
17. Keller, *The Story of My Life* (Airmont), 127.
18. JEC to AS, February 1, 1894, AFB.
19. For an understanding of theories regarding "nervous conditions" at the time, see John F. McDermott, "Emily Dickinson's 'Nervous Prostration' and Its Possible Relationship to Her Work," *Emily Dickinson Journal* 9, no. 1 (Spring 2000): 71–86. "Nervous prostration or exhaustion" was subsumed under the accepted medical diagnosis of neurasthenia. According to a prominent neurologist at the time, George M. Beard, "nervousness was an unfortunate byproduct of the teeming cities and their attendant problems was that people spent too much of this 'nervous energy' and when it was depleted, they got sick with a condition called neurasthenia; a direct consequence of modern life." The only cure was withdrawal from the pressures of urban life, rest, and a simpler, healthy lifestyle. Neurasthenia was almost a badge of social status. Beard's book *American Nervousness: Its Causes and Consequences* (New York: G. P. Putnam's Sons, 1881), espoused this prominent theory of neurasthenia. Beard's work was later summarized by Julie Beck in "'Americanitis': The Disease of Living Too Fast," *Atlantic*, March 11, 2016, https://www.theatlantic.com.
20. Lash, *Helen and Teacher*, 167.
21. Ibid., 166.
22. HK to Frank B. Sanborn, September 28, 1906, AFB.
23. JEC to NBH, December 6, 1933, AFB.

CHAPTER SIX: AWAY AND BACK TO BOSTON, 1894–1896

1. Dorothy Herrmann, *Helen Keller: A Life* (Chicago: University of Chicago Press, 1999), 90.
2. Helen Keller, "In Memoriam: William Wade," *Outlook for the Blind*, Autumn 1913, 47–49.
3. Susanna Coit, archives and research library assistant, Perkins Archives, communication with author, November 8, 2018.

4. Patricia J. Fanning, *Artful Lives: The Francis Watts Lee Family and Their Times* (Amherst: University of Massachusetts Press, 2016), 154.
5. Joseph P. Lash, *Helen and Teacher: The Story of Helen Keller and Anne Sullivan Macy* (Reading, MA: Addison-Wesley, 1980), 164.
6. Kim E. Nielsen, *Beyond the Miracle Worker: The Remarkable Life of Anne Sullivan Macy and Her Extraordinary Friendship with Helen Keller* (Boston: Beacon, 2009), 140–142.
7. Ibid., 128.
8. Edwin S. Grosvenor and Morgan Wesson, *Alexander Graham Bell: The Life and Times of the Man Who Invented the Telephone* (New York: Harry N. Abrams, 1997), 157.
9. Ibid., 158.
10. Nielsen, *Beyond the Miracle Worker,* 130.
11. AGB to AK, July 20, 1894, AGB, LOC.
12. Helen Keller, *The Story of My Life: With Her Letters (1887–1901) and a Supplementary Account of Her Education, Including Passages from the Reports and Letters of Her Teacher, Anne Mansfield Sullivan* (New York: Doubleday, Page, 1921), 386.
13. "A Bright Blind Girl: Helen Keller of Boston Comes to a School in New York," *New York Times*, January 6, 1895.
14. Keller, *The Story of My Life,* 82.
15. The Tadoma Method is rarely used by people who are deafblind in the U.S. today, according to Haben Girma, communication with author, February 2, 2021.
16. Nielsen, *Beyond the Miracle Worker,* 137.
17. HK to MA, April 21, 1895, Anagnos-Sullivan-Keller Collection, Perkins Archives.
18. AS to JH, n.d. [1895], AFB.
19. JH to AS, n.d. [probably 1895], AFB.
20. Nielsen, *Beyond the Miracle Worker,* 145.
21. Ibid.
22. Keller, *The Story of My Life,* 138.
23. Ibid., 139.
24. Herrmann, *Helen Keller,* 103–109.
25. Mark Twain to HK, March 17, 1903, AFB.
26. Nielsen, *Beyond the Miracle Worker,* 139.
27. *Boston Transcript,* January 17, 1896.
28. Nielsen, *Beyond the Miracle Worker,* 142.
29. Keller, *The Story of My Life,* 83.
30. "A Beacon Light," letter to the editor, *Boston Transcript,* March 15, 1895.
31. "A History of the Youth's Companion and Pledge of Allegiance with Collectors' Notes," Collecting Old Magazines, http://www.collectingoldmagazines.com.
32. The books were sold as a set for $1.50.
33. J. L. Gilder and J. B. Gilder, eds., "Note," *The Critic,* September 19, 1896, 179.
34. "Author of the 'Listener' Column: Complimentary Dinner Given to Mr. Joseph Edgar Chamberlin," *Boston Herald,* September 13, 1896.

35. HK to JLC, July 7, 1935, copy in author's possession. According to Helen Keller, she used the Tadoma Method most often when speaking with Ed Chamberlin.
36. Joseph Edgar Chamberlin, *Listener in the Town* (Boston: Copeland and Day, 1896), 9–10.
37. Ibid., 10.
38. Ibid., 31.
39. Ibid., 34–35.
40. Ibid., 36–39.
41. Ibid., 10–11.
42. Joseph Edgar Chamberlin, *Listener in the Country* (Boston: Copeland and Day, 1896), 45–48.
43. Ibid., 3, 18, 24.
44. Ibid., 83–84.
45. Ibid., 98–104.
46. HK to JH, July 15, 1896, in Keller, *The Story of My Life,* 234.
47. Joseph Edgar Chamberlin, *Nomads and Listeners of Joseph Edgar Chamberlin,* ed. Samuel M. Waxman (Cambridge, MA: Riverside Press, 1937), xiv.
48. HK to JLC, July 5,1935, copy in the author's possession.
49. HK to JH, July 15, 1896 in Keller, *The Story of My Life,* 236.
50. IAC to FHD, May 14, 1899, Chamberlin Correspondence, reel 4951, F. Holland Day Papers, 1858–1977, Manuscripts Division, Library of Congress, Washington, DC.
51. *Boston Herald,* July 4, 1896.
52. HK to JEC, February 2, 1934, AFB.
53. Patricia J. Fanning, *Through an Uncommon Lens: The Life and Photography of F. Holland Day* (Amherst: University of Massachusetts Press, 2008), 34–35.
54. Ibid., 42.
55. LIG to FHD, September 23, 1897, quoted in ibid., 94.
56. Ibid.
57. Ibid., 36.
58. Patricia J. Fanning, conversations with author, 2015–2018.
59. Fanning, *Through an Uncommon Lens,* 85.
60. "F. Luis Mora (1874–1940)," Spellman Gallery, https://www.spellmangallery .com.
61. Helen M. Chesnutt, *Charles Waddell Chesnutt: Pioneer of the Color Line* (Chapel Hill: University of North Carolina Press, 2011), 145.
62. HK to IAC, September 10, 1896, AFB.
63. Helen Keller, *The World I Live In,* ed. Roger Shattuck (New York: New York Review of Books, 2003), 10.
64. Nella Braddy Henney, "Helen Keller at 75: 'Tranquil and Unafraid,'" *New York Times,* June 26, 1955.
65. Keller, *The World I Live In,* 11.
66. Ibid., 31.
67. Ibid., 44.
68. Nielsen, *Beyond the Miracle Worker,* 146; Grace Powers Thomas, ed., *Where to Educate: A Guide to the Best Private Schools, 1898–1899* (circa 1899; reprint N.p.: Palala Press, 2016), 149–150.

69. Arthur Gilman, notes on Helen Keller, 1896, Helen Keller and Arthur Gilman Collection, Perkins Archives.
70. Ibid.
71. Ibid.
72. Nielsen, *Beyond the Miracle Worker,* 144.
73. Sara Day, *Coded Letters, Concealed Love: The Larger Lives of Harriet Freeman and Edward Everett Hale* (Washington, DC: New Academia, 2014), 183.
74. Lash, *Helen and Teacher,* 782.
75. Ibid.
76. AS to JH, September 10, 1896, AFB.
77. Ibid.
78. Fanning, *Artful Lives,* 50.
79. HK to IAC, September 10, 1896, AFB.

CHAPTER SEVEN: THE CAMBRIDGE SCHOOL

1. JH to AGB, December 27, 1897, AFB.
2. Helen Keller, *The Story of My Life* (New York: Airmont, 1965), 53.
3. Joseph P. Lash, *Helen and Teacher: The Story of Helen Keller and Anne Sullivan Macy* (Reading, MA: Addison-Wesley, 1980), 209.
4. Ibid.
5. Arthur Gilman, *The Cambridge of Eighteen Hundred and Ninety-Six: A Picture of the City and Its Industries Fifty Years after Its Incorporation* (Cambridge, MA: Riverside Press, 1896), 214, 215.
6. Arthur Gilman obituary, *New York Times*, December 28, 1909.
7. Gilman, *The Cambridge of Eighteen Hundred and Ninety-Six,* 214.
8. Ibid., 215.
9. Ibid., 216.
10. Ibid., 215.
11. Lash, *Helen and Teacher,* 211.
12. Ibid.
13. AG to EH, December 1896, Helen Keller and Arthur Gilman Collection, Perkins Archives.
14. Lash, *Helen and Teacher,* 210.
15. AG to HK, September 24, 1897, AFB.
16. Kim E. Nielsen, *Beyond the Miracle Worker: The Remarkable Life of Anne Sullivan Macy and Her Extraordinary Friendship with Helen Keller* (Boston: Beacon, 2009), 147.
17. "Helen Keller's Studies," *Boston Transcript,* April 5, 1897.
18. Lash, *Helen and Teacher,* 210–211.
19. AG to AS, April 26, 1897, AFB.
20. Lash, *Helen and Teacher,* 213.
21. Keller, *The Story of My Life,* 53.
22. HK to KK, July 9, 1897, AFB.
23. HK to JH, July 9, 1897, AFB.
24. Ibid.
25. J. E. Chamberlin, "Helen Keller," *Boston Transcript,* April 7, 1897, reprinted in Joseph Edgar Chamberlin, *Nomads and Listeners of Joseph Edgar*

Chamberlin, ed. Samuel M. Waxman (Cambridge, MA: Riverside Press, 1937), 150–152.

26. HK to JLC, July 7, 1935, copy in author's possession.
27. HK to AP, September 23, 1897, AFB.
28. HK to AG, July 17, 1897, Helen Keller and Arthur Gilman Collection.
29. Nielsen, *Beyond the Miracle Worker,* 148.

CHAPTER EIGHT: THE GILMAN AFFAIR

1. Laurie Lawlor, *Helen Keller: Rebellious Spirit* (New York: Holiday House, 2001), 79.
2. Helen Keller, *The Story of My Life* (New York: Airmont, 1965), 55.
3. Ibid.
4. Ibid., 55–56.
5. AG to EH, October 22, 1897, AFB.
6. EH to JEC, probably November 1897, AFB.
7. EH to JEC and IAC, December 1, 1897, AFB.
8. Dorothy Herrmann, *Helen Keller: A Life* (Chicago: University of Chicago Press, 1999), 154; WW to AG, March 28, 1898, Helen Keller and Arthur Gilman Collection, Perkins Archives.
9. KK to AS, November 28, 1897, AFB.
10. Kim E. Nielsen, *Beyond the Miracle Worker: The Remarkable Life of Anne Sullivan Macy and Her Extraordinary Friendship with Helen Keller* (Boston: Beacon, 2009), 151.
11. Helen Keller, *Teacher: Anne Sullivan Macy* (1955; reprint Westport, CT: Greenwood Press, 1985), 81.
12. AG to KK, December 8, 1897, AFB.
13. AG to KK, draft, December 8, 1897, AFB.
14. Ibid.
15. Nielsen, *Beyond the Miracle Worker,* 133.
16. Ibid., 151.
17. Keller, *Teacher,* 81.
18. Ibid.
19. Howells House was a residence hall that had formerly been the home of the writer William Dean Howells.
20. Joseph P. Lash, *Helen and Teacher: The Story of Helen Keller and Anne Sullivan Macy* (Reading, MA: Addison-Wesley, 1980), 225.
21. JEC to NBH, December 6,1933, Nella Braddy Henney Collection, Perkins Archives.
22. Ibid.
23. Ibid.
24. EH to AG, December 9, 1897, AFB.
25. AG to EH, December 11, 1897, AFB.
26. Ed sent several communications to Gilman on December 11 inquiring as to Keller's arrival time and offering to meet her at Park Street Station for the ride to Red Farm.
27. KK to JH, December 28, 1897, AFB.
28. LDF to AS, December 1897, AFB.

29. LDF to AS, December 15, 1897, AFB.
30. LDF to AS, December 16, 1897, AFB.
31. Ibid.
32. Ibid.
33. AG to JEC, December 17, 1897, AFB.
34. JEC to AG, December 18, 1897, Helen Keller and Arthur Gilman Collection.
35. EH to JEC, December 19, 1897, AFB.
36. AG to JEC, December 24, 1897, AFB.
37. HK to JH, "A Terrible Extreme," transcribed by JEC, December 27, 1897, AFB.
38. EH to JEC, 1897, AFB.
39. JH to AGB, December 27, 1897, AGB, LOC.
40. JH to JEC, December 28, 1897, AFB.
41. JH to JEC, December 29, 1897, AFB.
42. Ibid.
43. Nielsen, *Beyond the Miracle Worker,* 152.
44. AG to AGB, January 3, 1898, AGB, LOC.
45. AGB to AC, n.d., AFB.
46. JEC to AG, January 4, 1898, Helen Keller and Arthur Gilman Collection.
47. AG to JEC, January 6, 1898, AFB.
48. EH to JEC, January 12, 1898, AFB.
49. AS to JH, January 14, 1898, AFB.
50. George Hodges to "Mr. Greer," January 18, 1898, AFB.
51. "SCH" to AG, n.d.; other examples, Helen Keller and Arthur Gilman Collection.
52. Lash, *Helen and Teacher*, 217.
53. HK to JH, "A Terrible Extreme," transcribed by JEC, December 27, 1897, AFB.

CHAPTER NINE: "THE HAPPIEST MONTHS"

1. *Boston Transcript,* January 13, 1898.
2. HK to AP, January 4, 1898, AFB.
3. HK to JH, July 9, 1897, AFB.
4. HK to JH, February 9, 1898, AFB.
5. HK to EH, February 20, 1898, in Helen Keller, *The Story of My Life* (New York: Airmont, 1965), 136–137.
6. Helen Keller, Journal, March 11, 1898, AFB.
7. HK to EH, April 12, 1898, in Helen Keller, *The Story of My Life: With Her Letters (1887–1901) and a Supplementary Account of Her Education, Including Passages from the Reports and Letters of Her Teacher, Anne Mansfield Sullivan* (New York: Doubleday, Page, 1921), 242.
8. Helen Keller, *Teacher: Anne Sullivan Macy* (1955; reprint Westport, CT: Greenwood Press, 1985), 69–70.
9. Ibid., 101.
10. Ibid., 87, 74, 85.
11. Ibid., 94–95.
12. Ibid., 101–103.

13. Ibid., 87, 86.
14. Ibid., 85–87.
15. Ibid., 92–93.
16. Ibid., 84.
17. Helen Keller, "Joseph Edgar Chamberlin," *American Magazine,* February 1912, 421–422.
18. "Trachoma," World Health Organization, August 11, 2020, https://www.who.int.
19. Keller, *Teacher,* 57–58.
20. IAC to JH, June 10, 1898, AFB.
21. EEH to Harriet Freeman, June 19, 1898, Special Correspondence, Hale Family Papers, Manuscript Division, Library of Congress, Washington, DC.
22. Helen Keller, Journal, July 1, 1898, AFB.
23. HK to JH, July 6, 1898, AFB.
24. HK to JH, November 26, 1900, in Keller, *The Story of My Life* (Doubleday), 267.
25. Christopher Daly, *Covering America: A Narrative History of a Nation's Journalism* (Amherst: University of Massachusetts Press, 2012), 133.
26. Joseph Edgar Chamberlin, "Spanish Bravery at Caney," *American Monthly Review of Reviews,* September 1898, 325.
27. "The Newspaper Correspondents in the War," *American Monthly Review of Reviews* 18 (August 1898): 538–541.
28. Joseph Edgar Chamberlin, "Reflections on Cuba and the Spanish-American War," in Joseph Edgar Chamberlin, *Nomads and Listeners of Joseph Edgar Chamberlin,* ed. Samuel M. Waxman (Cambridge, MA: Riverside Press, 1937), 161–162.
29. Ibid., 161–167.
30. Lash, *Helen and Teacher,* 246.
31. Ibid., 310–311.
32. Keller, *Story of My Life* (Airmont), 139.
33. Ibid., 124.

CHAPTER TEN: RADCLIFFE ASPIRATIONS

1. HK to EH, February 20, 1898, in Helen Keller, *The Story of My Life* (New York: Airmont, 1965), 56.
2. Ibid., 140.
3. HK to JH, December 11, 1898, AFB.
4. HK to JH, December 22, 1898, AFB.
5. HK to JH, January 7, 1899, AFB.
6. HK to JH, February 3, 1899, AFB.
7. HK to EH, March 5, 1899, AFB.
8. HK to JH, April 11, 1899, AFB.
9. HK to JH, April 30, 1899, AFB.
10. Joseph Edgar Chamberlin, "Helen Keller as She Really Is: An Intimate Glimpse of the Wonderful Deaf and Blind Girl," *Ladies' Home Journal,* May 1899, reprinted in *American Annals of the Deaf* 44, no. 4 (June 1899) 286–301.
11. HK to JH, May 17, 1899, AFB.

12. Helen Keller, *The Story of My Life: With Her Letters (1887–1901) and a Supplementary Account of Her Education, Including Passages from the Reports and Letters of Her Teacher, Anne Mansfield Sullivan* (New York: Doubleday, Page, 1921), 93–95.
13. HK to AP, July 7, 1899, AFB.
14. HK to JH, September 4, 1899, AFB.
15. IAC to FHD, September 5, 1899, Chamberlin Correspondence, reel 4951, F. Holland Day Papers, 1858–1977, Manuscripts Division, Library of Congress, Washington, DC.
16. Angel De Cora to "Mrs. Clapp," September 27, 1899, Angel De Cora student file, Hampton University Archives, Hampton, Virginia; transcription courtesy of Linda M. Waggoner.
17. JEC to FHD, September 18, 1899, Chamberlin Correspondence, reel 4951, F. Holland Day Papers.
18. Helen Keller to Zitkala-Ša, August 25, 1919, "Letter by Helen Keller," Science Views, https://scienceviews.com.
19. Linda M. Waggoner, *Firelight: The Life of Angel De Cora, Winnebago Artist* (Norman: University of Oklahoma Press, 2008), 89.
20. "Zitkala-Sa *Red Bird* (1876–1938)," Akta Lakota Museum and Cultural Center, http://aktalakota.stjo.org.
21. Jan McCoy Ebbets, "Paying Tribute to Smith's First Known Native American Graduate, *NewsSmith,* Smith College, Fall 2003, https://www.smith.edu.
22. Elizabeth Hutchinson, *The Indian Craze: Primitivism, Modernism and Transculturation in American Art, 1890–1915* (Durham, NC: Duke University Press, 2009), 9.
23. Ibid., 195.
24. Kim E. Nielsen, *Beyond the Miracle Worker: The Remarkable Life of Anne Sullivan Macy and Her Extraordinary Friendship with Helen Keller* (Boston: Beacon, 2009), 32.
25. Joseph Edgar Chamberlin, *John Brown, Beacon Biographies of Eminent Americans,* ed. M. A. DeWolfe Howe (Boston: Small Maynard, 1899), ix–x.
26. Ibid., 129.
27. LDF to HK, August 6, 1899, AFB.
28. HK to LDF, October 20, 1899, in Keller, *The Story of My Life* (Doubleday), 146.
29. HK to AP, October 20, 1899, AFB.
30. Nielsen, *Beyond the Miracle Worker,* 159.
31. AS to JH, October 1899, AFB.
32. AS to JH, n.d., probably 1899, AFB.
33. Merton A. Keith, "Helen Keller Souvenir: No. 2, 1892–1899," in *Commemorating the Harvard Final Examination for Admission to Radcliffe College, June 29–30, 1899* (Washington, DC: Volta Bureau, 1899), 5–6.
34. WW to AGB, October 31, 1899, AGB, LOC.
35. Unknown to AGB, November 21, 1899, AGB, LOC.
36. HK to JH, December 1, 1899, AFB.
37. WW to AG, August–December 1899, Helen Keller and Arthur Gilman Collection, Perkins Archives.
38. HK to WW, December 5, 1899, AGB, LOC.

CHAPTER ELEVEN: DREAMS AND CHALLENGES

1. IAC to JH, December 15, 1899, AFB.
2. IAC to HK and AS, December 20, 1899, AFB.
3. HK to JH, January 13, 1900, AFB.
4. HK to JH, March 12, 1900, AFB.
5. HK to JH, April 22, 1900, AFB.
6. HK to Radcliffe College, May 5, 1900, AFB.
7. HK to AGB, June 2, 1900, AGB, LOC.
8. Helen Keller, *The Story of My Life* (New York: Airmont, 1965), 151.
9. JEC to Dean Agnes Irwin, August 31, 1900, Helen Keller Papers, Arthur and Elizabeth Schlesinger Library on the History of Women in America, Radcliffe Institute for Advanced Study, Harvard College, Cambridge, MA.

CHAPTER TWELVE: BATTLE LINES

1. "Helen Keller at Radcliffe—The Blind Deaf-Mute Passes the Examination and Is Admitted," *New York Times,* October 8, 1900.
2. Helen Keller, *The Story of My Life* (New York: Airmont, 1965), 58–59.
3. Ibid.
4. AP to AGB, October 5, 1900, AGB, LOC.
5. Kim E. Nielsen, *Beyond the Miracle Worker: The Remarkable Life of Anne Sullivan Macy and Her Extraordinary Friendship with Helen Keller* (Boston: Beacon, 2009), 165–167, provides a clear summary of events involving Ida Chamberlin and her plans for a school for the deaf and blind, to be headed by Helen and Annie.
6. AP to AGB, October 5, 1900, AGB, LOC.
7. AGB to AP, October 13, 1900, AGB, LOC.
8. IAC to AGB, October 17, 1900, AGB, LOC.
9. IAC to EEH, October 17, 1900, AGB, LOC.
10. IAC to AP, November 1, 1900, AGB, LOC.
11. AP to IAC, n.d., transcription in "Letter from Ida Chamberlin to Annie C. Pratt, November 15, 1900," Alexander Graham Bell Family Papers, Library of Congress, Washington, DC, https://www.loc.gov.
12. IAC to AP, November 15, 1900, in "Letter from Ida Chamberlin to Annie C. Pratt, November 15, 1900," Alexander Graham Bell Family Papers.
13. Joseph P. Lash, *Helen and Teacher: The Story of Helen Keller and Anne Sullivan Macy* (Reading, MA: Addison-Wesley, 1980), 256–257.
14. HK to JH, November 26, 1900, in Helen Keller, *The Story of My Life: With Her letters (1887–1901) and a Supplementary Account of Her Education, Including Passages from the Reports and Letters of Her Teacher, Anne Mansfield Sullivan* (New York: Doubleday, Page, 1921), 267.
15. Ibid.
16. Keller, *The Story of My Life* (Airmont), 152–153.
17. Ibid.

CHAPTER THIRTEEN: CRISIS

1. JEC to AP, November 26, 1900, AGB, LOC.
2. IAC to AGB, December 2, 1900, AGB, LOC.
3. AP to AGB, December 6, 1900, AGB, LOC.

4. EEH to AGB, December 14, 1900, AGB, LOC.
5. IAC to AGB, December 18, 1900, AGB, LOC.
6. HK to JH, December 23, 1900, AGB, LOC.
7. HK to LDF, December 24, 1900, AFB.
8. IAC to AP, undated letters, probably mid- to late December 1900, AGB, LOC. The letters were bundled together in a packet labeled "Bessie," with a request for the addressee to put the letters with others previously filed.
9. AS to AP, December 26, 1900, AGB, LOC.
10. Ibid.
11. HK to EH, December 27, 1900, AFB.
12. IAC to AP, December 28, 1900, AGB, LOC.
13. IAC to AP, January 12, 1901, AGB, LOC.
14. Bright's Disease is now considered an archaic medical diagnosis. Symptoms and treatment of the disease in women at the time are discussed extensively in Henry B. Millard, *A Treatise on Bright's Disease of the Kidneys: Its Pathology, Diagnosis, and Treatment* (New York: William Wood, 1893), 130–138. For a summary of symptoms and treatments for Bright's Disease, see "Bright's Disease," Wikipedia, http://en.wikipedia.org.
15. Millard, *Treatise on Bright's Disease,* 130–138.
16. HK to JH, February 8, 1901, AFB.

CHAPTER FOURTEEN: UPHEAVAL AND RECOVERY

1. HK to JH, March 11, 1901, AFB.
2. The St. Paul relative must have been someone other than Ed's brother, George Campbell Chamberlin, as he left St. Paul, Minnesota, to return to Vermont in 1893 and died there in November 1896. See Frederic P. Wells, *History of Newbury, Vermont, 1704–1902* (St. Johnsbury, VT: Caledonian, 1902), 504.
3. AGB to Mabel Hubbard Bell, March 15, 1901, AGB, LOC.
4. Kim E. Nielsen, *Beyond the Miracle Worker: The Remarkable Life of Anne Sullivan Macy and Her Extraordinary Friendship with Helen Keller* (Boston: Beacon, 2009), 167.
5. HK to JH, March 24, 1901, AFB.
6. HK to JH, April 16, 1901, AFB.
7. IAC to FHD, May 23, 1901, Chamberlin Correspondence, reel 4951, F. Holland Day Papers, 1858–1977, Manuscripts Division, Library of Congress, Washington, DC.
8. "Perhaps one marriage in ten contracted in the early 1890s would end in divorce." See Patricia J. Fanning, *Artful Lives: The Francis Watts Lee Family and Their Times* (Amherst: University of Massachusetts Press, 2016), 53. Likewise, "unions were not dissolved quickly or lightly." See David I. Macleod, *The Age of the Child: Children in America, 1890–1920.* (New York: Twayne, 1998), 15. However, "it was recognized that the death of a child created extraordinary strain on a marriage and there was a high incidence of divorce among couples who had lost a child." Fanning, *Artful Lives,* 102.
9. WW to AG, April 5, 1901, Helen Keller and Arthur Gilman Collection, Perkins Archives.
10. WW to AG, April 18, 1901, Helen Keller and Arthur Gilman Collection.

11. WW to AG, May 25, 1901, Helen Keller and Arthur Gilman Collection.
12. HK to JH, May 26, 1901, AFB.
13. HK to JH, June 21, 1901, AFB.
14. Joseph P. Lash, *Helen and Teacher: The Story of Helen Keller and Anne Sullivan Macy* (Reading, MA: Addison-Wesley, 1980), 257.
15. Helen Keller, *Teacher: Anne Sullivan Macy* (1955; reprint Westport, CT: Greenwood Press, 1985), 99–100.
16. Helen Chamberlin Dodd and Walter Sedgwick Dodd married on June 17, 1899, with Edward Everett Hale officiating under a massive oak tree near Red Farm. Helen had graduated from the Massachusetts Institute of Technology in 1896 with high honors from the School of Architecture. After 1900, she and Walter lived in Vermont. She authored "The Healthful Farm House" (Boston, MA: Whitcomb and Barrows, prior to 1911) and many other published articles.
17. Frances Parkinson Keyes, *Roses in December* (New York: Avon Books, 1970), 212.
18. Ibid., 212–213.
19. *New York Evening Mail,* November 16, 1904. Ed Chamberlin joined the *Mail and Express* staff in 1901 and worked for the paper until 1915. The *Mail and Express* went through a number of name changes. Founded in 1867 as the *New York Evening Mail,* after several name changes it was renamed the *Mail and Express* in 1881, which it remained until 1904, when it became the *New York Evening Mail* once again. See "New York Evening Mail," Wikipedia, https://en.wikipedia.org.

CHAPTER FIFTEEN: THE INTERVENING YEARS, 1901–1915

1. JEC to HK, September 1, 1902, AFB.
2. Angel De Cora to Cora Folsom, October 1902, Angel De Cora student file, Hampton University Archives, Hampton, Virginia; transcription courtesy of Linda M. Waggoner.
3. Linda M. Waggoner, conversation with the author, January 2019.
4. Linda M. Waggoner, *Fire Light: The Life of Angel De Cora, Winnebago Artist* (Norman: University of Oklahoma Press, 2008), 127.
5. U.S. Federal Population Census, June 1905, New York State, New York County, Manhattan Borough, 21st Assembly District, 16th Election District, Block A, page 9, entries 43, 45.
6. Waggoner, *Fire Light,* 128.
7. Ibid., 134.
8. Helen Keller, *The Story of My Life: With Her letters (1887–1901) and a Supplementary Account of Her Education, Including Passages from the Reports and Letters of Her Teacher, Anne Mansfield Sullivan* (New York: Doubleday, Page, 1921), dedication.
9. *Boston Herald,* March 15, 1903.
10. AGB to John Macy, April 2, 1903, AGB, LOC.
11. Ibid.
12. Joseph P. Lash, *Helen and Teacher: The Story of Helen Keller and Anne Sullivan Macy* (Reading, MA: Addison-Wesley, 1980), 299, 303.

13. Ibid., 313.
14. "Helen Keller Breaks Down," *New York Times*, June 25, 1904.
15. Lash, *Helen and Teacher*, 314.
16. Ibid., 313.
17. John Gregg, "The House Helen Keller Loved," *Boston Globe*, February 22, 1998.
18. Lash, *Helen and Teacher*, 310.
19. "Helen Keller's Big Audience," *New York Times*, October 19, 1904.
20. HK to JEC, September 10, 1930, in COKH article.
21. "New York Evening Mail," Wikipedia, https://en.wikipedia.org.
22. Christopher Gray, "Refined in an Era of Superlatives: An Early New York City Skyscraper Remembered," *New York Times*, October 24, 2014.
23. Christopher Daly, *Covering America: A Narrative History of a Nation's Journalism* (Amherst: University of Massachusetts Press, 2012), 113.
24. Gray, "Refined in an Era of Superlatives."
25. See, for example, *New York Evening Mail*, February 17–April 22, 1913.
26. Carol Willis, "Mail and Express," in "News Paper Spires: From Park Row to Times Square," Skyscraper Museum: News Paper Spires Walkthrough, 1997–2021, http://skyscraper.org.
27. U.S. Federal Population Census, 1910, New Jersey, Bergen County, Rutherford Borough, District 6, Ward 4, Sheet 9.
28. Joseph Edgar Chamberlin, *The Only Thing for a Man to Do: The Story of Raymond Chamberlin, Private* (Boston: N.p., 1921), 8.
29. For example, he was listed as a contributing writer in the *Harper's Weekly*, July 19, 1902 edition.
30. J. E. Chamberlin, "A Day with Helen Keller: Joseph Edgar Chamberlin in the Sunday Magazine," *Colorado Springs Gazette*, June 19, 1906.
31. HK to JEC, May 3, 1906, copy in author's possession.
32. HK to JEC, June 23, n.d., copy in author's possession.
33. Joseph Edgar Chamberlin, *The Ifs of History: How the World Might Have Changed If Things Had Gone Slightly Differently* (Philadelphia: H. Altemus, 1907).
34. J. E. Chamberlin, "Lincoln's Use of Scripture," *New York Evening Mail and Express*, February 6, 1909.
35. *Evening Mail* (New York), February 27, 1913.
36. Tom Vitale, "'Armory Show' That Shocked America in 1913, Celebrates 100," *NPR Weekend Edition*, February 17, 2013, National Public Radio.
37. J. E. Chamberlin, quoted in Jonathan Green, ed., *Camera Work: A Critical Anthology* (New York: Aperture, 1973), 175.
38. JEC to FHD, probably May 14, 1913, Chamberlin Correspondence, reel 4951, F. Holland Day Papers, 1858–1977, Manuscripts Division, Library of Congress, Washington, DC. Clarence H. White was a photographer who was a friend of F. Holland Day, Edward Steichen, and Alfred Stieglitz.
39. Joseph Edgar Chamberlin, "Foolish Question: Who Is Goldberg?" *Vanity Fair*, December 1914, http://www.oldmagazinearticles.com.

40. Emily Wilson, "The Story behind Rube Goldberg's Complicated Contraptions," *Smithsonian Magazine,* May 1, 2018, https://www.smithsonianmag.com.
41. Helen Keller, *The World I Live In,* ed. Roger Shattuck (New York: New York Review of Books, 2003), xxiv.
42. Helen Keller, "John Hitz as I Knew Him," *Outlook for the Blind,* July 1, 1908, 64–67, reprinted from American Association to Promote the Teaching of Speech to the Deaf, *The Association Review,* June 1908.
43. Helen Keller, "In Memoriam: William Wade," *Outlook for the Blind,* Autumn 1913, 47–49.
44. Nella Braddy Henney, quoted in Helen Keller, *Teacher: Anne Sullivan Macy* (1955; reprint Westport, CT: Greenwood Press, 1985), 15.
45. Henrietta Edson to Angeline Allison, August 28, 1914, copy in possession of Will and Luz Schick, courtesy of Barbara Werner.
46. Helen Keller, "Joseph Edgar Chamberlin," *American Magazine,* February 1912, 421–422.
47. JEC to LIG, December 26, 1895, Louise Imogen Guiney Papers, Holy Cross College Archives, Worcester, Massachusetts.
48. Kim E. Nielsen, *Beyond the Miracle Worker: The Remarkable Life of Anne Sullivan Macy and Her Extraordinary Friendship with Helen Keller* (Boston: Beacon, 2009), 140.
49. JEC to FHD, probably May 14, 1913, Chamberlin Correspondence, Reel 4951, F. Holland Day Papers.
50. In the 1910 U.S. Census, when they were living in Rutherford Borough, New Jersey, the Chamberlins reported eleven children in the category "number born." Four children were listed under "number now living." Those would have been Helen, Betty, Raymond, and Dolly. Adopted son Philip moved to California sometime in the early part of the century. U.S. Federal Population Census, 1910, New Jersey, Bergen County, Rutherford Borough, District 6, Ward 4, Sheet 9.
51. "Mrs. J. E. Chamberlin, Authoress, Is Dead," *Pawtucket [RI] Times,* February 19, 1914.
52. HK to KK, July 9, 1897, AFB.
53. HK to "Mrs. Fuller" (not LDF), January 24, 1930, AFB.
54. "J. E. Chamberlin Married," *American Art News,* June 12, 1915, 8.
55. Salary research conducted by Will Schick, biographer of Charles J. Edson, communication with author, May 23, 2019.
56. *Mail and Express* Company Records, 1914–1916, packages 10–13, New York Public Library.
57. Dolly Boshco, memoir, copy in author's possession.
58. "Honor Joseph Edgar Chamberlin," *New York Tribune,* August 27, 1915.
59. O. O. McIntyre, "New York Day-by-Day," *Washington Herald,* October 15, 1915.
60. JEC to R. W. Gilder, December 17, 1896, *Century* Company Records, 1870–1930, New York Public Library.

61. J. E. Chamberlin, "The Enlisted Yarn Spinner," *Sioux City [IA] Journal*, May 28, 1899.
62. J. E. Chamberlin, *A History of the Boston Transcript: Its First Hundred Years* (New York: Houghton Mifflin, 1930), 167.
63. Daly, *Covering America*, 186.

CHAPTER SIXTEEN: SOULS TRIED AND GREATENED

1. Joseph Edgar Chamberlin, *The Only Thing for a Man to Do: The Story of Raymond Chamberlin, Private* (Boston: N.p., 1921), 13.
2. Ibid.
3. Joseph P. Lash, *Helen and Teacher: The Story of Helen Keller and Anne Sullivan Macy* (Reading, MA: Addison-Wesley, 1980), 414, 415, 417.
4. Chamberlin, *The Only Thing for a Man to Do*, 16–17.
5. Ibid., 20–21.
6. Ibid., 27.
7. J. E. Chamberlin, *A History of the Boston Transcript: Its First Hundred Years* (New York: Houghton Mifflin, 1930), 218–219.
8. Chamberlin, *The Only Thing for a Man to Do*, 36.
9. Ibid., 58–59.
10. Chamberlin, *The Only Thing for a Man to Do*, 61.
11. Ibid., 65.
12. Ibid., 74.
13. Ibid., 85.
14. Ibid., 85, 86, 90, 93.
15. Ibid., 93.
16. Raymond Boshco to Brooke Schumm, Jr., March 5, 1998, copy in author's possession.
17. Chamberlin, *The Only Thing for a Man to Do*, 99.
18. "Helen Keller Warns Germany's Students; Says Burning of Books Cannot Kill Ideas," *New York Times*, May 10, 1933. See also Helen Selsdon, "Helen Keller's Words: 80 Years Later . . . Still as Powerful," AFB blog, May 9, 2013, https://www.afb.org.

CHAPTER SEVENTEEN: RECONNECTION

1. "More than 90 Years of Advocacy and Support for People with Vision Loss," American Foundation for the Blind, http://afb.org.
2. Edwin S. Grosvenor and Morgan Wesson, *Alexander Graham Bell: The Life and Times of the Man Who Invented the Telephone* (New York: Harry N. Abrams, 1997), 13.
3. JEC to HK, February 27, 1934, AFB.
4. JEC to HK, May 9, 1930, AFB.
5. HK to JEC, September 10, 1930, in COKH article.
6. Ibid.
7. JEC to HK, November 29, 1930, AFB.
8. Joseph Edgar Chamberlin, *Nomads and Listeners of Joseph Edgar Chamberlin*, ed. Samuel M. Waxman (Cambridge, MA: Riverside Press, 1937), xiv.

9. J. E. Chamberlin, *A History of the Boston Transcript: Its First Hundred Years* (New York: Houghton Mifflin, 1930), 11.
10. T. S. Eliot, "The Boston Evening Transcript," in *Collected Poems, 1909–1962* (Boston: Houghton Mifflin Harcourt, 1962).
11. JEC to NBH, June 10, 1927, Nella Braddy Henney Collection, Perkins Archives.
12. JEC to NBH, December 6, 1933, AFB.
13. Helen Keller, *Teacher: Anne Sullivan Macy* (1955; reprint Westport, CT: Greenwood Press, 1985), 113–114.
14. "The Listener," *Boston Transcript,* January 5, 1934.
15. HK to JEC, February 2, 1934, AFB.
16. Helen Keller, "Helen Keller Warns Germany's Students; Says Burning of Books Cannot Kill Ideas," *New York Times,* May 10, 1933.
17. Ibid.
18. "A Humanitarian and Her Teacher Arrive," *New York Times,* September 29, 1934.
19. HK to JEC, February 2, 1934, AFB.
20. JEC to HK, February 27, 1934, AFB.
21. HK to JEC, April 15, 1934, copy in author's possession.

CHAPTER EIGHTEEN: A GENTLE INFLUENCE

1. HK to M. C. Miguel, February 10, 1935, AFB.
2. Ibid.
3. Joseph Edgar Chamberlin, Death Record, Hanson, Massachusetts, July 6, 1935, *Massachusetts, U.S., Town and Vital Records, 1620–1988,* Ancestry.com, http://www.ancestry.com.
4. HK to Jenny LeRoyer Chamberlin, July 6, 1935, copy in author's possession.
5. "J. E. Chamberlain Is Dead in 83rd Year," *Editor and Publisher,* July 13, 1935, 32; *New York Herald Tribune,* July 9, 1935; "A Great Columnist," *Berkshire Evening Eagle* (Pittsfield, MA), July 20, 1935.
6. JLC to HK, January 18, 1936, AFB.
7. C. L. Edson, unpublished manuscript, 1936, Charles Leroy Edson Papers, Kansas Historical Society, Topeka; transcription courtesy of Will and Luz Schick.
8. Samuel Montefiore Waxman was a professor of Romance languages at Boston University.
9. Samuel M. Waxman, "Joseph Edgar Chamberlin," in Joseph Edgar Chamberlin, *Nomads and Listeners of Joseph Edgar Chamberlin,* ed. Samuel M. Waxman (Cambridge, MA: Riverside Press, 1937), xv–xvi.
10. HK to AP, January 4, 1898, AFB.

AFTERWORD

1. "A Great Columnist," *Berkshire Evening Eagle* (Pittsfield, MA), July 20, 1935.

INDEX

Fig. refers to gallery pages. See page 257 for name abbreviations.

ableism, 49, 263n8
abolitionism, 8, 10–12, 24, 44, 171–73; "Secret Six" conspirators, 148–49; Underground Railroad, 11–12. *See also* Brown, John
Albert Arnold Sprague Memorial Hall (Yale University), 19
Alcott, Louisa May, 34
Alden, Annie, 62
Alden, Henry M., 90, 174
"Alice Early Libel Suit," 21–22
American Annals of the Deaf, 54–55
American Association to Promote the Teaching of Speech to the Deaf Convention, 82
American Foundation for the Blind, 233
American Magazine, 218–21
American Notes (Dickens), 27
Anagnos, Michael (MA): AS and, 26, 64; on Cambridge School affair, 124–25; director, Perkins Institution, 7; HK and AS to Boston, 32–33, 36–37; on HK and Perkins, 35, 37–38, 72, 80; Kindergarten, 55; media coverage of HK, 72; publicity for Perkins Institution, 37–39, 84; recommends AS for HK, 28–29; reports on HK progress, 30–32. *See also* Frost King affair
Anne Sullivan Macy (Henney), 238–40
association to aid deaf and blind, 177, 181, 183–84
Atlantic Monthly, 82, 147
Atwood, Charles, 15, 17–22
Atwood, Helen Beebe, 18
Atwood, Sophia Gilman, 18, 221
Aunt Ida. *See* Chamberlin, Ida Atwood
Aunt Polly. *See* Pratt, Annie
Autocrat of the Breakfast Table, The (Holmes), 213

Beacon Biographies of Eminent Americans, 148
Bell, Alexander Graham (AGB), 153, 261n7; association to aid deaf and blind, 171–73, 177–78; AS telegram on AG, 114; on AS vision problems, 132; background and family, 51; Bridgman and, 27; Cambridge School affair report, 120–22; death of, 233; on disappearance of JEC, 192–93; HK and, 28, 33, 78–79, 83; HK book dedication, 205; to Macy praising AS, 205–6; on teaching methods, 81, 206. *See also* Frost King affair; Helen Keller School; Volta Bureau for the Deaf
Bell, Mabel Hubbard, 51, 77, 192
Bellamy, Francis, 24
Berkshire Evening Eagle, 247
Beth or Betty. *See* Chamberlin, Elisabeth
Birdie and the Frost Fairies (Canby), 46–50
Bonnin, Gertrude. *See* Zitkala-Ša
Boston Daily Advertiser, 23, 56
Boston Daily Globe, 57–58
Boston Daily Journal, 48

Boston Evening Transcript, 260n50, 263n19; on Cambridge School, 126; editorial page, 224; on HK, Perkins, 53; on HK Cambridge School, 102; on HK news, 153; HK Radcliffe examination article, 150; JEC at, 3, 7, 23; JEC leaves *Transcript*, 196; largest New England daily, 23; MA and Perkins, 84; on Perkins School, 141; on Spaulding, 83. *See also* "Listener" columns; "Nomad, The"
Boston Herald, 85, 90, 205
Boston Tercentenary Book, 233–36
Bridgman, Laura, 27–29, 37, 56, 84
Bright's Disease, 188–89, 274n14
Brooks, Phillips, 34–35, 52–53, 96–97, 148
Brown, John, 8, 148–49, 219
Burnham, Charles, 19

Cambridge School for Young Ladies, 95–96, 98–101, 108–9, 113–26, 128, 153
Canby, Margaret, 46–47, 49–50, 52, 54–55, 60
Carlisle Indian School, 205
Century magazine, 223–24
Chamberlin, Abner, 9, 12
Chamberlin, Adaline, 10, 21
Chamberlin, Charles (Charley) (son), 21, 25, 41–42, 46, 221, 252
Chamberlin, Corda, 25, 62–63, 67, 221–22, 252, 264–65n7
Chamberlin, Elisabeth (Beth), 25, 45, 62, 92, 127, 140, 185, 190–91, 194, 199; portrait, fig. 5
Chamberlin, Everett, 12–13, 18, 20
Chamberlin, George, 12–14, 274n2
Chamberlin, Helen, 71, 85, 190, 198–99, 275n16
Chamberlin, Ida Atwood (IAC): background and family, 8–9, 18–20, 89; burial of, 252; in Chicago, 22; colonial heritage, 18; death of, 222; on disappearance of JEC, 191–93; editorial career, 210; HK and, 85, 93, 117, 126–27, 129; ill health and pregnancies, 63, 66, 146–47, 151, 159, 163–64, 180, 187–90; marriage and family, 17, 20–21, 22, 25, 46, 66, 89, 189–90, 197–98; in Newbury, 197–99; portrait, fig. 3; at Red Farm, 1, 42–43, 45, 92. *See also* Helen Keller School
Chamberlin, Ida Atwood (IAC), letters: to AGB on association to aid deaf and blind, 184; to AGB on AS vision, 183; to AGB on Helen Keller School, 172–74, 180–83; to AP on Helen Keller School, 174–75; to AP on tension over Helen Keller School, 187–89; to FHD on estrangement from JEC, 195; to HK on "The Helen Keller School," 161–63; to JH on AS vision problems, 132–33; to JH on "The Helen Keller School," 159–61
Chamberlin, Jenny LeRoyer (JLC), 3–4, 233–34, 243, 245–46, 247–48
Chamberlin, Joseph, 9
Chamberlin, Joseph Edgar (JEC), 1, 3, 23; antislavery and abolitionism of, 11–12, 148–49; AS and, 8; AS telegram on AG, 114; background and family, 2–3, 9–10, 14, 20–21; biography of Brown, 148–49; Cambridge School affair, 114, 122; in Chicago, 14–19, 20; at *Chicago Evening Post*, 14–16, 18–19; at *Chicago Times*, 17, 20–21; "Cuban Fever," 135; "cur" and "dupe" by WW, 155; at *Daily Advertiser*, 23; at *Daily Journal* (Indianapolis),

17; death and burial, 245–47, 252; De Cora and Zitkala-Ša and, 148; disappearance from Red Farm, 191–93, 194–95, 196, 248, 274n2, 274n8; at *Evening Record*, 23; fame in Northeast, 7–8; family of, 22, 210, 277n50; family with IAC, 25; German immigrants and, 14; HK and, 3, 104; HK article for *Sunday Magazine*, 210–14; introduction to HK and AS, 36; on loss of Charley, 46; MA and, 73, 85; marriage to IAC, 17; marriage to Nilda, 222; meeting HK and AS, 7; nervous breakdown, 22, 71–72, 265n19; in New York, 197, 200–201, 204, 209–10; Perkins Institution and, 84; portrait, fig. 4–fig. 6; Raymond in WWI article, 228; at Red Farm, 262n2; Rube Goldberg article, 216; traveling war correspondent, 131, 134–35. See also *Boston Evening Transcript*; Frost King affair; "Listener" columns; *New York Mail and Express*; *Nomads and Listeners*; *Youth's Companion*

Chamberlin, Joseph Edgar (JEC), letters: to AG on Cambridge School affair, 118; to AP on IAC's health, 179; to AS on devotion to HK, 67–68; to AS on HK education, 54; to AS on *Youth's Companion* sketch, 71; to FHD on family, 216; to FHD on Zitkala-Ša, 147; to HK on *Boston Tercentenary Book*, 234–35; to HK on Ramapo camping and plagiarism, 202–3; to HK on their friendship, 236–37, 242–43; to HK on *Youth's Companion* sketch, 62–64, 66; to HK poem in "Olde English," 63; to Irwin on HK Radcliffe admission, 166–67; to MA, friendship, 57, 85

Chamberlin, Leonilda Farness Lowry (Nilda), 222, 233

Chamberlin, Martha Ann, 9, 20

Chamberlin, Mary Eleanor (Dolly), 9, 85, 127, 139, 190–91, 195, 210, 223, 231

Chamberlin, Mary Haseltine, 13

Chamberlin, Philip, 22, 46, 190, 260n47, 277n50

Chamberlin, Preston, 10, 12–13, 227

Chamberlin, Raymond, 66–67, 71, 127, 138–39, 190–91, 195; death of, 230–32; love of outdoors, 210; at *New York Evening Mail*, 223; at *Transcript*, 224; in WWI, 227–28

Chamberlin, Richard, 9

Chesnutt, Charles Waddell, 93, 148

Chicago and the Great Conflagration (Everett Chamberlin), 20

Chicago Evening Post, 13–16, 18–19

Chicago Sunday Times, 17–18

Chicago Times, 17, 20; "Alice Early Libel Suit," 21–22

Chicago Tribune, 20

Civil War, 8, 12–13, 28

Clement, E. H., 53, 224

Cleveland, Grover, 33

Coolidge, Elizabeth Sprague, 19

Copeland, Herbert, 91

Copeland & Day, 91–92

Curtis, Natalie, 205

Daily Journal (Indianapolis), 17

Darling, Richard, 200

Day, Fred Holland (FHD), 91–92, 147, 216

deafblindness, 2, 27–29, 37, 49, 52–53, 68–69, 77, 172–73, 257–58n1, 260n6. *See also* manual alphabet; Perkins Institution for the Blind

De Cora, Angel, 147–48, 188, 193, 204–5

Dickens, Charles, 27, 260n6
Dickinson, Emily, 84
Dodd, Walter Sedgwick, 198–99, 275n16
Dolly. *See* Chamberlin, Mary Eleanor "Dolly"

Editor and Publisher magazine, 247
Edson, Charles J., 218, 248
Eliot, T. S., 237
Evening Record, 23

Ford, Daniel Sharp, 64, 66, 84
Freeman, Harriet E., 35
Frost King affair, 46–61, 63–64, 124–25, 151
Fuller, Lucy Derby (LDF), 112–14, 117, 150
Fuller, Sarah, 79
Fuller, S. Richard, 112

Gilder, R. W., 224
Gilman, Arthur (AG), 95–96, 99–102, 111–16, 121–22; to AS on HK education, 102–3; to EH on AS and Cambridge School, 109–10; to JEC on separating AS and HK, 118–21; to WW on JEC family situation, 196
Gilman, Stella, 99–100
Goodson Gazette, 47
Greer, David H., 174–75, 177
Guiney, Louise Imogen (LIG), 91–92

Hale, Edward Everett (EEH), 112; association to aid deaf and blind, 181; Brooks and, 35, 43; death of, 217–18; Helen Keller School and, 174; HK and, 35–36; Indian Rights Movement and, 147; at literary dinner for JEC, 85; marriage ceremony, 208, 275n16; at Red Farm, 43, 90, 133
Harper's magazine, 82, 90
Harper's Weekly, 210
"Helen Keller as She Really Is" (J. E. Chamberlin), 141–51
Helen Keller School, 168–78, 180–87, 192, 194, 198
Henney, Nella Braddy (NBH), 94, 218, 237–40
History of the Boston Transcript, A (J. E. Chamberlin), 237
Hitz, John (JH): Cambridge School affair, 120–22; death of, 217; on Helen Keller School, 217; spirituality, 97; on teaching methods, 81; at Volta Bureau, 52; "Wonder-child," 55. *See also* Frost King affair
Holmes, Oliver Wendell, 36, 52, 56, 213
Hopkins, Sophia, 37, 47, 96, 111, 115
Howe, Julia Ward, 52, 149
Howe, Samuel Gridley, 8, 26–27, 29, 36, 148
Howells, William Dean, 82, 85, 174, 210
How I Became a Socialist (H. Keller), 241
Humason, Thomas A., 80, 102
Hutchinson, Elizabeth, 148
Hutton, Eleanor (EH), 82, 99, 102, 109–10, 115, 118–20, 123
Hutton, Laurence, 82

Ifs of History, The (J. E. Chamberlin), 214
Illustrated American, 72
Indian Rights Movement, 147–48
Indians' Book, The (De Cora), 205
Irwin, Agnes, 124, 126, 149–51, 166–67, 182–83

"Joseph Edgar Chamberlin" (H. Keller), 218–21

Keith, Merton, 124, 127–28, 137, 144, 152, 155–56
Keller, Arthur, 26, 77, 97; AGB and, 28

Keller, Helen (HK), 250; advisory committee, 177–78; AG and Cambridge School affair, 114; AGB and, 77–79; AGB meeting (1888), 33; AS and, 31–32; assistive frame, 258n2; AS "Teacher" and, 69–70, 129; in Boston, 32–35, 85, 137, 245; in Cambridge, 147; Cambridge School and, 99, 101, 126; Cambridge School affair, 118–20, 125; death of, 250; early years, 2, 26, 68–70; education expenses, 77–79, 99, 102, 110; EEH and, 35–36, 43; on father's death, 97–98; fever and deafblindness, 28, 69; in Forest Hills, New York, 233; at Howells House, 114, 269n19; JEC and, 36, 40, 135–36, 217–21, 247–48; JH and, 78; Kindergarten fundraiser, 55–56, 264n30; lecture touring, 221; MA and, 72, 80; media fascination with, 31–32; on Nazi Germany, 241; in New York, 82–83; Perkins Institution and, 35–37, 262n3; portrait, fig. 7; portrait with AS, fig. 2; Radcliffe cum laude, 207–8; reading a Braille book, fig. 1; at Red Farm, 42–44, 85, 90, 93–95, 104–7, 117, 128, 134, 136, 154, 269n26; in Scotland, 234, 240, 242–44; on senses of smell and touch, 94–95, 142–43, 212–13; snow, 40–41, 127–28; "souvenir," 146, 152; spirituality, 97; summer cottage rental, 141–45; Wrentham home purchase, 208; writing with assistive wooden frame, 37; WW and, 77; WWI neutrality, 227–28, 232; *Youth's Companion* sketch, 60–61, 64, 68–70, 264n3. *See also* Frost King affair; Helen Keller School; Radcliffe College

Keller, Helen (HK), letters: to AGB on summer plans, 165–66; to AG on Red Farm summer, 107; to AP for AS, 106–7; to AP on AG, 126; to AP on rental cottage, 150–51; to AP on summer cottage, 145–46; to EH on AS vision problems, 140; to EH on helping deafblind children, 187; to EH on Radcliffe admission, 166; to EH on Red Farm and tutor, 128, 137; to FHD on American Indian visitors, 147; to HK on "souvenir," 146; to IAC on father's death, 98; to JEC on *Anne Sullivan Macy* review, 240–41; to JEC on articles about her, 214; to JEC on *Boston Tercentenary Book*, 234–35; to JEC on Red Farm, 91; to JH on AS vision problems, 139–40, 154; to JH on Beth, 194; to JH on Chamberlin family, 197; to JH on Christmas plans, 138–39; to JH on cottage rental, 141–44; to JH on Helen Keller School, 175–78; to JH on IAC and Helen Keller School, 185; to JH on IAC's health, 163–64, 190, 194; to JH on JEC disappearance, 191, 194; to JH on Radcliffe preparation, 137; to JH on Red Farm, 89–90, 104–5, 126–28, 134; to JH on Red Farm Thanksgiving, 154; to JH on rental cottage and future, 163–64; to JH on *Youth's Companion* sketch, 65; to JLC on death of JEC, 245–46; to JLC on JEC and AS, 243; to LDF on Radcliffe admission, 150; on Uncle Ed's death, 4; to WW in anger, 155–56

Keller, Kate (KK), 26–28, 35, 37, 98, 102, 111–16, 118
Keller, Mildred, 28, 69, 101–4
Keller, Phillips Brooks, 34
Kennedy, William Sloane, 58
Keyes, Frances Wheeler, 199–200

Ladies' Home Journal, 136, 141–42, 202–3, 205, 208
Lend a Hand (magazine), 55
Lincoln, Abraham, 12–13, 214–15
lip-reading and speech, 79–80, 85; Tadoma Method, 80, 266n15
"Listener" columns, 3, 7, 24–25, 233; *Anne Sullivan Macy* review, 238–39; companion books, 84–85; Cuban War observations, 134–35; fundraising for HK, 105–6; HK and Brooks on spirituality, 53; on Kindergarten fundraiser, 55–56; "The Listener in the Country," 23, 88; "The Listener in the Town," 23, 86; "A Little World," 86–87; "Lost in the Fells," 88–89; "The Nomad," 23; Perkins Kindergarten article, 52–53; "The Victim," 87–88

Macy, John, 202, 208, 221
manual alphabet, 29–30, 33, 58, 70, 99
"Man without a Country, The" (Hale), 43
McIntyre, O. O., 223
Mentor (magazine), 46, 156
Migel, M. C., 233
Miracle Worker, The (movie), 2
Mitchell, Lucy Sprague, 19
Mora, F. Luis, 92–93

New England Institution for the Education of the Blind, 27
New York Armory Art Show, 215
New York Evening Mail. See *New York Mail and Express*
New York Herald Tribune, 247
New York Mail and Express, 197, 200–201, 204, 209, 215, 223, 275n19
New York Times, 38, 79, 168, 207–8, 241
New York World, 156
Nielsen, Kim, 82
"Nomad, The," 224, 230
Nomads and Listeners (J. L. Chamberlin), 248–51
North Alabamian, 28

Only Thing for a Man to Do, The (J. E. Chamberlin), 231–32
Outlook for the Blind, 217
Out of the Dark (H. Keller), 218
"Over There" (J. E. Chamberlin), 229

Pawtucket [RI] Times, 222
Perkins, Thomas H., 27
Perkins Institution for the Blind: annual report (1888), 37–38; AS and, 26, 29, 64, 238; board members, 35; commencements and HK, 57, 68; founded by Samuel Gridley Howe, 8; "Frost King Affair," 47; fundraising for, 7, 33–34, 83–84; history of school, 27; HK and, 65, 72, 205; HK at commencement, 35; HK visit (1888), 33–34; JEC defense of HK, 58; Kellers seek teacher, 28; Kindergarten, 52–53, 55, 83–84; MA and AS, 64; piano tuning skill, 57; premier program for deafblind, 2; publicity for school and disabled, 48–49; reports on HK progress, 31–32; Spaulding and, 79; teaching methods of, 257–58n1, 258n2. *See also* Frost King affair; *Mentor*
Pratt, Annie (AP), 137; to AGB on Helen Keller School, 180–82;

AS telegram on AG, 114; Helen Keller School and, 170, 175. *See also* Frost King affair
Public Forum, 134–35
Puritanism, 13–14

Radcliffe College: to the Academic Board, 164–65; entrance exams, 144–45; entrance exams, algebraic symbols, 153; history of, 100; HK admission to, 145, 149, 168–69; HK and AS at, 2, 168; preparation for, 83, 96, 103–4, 126, 137. *See also* Keith, Merton
Red Farm, 1, 250–51; AS fingerspelling to HK at, 44–45; Bunker Hill Day picnics, 90; Cambridge School affair sanctuary, 117, 126; De Cora and Zitkala-Ša at, 147; entertaining famous at, 43–44, 89–90; HK and AS full time residence, 126; invitation to HK and AS, 8; photograph, fig. 8; photography of, 92; rental of, 42
Rice, Ruby, 175
Robin, Willie Elizabeth, 52, 84
Roses in December (Keyes), 199
Ruggles, Samuel Preston, 27
Rumely, Edward, 223

Sanborn, Frank B., 26, 48, 58, 149
Sanderson family, 200
Sargent, Louise Peabody, 92
Silent Educator, 58
"Song of the Stone Wall, The" (H. Keller), 218
Spaulding, John P. (King John), 79, 83
Sprague, Albert Arnold, 19
Sprague, Lucia Atwood, 19
Sprague, Nancy Ann Atwood, 19–20, 169
Sprague, Otho, 19
Sprague, Warner & Co., 19
St. Botolph's Club of Boston, 90
Stieglitz, Alfred, 92
St. Nicholas (magazine), 55, 77
Storey, Wilbur F., 19, 21–22
Story of My Life, The (H. Keller), 144, 176, 205–6, 217, 232, 235
Stringer, Tommy, 52–53, 83–84, 160
Sullivan, Annie (AS), 2; abolitionist views, 8; AG seeks to dismiss AS, 111–12; biography of, 237–38; calls HK "Baby," 35; Cambridge School and, 99; death of, 248; discipline and, 29–30; on education, 85; first description of HK, 29; Helen Keller School and, 170–72, 185–87; HK and, 68; HK and AS leaving Cambridge School, 118; on HK education, 198; HK education articles, 54, 58, 61; JEC and, 36, 39–40; MA and, 64; marriage to Macy, 208–9, 221; media coverage of HK, 38–39; portrait with HK, fig. 2; at Red Farm, 42, 93, 128–30; Samuel Gridley Howe's techniques with deafblind, 28–29; teaching methods, 80–81; Tewksbury Almshouse and, 26, 31, 48, 198, 238; trachoma and vision problems, 26, 131–33, 139–41, 169, 222, 233; WW on AS teaching methods article, 153
Sullivan, Annie (AS), letters: to AGB on Helen Keller School, 198; to AP on tension over Helen Keller School, 186–87; to JH on Cambridge School affair, 123–24; to JH on HK father's death, 97; to JH on Radcliffe admission, 151–52; to JH on '"souvenir," 152; to JH on Wright-Humason School, 80–81; to JH on *Youth's Companion* sketch, 68; to MA on HK education sketch, 61; to MA on progress with HK, 30–32; Perkins school apology, 48. *See also* Frost King affair

Sullivan, Jimmie, 26, 31, 240
Swedenborg, Emanuel, 97

"Teacher." *See* Sullivan, Annie
Thomas, Edith, 52, 84
Thomson, Polly, 222, 234–35, 240, 243–45, 248–50
Torrey, Bradford, 44
Twain, Mark, 44, 82–83, 217

Uncle Ed. *See* Chamberlin, Joseph Edgar
Unitarian movement, 34–35, 43, 97

Vanity Fair, 216
Vining, Eugene C., 144
Virginia Institution for the Education of the Deaf, Dumb and Blind, 47
Volta Bureau for the Deaf, 52, 161

Wade, William (WW), 77, 102, 111, 125, 153–56, 196, 218
Waggoner, Linda M., 147
Walsh, Justin E., 21
Warner, Ezra J., 19
Watson, Thomas, 51
Waxman, Samuel M., 8, 248–50, 279n8
Whitman, Walt, 58, 130
Whittier, John Greenleaf, 36
Wilkins, Mary, 44
World I Live In (H. Keller), 216–17
World War I (WWI), 227–32
Wright, John D., 80
Wright-Humason School for the Deaf, 79–81, 83, 122

"Your Souls Will Be Tried and Greatened" (J. E. Chamberlin), 230
Youth's Companion, 84, 202; HK education sketch, 54, 61–66, 68–72

Zitkala-Ša (Red Bird), 147–48, 188, 193, 204